The Future of
Catholic Leadership

Responses to

the Priest Shortage

Dean R. Hoge

Sheed & Ward

Sheed & Ward™ is a service of the National Catholic Reporter Publish-
ing Company, Inc.

Library of Congress Catalog Card Number: 87-50320

ISBN:1-55612-074-5

Published by: Sheed & Ward
            115 E. Armour Blvd. P.O. Box 414292
            Kansas City, MO 64141-4292

To order, call: (800) 333-7373

Contents

Acknowledgments

In preparing this book I have acquired many debts, and it is a pleasure to acknowledge them. The Lilly Endowment, Inc. gave me financial support for the new research in 1985, and The Catholic University of America released me from teaching for a semester to supervise data collection.

I am also grateful for the support of many individuals. The Advisory Committee for the project provided ideas, reactions, and correctives. The members were Ruth Doyle, Office of Pastoral Research, Archdiocese of New York; Sr. Nadine Foley, O.P., Prioress General of the Adrian Dominican Sisters; Dr. David Grissmer, Rand Corporation; Dr. Eugene Hemrick, Director of Research, United States Catholic Conference; Rev. John Kinsella, Department of Planning, National Conference of Catholic Bishops/United States Catholic Conference; Dr. Joseph Komonchak, Department of Religion, Catholic University; Ms. Dolores Leckey, Executive Director, Secretariat of the Laity, National Conference of Catholic Bishops; Rev. Philip Murnion, National

Pastoral Life Center, NY; Dr. Paul Philibert, Department of Religion, Catholic University; Dr. Raymond Potvin, Department of Sociology, Catholic University; and Dr. Michael Welch, Department of Sociology, University of Notre Dame. In addition Rev. Robert Sherry, Executive Director, Secretariat for Priestly Formation, National Conference of Catholic Bishops, Francis Butler, FADICA, and Fred Hofheinz of the Lilly Endowment offered important advice. Dr. David Leege of the University of Notre Dame, who was a visiting scholar at Catholic University in 1985-86, read early papers and offered help in many discussions.

Dr. Joseph Shields and Dr. Mary Jeanne Verdieck of the National Catholic School of Social Service, Catholic University, were my collaborators in carrying out the priest survey and analyzing the data. We were aided by Dr. Richard Schoenherr of the University of Wisconsin, who directed the 1970 priest survey, and by Msgr. Colin MacDonald, Executive Director, Secretariat for Priestly Life and Ministry, National Conference of Catholic Bishops.

Susan James and Sr. Donna Watzke assisted in the data collection, and Kathleen Ferry and Barbara Williams assisted in researching portions of the final manuscript. Raymond Potvin, William D'Antonio, Paul Philibert, Colin MacDonald, Fred Hofheinz, and Zeni Fox read earlier drafts of the manuscript or chapters of it, and offered helpful suggestions. None of these persons — advisors or commentators on earlier drafts — have any responsibility for the outcome. I accept responsibility.

Finally, I thank my wife Josephine for her forbearance during the whole project, for which she deserves a medal.

D.H.
Autumn 1986

Preface

Since the close of the Second Vatican Council in December 1965, there has been a steady outpouring of books, articles, position papers, conference reports, and speeches on one or another aspect of the crisis of postconciliar Catholicism.

It has been a church marked by a weakening of its authority structure, by a decline in traditional devotional practices, by instability in marriage, by theological dissent and catechetical uncertainty, by a decrease in attendance at weekly Mass and an even sharper decline in the reception of the sacrament of Reconciliation, and especially by a precipitous dropoff in vocations to the ordained priesthood and religious life.

Unfortunately, efforts to interpret these and other postconciliar developments have sometimes been marred by ideological self-interest. Progressives and conservatives alike occasionally shape the "evidence" to support judgments already formed. They manifest a supreme indifference to data, making assumptions without research, and drawing conclusions without ever having tested them.

Dean R. Hoge's work over the years, and especially this one, has been a refreshing exception to that practice. He has consistently addressed one of the most serious problems in the postconciliar Catholic Church — the decline in vocations to the priesthood, or presbyterate — in a thoroughly scholarly and scientifically objective manner.

His thesis is that the shortage of priests in the United States is an institutional problem, not a spiritual problem. As such, it cannot be solved by prayer, fasting, and penance. But neither can it be solved by more imaginative advertising campaigns or more angelic-looking vocations directors. Because it is an institutional problem, it can be solved only through institutional measures.

Such measures, however, will require institutional leadership — from the bishops in particular. Fortunately, most of the bishops are so confused on the matter that they are really open to any reasonable suggestions.

Indeed, the bishops know that this problem isn't simply going to disappear, that God isn't going to pull any rabbits out of a miter. Therefore, to do nothing, i.e. to choose none of the eleven options Dean Hoge describes in this book, is to allow one of two fundamentally unacceptable options to prevail by default: either local communities will simply have to get along without the Eucharist, or lay members themselves will assume Eucharistic leadership and Catholicism in the United States will gradually be replaced by a new form of American high-church congregationalism.

If the bishops and other responsible parties do not want either of these two possiblities to occur, then they should heed the words of Archbishop John F. Whealon, of Hartford: "There is no doubt that much hard thinking, planning and even experimentation should be done *now* to prepare for the future."

This book should be read by every bishop, every vocation director, every member of every seminary staff, every person involved in the recruitment, formation, and evaluation of ministers of every kind, and any and every individual who has ever written or lectured or just "sounded off" on the so-called vocations crisis.

When the Lilly Endowment initially funded this important project, it suggested that it be "practical, realistic, and helpful." This book meets all three requirements. And more.

But now it has to be read, pondered, discussed, and acted upon. Especially acted upon.

Richard P. McBrien
University of Notre Dame

Introduction

This book is a summary of three years of research on the priest shortage. The work began in 1983 when I was asked by the Lilly Endowment if I would coordinate a review of literature on vocations. I said yes, and soon a group at Catholic University received a grant from the Endowment. We assembled a team of collaborators and advisors,[1] then for five months we gathered all possible materials, read them, discussed our findings, and finally we published the book *Research on Men's Vocations to the Priesthood and the Religious Life.*[2]

This experience led us to some conclusions about the nature of the problem and about new research which would aid church leaders in future planning. In the final chapter of the book we proposed a new survey of Catholic youth to get their attitudes about vocations, we proposed trend studies of Catholic adults to plot their feelings about their sons entering the priesthood, and we suggested a study of seminarians.

In 1984 the Lilly Endowment showed interest in supporting new research, and I worked with collaborators in designing new studies which
would have maximal value in coming years. The Endowment solicited
ideas from other researchers as well, and in summer 1984 it made a series
of grants, including one to me. So I devoted as much time as possible
during the latter part of 1984 and all of 1985 to the new research. I was
relieved of all teaching duties at Catholic University between January and
August 1985 so that I could concentrate on the nationwide Catholic college
student survey. By late summer all the data gathering was done, and for
the last year my collaborators and I have been analyzing data and writing
reports.[3]

Meanwhile, the Lilly Endowment made a grant to the National Catholic
Educational Association for a series of surveys of seminarians, the first of
which was in autumn 1984. Rev. Eugene Hemrick and I carried out the
data analysis and wrote the report *Seminarians in Theology: A National
Profile*.[4]

In the present book I summarize the research as of mid-1986, and I
review related work by other researchers and observers. The focus is on
future leadership at the parish level. Numerous assumptions and early
decisions informed the research and the writing of this book, and the reader
would benefit from a discussion of the main ones here at the beginning.
Therefore I will explain six of them and try to argue that they are reasonable.

Six Assumptions

1. The vocation shortage is long-term, not just temporary. We came to
this conclusion after reviewing the literature in 1983, and I continue to
believe it. The trend lines in the United States are similar to those in other
modern nations, indicating that something basic underlies all of them.
Whatever caused the downturn in vocations in the 1960s and 1970s has not
gone away, and the most probable projection into the future is one of increased vocation shortage. I accept Richard Schoenherr's projection which
foresees a decline in active priests in the United States by about 40 percent

from 1980 to 2000.[5] The future flow of men into seminaries is of course unknown, but the present gradual diminution of numbers has been a constant trend for almost a decade, and no change is in sight.

The social pressures causing the downturn in vocations are pervasive and strong, and the Church is powerless to reverse them. The most that can be done is to maximize the number of vocations available in the new social context. The Church must be realistic about the new social context in which it finds itself today — which it cannot undo — and develop strategies for Christian mission in this setting.

Since the prospect for a major increase in vocations is zero, responsible church leaders should look at other options for furnishing the best possible parish leadership in the future. Vocations personnel should be encouraged to do their best, while at the same time other efforts to select and train leadership should be started. Multiple approaches are the best policy.

2. Church-serving sociological research should address practical topics facing church leaders today. Therefore, our work is practical and applied, not theoretical or academic. We also have a bias that data must be reliable, even if this introduces other limitations. Limited reliable data is more valuable than farther-reaching but less defensible information.

The nature of the problem of priest shortage is basically one of clarifying the options which seem to be available. The advisory committee for the research discussed the options we could identify, and we soon found that we were divided on the question of how many we should investigate. Some members argued that options to which the Vatican is presently opposed should be off limits, since discussion of them would be offensive and would close many ears to anything else we may have to say. For example, the idea of optional celibacy for diocesan priests is widely talked about in Catholic literature today, but the Vatican is opposed even to discussing it. Other members argued that we should include such options in our purview, since information regarding them would be important for orienting future church leaders. We finally decided to include them. But

we concluded it would not be useful to investigate other options which
would require some theological reformulation, such as changes in the
theology of sacraments. Our research is limited to consideration of options
within the domain of church discipline, and it does not touch the area of
sacred dogma.

3. The most useful sociological research produces reliable information
without taking any positions on what leaders should do. The attitude we
adopted in the 1984 book seems appropriate:

> Research can be likened to the instruments and dials in the cock-
> pit of an airliner, which tell the pilot about internal and external
> conditions but don't determine where he should fly. Where the
> Church should go is a theological question, to be decided in
> prayer and study by Catholic leaders. The role of research is
> merely to provide information and interpretation of current condi-
> tions.[6]

I am not arguing that value-free sociology is possible, for it is not. Sub-
tle biases creep into even the most controlled investigations. But I hope to
minimize biases wherever possible. Decisions will have to be made in
years ahead, but they are not mine to make, and I am merely offering information to aid the decision-makers.

4. The American Catholic community is in the midst of a long assimilation process from immigrant enclave to mainstream middle-class
culture. This process has been moving rapidly in the past twenty years,
and it shows no signs of slowing. Nor has it reached its end. Very pervasive cultural influences are affecting the Catholic community today,
pushing the institutional Church in the general direction of middle-class
Protestant churches. The nearest Protestant denominations in sight are the
Episcopalians and Lutherans (minus the Missouri Synod Lutherans), and
the assimilation process is slowly moving the Catholic community in that
direction. In this situation Catholic leaders would benefit from descriptions of church life in those denominations, since social pressures will

make tomorrow's Catholics more and more like today's Episcopalians and Lutherans. For this reason we have included Protestant research in this book, especially Episcopalian and Lutheran research when available.

5. The shortage of priests is an institutional problem, not a spiritual problem. This basic conclusion emerged from our 1983 research, and I am still certain it is true. Now I add a second part: . . . and it can be solved through institutional measures.

In 1983 we compared numbers of seminarians and clergy in various denominations in America and we found that all the middle-class Protestant denominations have a surplus of clergy. The Catholic Church alone has a shortage. Yet both mainline Protestants and Catholics live in the midst of the same mainstream American culture. Their young men attend many of the same colleges, watch the same television shows, participate in the same youth culture, and emerge with similar self-conceptions. The reason for the low enrollment in Catholic seminaries cannot be due to any putative cultural factor which distinguishes Catholics from mainline Protestants in America. It must be due to differences in institutional rules concerning clergy.

In addition there is abundant evidence that Catholic young people are strong in the faith and ready to serve Jesus Christ and the church in many ways. Applications to volunteer service programs are rising, and campus ministries are thriving. More and more laypersons would like to find employment in church ministries. As one observer has said, "The Church has a vocations crisis, not a personnel crisis." There is no evidence to support the often-heard complaint saying that Catholic young people have lost the faith and that for this reason vocations are down. The Catholic Church is not dying. Spiritually the Catholic faith is as alive as anytime in decades past. The problem of priest shortage lies at the institutional level, and it is best analyzed in sociological terms and addressed at this level.

Our research stresses sociological analysis more than psychological or theological. We have never seen evidence that psychological factors are explanatory for recent trends in church leadership; also on the theological level, we have little to add. Our main contribution is to depict the pressures coming up "from below," that is, from everyday influences of American culture being experienced by the Catholic population and in turn changing their church life. Well-constructed sociological studies have the ability to expose and describe the pervasive, vaguely-felt cultural pressures on the American church in the 1980s and 1990s.

6. The sixth assumption may sound picayune at first, but it turns out not to be. I assume that parishes as presently constituted will continue to be the backbone of Catholic religious life, and that social institutions as complex as present-day parishes require stable full-time professional leadership. There is talk today about emerging Christian base communities or new covenant communities, but at present they are small and scattered.

Parishes will continue to dominate the future, and they require trained leadership. I cannot take seriously the suggestions being made today about eliminating or greatly reducing paid parish staffs, or about eliminating the clergy-laity distinction. Various Catholics espouse some form of priest-hood of all believers and collective leadership, but sociologically I see no relevance of these ideas for structuring parish leadership. If non-clergyper-sons assume leadership roles, as for example in some priestless parishes today, social pressures will thrust clergy-like leadership roles upon them in keeping with traditional expectations. Parishes cannot run on volunteers. The most realistic expectation is no great change in leadership roles, sociologically speaking. Staff salary costs per 1,000 Catholics in the future will be no lower, and probably higher, than at present.

These assumptions influenced the new research in 1985, but they did not determine it in any strict sense. Readers of this book who do not find some of the assumptions convincing are respectfully urged to read on and not lay the book down. The new data we gathered is extensive, and its usefulness is not dependent on whether or not one agrees with all our assumptions.

The 1985 Research Studies

A few words here about the 1985 research studies will clarify the source of the new data and eliminate the need to repeat methodological details over and over. (Appendix A gives more complete details of research methods for persons interested.) In autumn 1984 the advisory committee for the research decided that the most useful new data would come from a survey of Catholic college students, a survey of adult Catholics, and a survey of priests. Each would be designed to fulfill several purposes, and a set of questions would be identical in all three surveys for purposes of comparing attitudes.

The college student survey was the most difficult to do. We decided on a telephone survey of a random sample of Catholic undergraduates in both Catholic and non-Catholic colleges and in addition we decided to get a survey of undergraduates who comprise the leadership of Catholic campus ministries and Newman Centers across the nation. The latter group would be especially interesting, since it probably includes a disproportionate number of future church leaders, both clergy and lay. I hired a sampling expert, Dr. John Robinson of the University of Maryland, to design a sample, and he randomly selected 33 colleges across the nation. Ten were Catholic and 23 were non- Catholic (state and private). In the first four months of 1985 I traveled to all 33, gathered lists of leaders from campus ministers, and set up telephone interviewing of the random samples. The available lists for sampling varied from place to place, calling for some variation in method. I hired interviewers to finish the job in each place, and they completed 607 interviews. Also we received 610 completed mailed questionnaires from campus ministry leaders (87.5% of all we sent out). Since Catholic colleges were oversampled, we down-weighted the data from Catholic colleges to produce overall nationwide data. A by-product of this study was a series of rich experiences and interviews with people in many parts of the country.

The adult survey was simply a nationwide random sample of adult Catholics 18 or older, sampled in a way which would closely repeat earlier surveys by Andrew Greeley. The Gallup Organization is known for reliable polling, so we purchased a Gallup telephone survey of 800 adult Catholics, carried out in June.

The priest survey was designed to repeat portions of a landmark 1970 survey. We adopted the same procedures used in 1970 except with a smaller sample and shorter questionnaire. Our sample included 28 dioceses and 27 religious orders. We sent out mail questionnaires to a 12.5% random sample in each diocese or order, and we received 1062 usable replies (89.0% of those sent out). The priest survey included retired priests and those serving outside of their diocese or the United States. Data collection was between April and August.

My Past Experience

My personal past has struck some people as unusual, and perhaps I should comment on it. I finished Harvard Divinity School with a B.D. degree but did not proceed to ordination. Rather, I decided to remain a Presbyterian layperson and devote myself to the sociology of American religion. I finished a Ph.D. in sociology, then taught for five years at Princeton Theological Seminary, where I undertook Protestant research. In 1974 I came to Catholic University. In 1979-81 I worked for the Bishops' Committee on Evangelization, gathering attitudes and personal histories of new converts, church dropouts, and former dropouts who have returned to church life (published in paperback in 1981: *Converts, Dropouts, Returnees: A Study of Religious Change Among Catholics*). Recently I have also done cross-denominational studies of church youth and religious education.[7]

Not being reared Catholic has disadvantages and advantages. The main disadvantage is a lack of personal experience with various facets of Catholic parish life. The advantages come from my acquaintance with Protestant church research and its increasing relevance for the Catholic community which, as I have said, is in a long-term process of assimilation to mainstream middle-class American culture. What I lack in direct experience I need to make up for with perspective. My views about parish life are not different from those of most of my Catholic colleagues, and in fact I have encountered such a range of attitudes in the last three years that I find myself only slightly to the liberal side of center.

All non-Catholic Americans have begun taking the Catholic Church more seriously during the past five years, and this is true of me also. With the bishops' pastoral letter on nuclear warfare, published on May 3, 1983, the Catholic Church gained immeasurable new respect and esteem, and the publication of the second pastoral letter on the American economy has earned it more respect and esteem. Events in 1986 in the Philippines, in which Catholic bishops risked their power for the liberation of their people, have been inspiring. And the new currents of Catholic thought and influence regarding Latin America are of world historical significance. I appreciate the opportunity I have to be of genuine service to the American Catholic community.

Part I:
The Problem and the Context

1

What is the Problem?

We began with the assumption that the declining number of priests available to serve American parishes is a major problem. With the facts of the decline we discovered no serious disagreement, but we did find an important lack of consensus among Catholics about the implications of the decline for the total mission of the Church. Different writers had quite different assessments of the situation. This chapter looks at the decline and the diverse attitudes toward it. First we review the factual data, then we look at the varying viewpoints about what is really the problem.

Trends in Numbers of Priests

Figure 1 depicts the total number of Catholics in the U.S. and the total number of priests each year since 1920. The total number of Catholics is estimated in two ways, first by the figures reported by American dioceses to the *Official Catholic Directory*, second by the number of self-identified Catholics indicated by the best nationwide polls. As the figure shows, the estimates in recent years from nationwide polls

3

Figure 1

Numbers of Catholics and Priests, 1920—1985

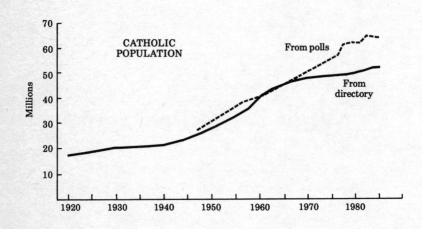

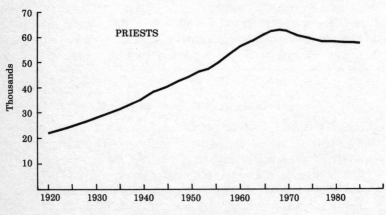

Sources: *Official Catholic Directory* and Gallup polls.
See Appendix Table B-1.

have been quite a bit higher than the reports to the *Official Catholic Directory*,probably because many persons who tell pollsters that they are Catholics do not take part in parish life enough to be visible to pastors when they make their estimates of active parishioners.

In general, the number of Catholics in the U.S. has increased steadily over the past 65 years, and the number of priests rose steadily to 1966, then levelled off and began to decline. The number of priests available to carry out parish leadership has declined more than Figure 1 suggests, since the figure includes retired priests. In a separate 1970 survey, 3 percent of the priests enumerated by the *Official Catholic Directory* were found to be retired, and in our 1985 survey it was 8 percent.[1]

The number of Catholics per priest is given in Table 1, using both estimates of the size of the total Catholic population. (For the data see Appendix B.) The main contributions of Table 1 are a de-emphasis on the alleged uniqueness of the 1950s and an absence of support for the sometimes-heard view that the present situation is only a "return to the period before the fifties." Actually the high number of priests in the late fifties was not solely a product of the overflowing seminaries at that

Table 1

Catholics Per Priest

Year	Using Official Catholic Directory reports on the Catholic population	Using nationwide poll estimates of the Catholic population
1920	806	
1930	717	
1940	603	
1947	596	646
1957	664	756
1967	747	756
1977	846	1056
1982	882	1116
1985	912	1123

time; the supply of priests had improved gradually for several decades. And the downturn in availability of priests since the early 1970s has been worse than anything experienced in the twentieth century. The two alternative ways of counting Catholics complicate our conclusions, yet they are less misleading, taken together, than either method taken alone.

Figure 2

Trends for Enrollment in Theology Programs, 1922-1980, and Trends in Ordinations, 1966-1980, with Projections to 1988 (indexed: 1970 = 100)

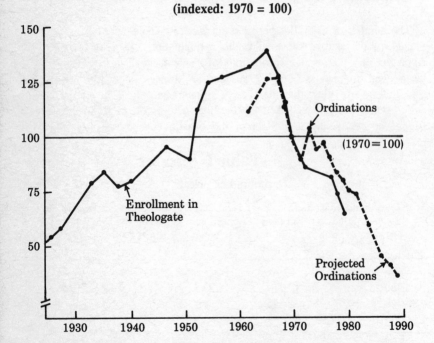

Source: Hoge, Potvin, and Ferry (1984); Schoenherr and Sorensen (1982). Ordination figures after 1980 are projections.

Figure 2 gives the numbers of seminarians in the theologate (the final four years prior to ordination) at different times between 1922 and the present, graphed with 1970 as the norm set at 100. Also the number of ordinations is shown. The upward trend in the 1950s and early 1960s is often interpreted as an unusual phenomenon of the 1950s and not to be taken as normative or normal. But when we look at the number of seminarians per 1,000 Catholics for these years, the argument loses its punch. The total Catholic Community was growing about as rapidly as the number of seminarians in the theologate, so the ratio does not change much. (See Appendix B, Table B-1.) The dramatic change is not the growth in the 1950s but the precipitous drop after 1965.

Figure 3 is a reproduction of Schoenherr and Sorensen's projections of the numbers of active diocesan priests available in the future. It does not include religious priests, but if it did the downward slope would be steeper, since the shortage of vocations is more extreme in the religious orders than in the dioceses. The projections were calculated in 1982, and since then a few years have elapsed which possibly could help us assess each of the three projections in the figure. But in reality not much can be learned in this respect, since detailed figures on active priests are not available. Dr. Schoenherr told us in July 1986 that all recent evidence he knows of supports the projections and that Series B is probably the best.[2]

There is no reason to doubt the projections in Figure 3. No analyst has done a better job or a more recent job than Schoenherr and Sorensen in 1982, and if anyone did, probably the projections would not be much different. The diminishing supply of active priests is a reality.[3]

The shortage is not evenly distributed in geographic terms. Observers agree that it is worst in the Southwest. It has not yet hit some large cities in the East, especially where Catholic colleges and other institutions have brought enough religious priests to town to help out. One frustrated bishop offered a revealing explanation of why the U.S.

Figure 3

Estimates of United States Active Diocesan Clergy Population, 1950-1975, and Projections, 1980-2000

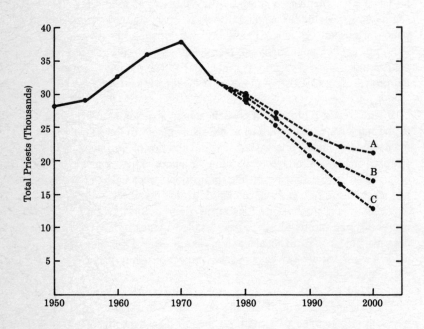

bishops have not been more aggressive in searching for alternatives in coping with the priest shortage: "Nothing will happen until the Eastern seaboard dioceses begin to feel the crunch."[4]

Figure 4 depicts the ages of priests in 1970 and 1985, based on nation-wide surveys.[5] Clearly the priesthood is composed of older and older men.

We are including Figure 5 because of all the recent concern about priestly resignations. Between about 1968 and 1973, resignations were a major worry of church leaders, and several research projects were

Figure 4

Ages of Priests in 1970 and 1985

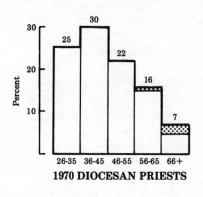

1970 DIOCESAN PRIESTS

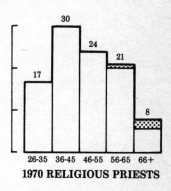

1970 RELIGIOUS PRIESTS

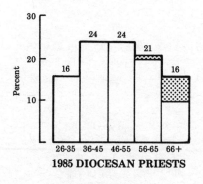

1985 DIOCESAN PRIESTS

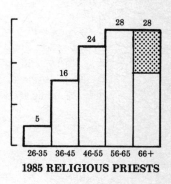

1985 RELIGIOUS PRIESTS

Retired Priests

launched to analyze the problem.[6]   After 1973 the resignations
diminished. The top part of Figure 5 depicts resignations of religious
priests in the U.S., and the bottom part depicts resignations of diocesan
priests. The sources of the data are different, and in addition the bottom
part is made up from data from three different sources. To get a sense of
percentage resignations in the top part, the 1970 figure represents 2.4
percent of all religious priests at that time, and the 1976 figure represents 1.3 percent. The best estimate of total resignations is that about 15
percent to 17 percent of all religious priests active in 1970 resigned in
the following decade, and about 12.5 percent to 13.5 percent of all
diocesan priests in 1970 resigned in the following decade.[7]

The priests who resigned, both diocesan and religious, tended to be
young men. In the 1970 survey Greeley found that 86 percent were 45 or
younger at the time of the survey (and even younger at the time they
resigned). [8]   Schoenherr found that the highest rate of resignation is in
the fifth to tenth year after ordination; few priests resign in the first five
years.

In recent research, Schoenherr discovered that the number of resignations is commonly under-reported by dioceses to the *Official Catholic
Directory,* partly because some priests resign in an unofficial way and
partly because a proportion of the resignees are granted leaves of absence by their bishops to think over what they want to do. These unofficial or pending cases tend to be under-reported, hence the number of
active priests shown in the directory is, on the average, higher than the
number actually available for service.

Concern about resignations has abated somewhat in recent years as
the numbers of resignations have ebbed. Probably the bulge in resignations in 1966 to 1973 was a specific product of that period of time -- just
after a large number of new ordinations and in the midst of rapid change
in the church.[9]   The most reasonable projection for the future is that

Figure 5

Resignation of Priests in the United States, 1966—1984

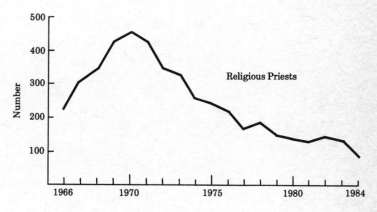

Source: Shields and Verdieck (1985), p. 11.

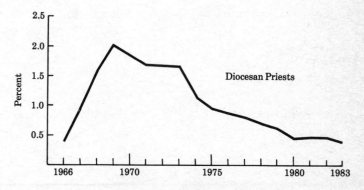

Sources: Greeley (1972) for data up till 1969; Schoenherr and
Sorensen (1982) for data in 1971 and 1973; *Statistical Yearbook of the Church* (Vatican) for later data. The data points
beginning in 1974 are slightly depressed, since they are
based on total priests, whereas the earlier data points are
based on active priests. Hence the decline in the early 1970s
is more extreme in the figure than in reality.

resignations will not rise, since there are simply not enough young priests in the system. Even if the age-specific rates remain roughly the same, the total number of resignations will gradually decline.

The International Situation

Figure 6 depicts trends in the availability of priests throughout the world from 1956 to 1983. It plots the number of priests (diocesan and religious) per 10,000 Catholics in 14 nations and continents. To make it more readable, the figure is broken into two parts, A and B, with the United States and similar industrialized western nations in Part A and other nations and continents in Part B. (The data is shown in the appendix, Table B-2.)

Figure 6, Part A

International Trends

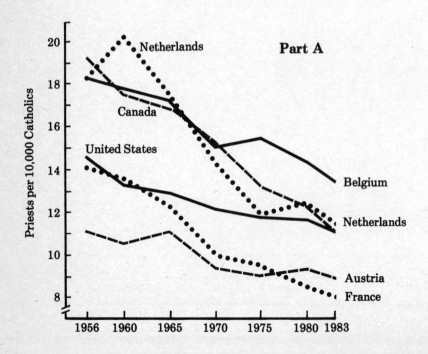

Most pertinent for the United States is Part A, which shows that all the industrialized nations are experiencing a decline in priests. The sharpest drops since 1956 have occurred in Netherlands, Belgium,

Figure 6, Part B

International Trends

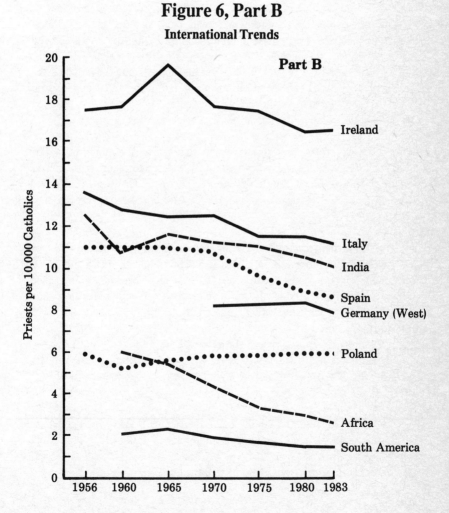

Part B

14 Future of Catholic Leadership

France, and Canada. Declines in the United States, Italy, and Austria
have been more gradual. (The data from West Germany is shown only
beginning in 1970, since earlier reports included both East and West
Germany, and the data from Great Britain is not shown since it is erratic
over time, thus probably unreliable.) We conclude that the problem of
priest shortage is much more widespread than just the United States,
and it arises from apparently similar sources in all the industrialized
western nations. In fact, the United States is unusual in the *gradualness*
of its decline, not vice versa; whatever its causes are, they afflict the
United States less than the nations of western Europe and Canada. And
the fairly constant straight-line plots in Figure 6 imply that the problem
is ongoing and basic to the social fabric. No reversal is in sight.

Part B of the figure shows other nations and continents. The
availability of priests varies very widely from place to place, with Ireland
having the highest and South America the lowest. Only in Poland was
there an increase in the priest-per-10,000-Catholic ratio over the past
two decades.

Worldwide data on rates of resignations from the priesthood since
1974 is shown in Appendix B, Table B-3. The trends are the same as we
saw in the United States — that resignations have been declining since
the early or middle 1970s. In the nine nations for which we have data
(eight in Europe and the United States), in all but one the resignations
have dropped down to less than one-third their level in the early 1970s.
The exception is Poland, where the rate was never high enough to be a
problem, and it has been consistently low. In general, future priestly
resignations will probably not be great enough to have much influence
on the availability of priests.

The priest-per-10,000-Catholic ratios in Figure 6 are influenced both
by the numbers of vocations and the numbers of Catholics. This point
must be remembered, since it helps prevent confusion regarding the effect of increasing vocations in some nations.

Recent reports tell of increases in vocations, mostly in the third world. A 1985 Vatican survey found that vocations reached an "all-time high" of 80,000 in 1984, which compares with their low point of about 60,000 in 1975. The increases were greatest in Philippines, Africa, South America, and Poland. Meanwhile, the United States, Canada, and most of Europe continued to experience decreases.[10] The increase in vocations in South America is due to greater receptivity by seminaries of men from all social classes, not just the educated classes, and also a surge of Catholic commitment in the lower and middle classes since the church's "preferential option for the poor."

In Africa the number of vocations has risen, but so has the total number of Catholics, and therefore the priest-per-laity ratio has continued to slide. The situation in Africa is exacerbated by the departure of foreign missionary priests, so that one scholar estimates that each year 200 fewer priests are available to serve 2 million *more* Catholics.[11] In world terms, then, the new vocations are coming more and more from areas away from the traditional European center of Catholicism, but the new vocations are not enough to reverse the worldwide downward trend in availability of priests. In 1970 there were 111.5 major seminarians per million Catholics in the world, but in 1984 the figure was only 95.6.[12]

Two current theories have been advanced about how to explain trends and variations in vocations. One is that vocations are numerous only in nations which are in a process of national or ethnic consciousness-raising while under foreign or dictatorial domination. This could account for large numbers in Ireland, Poland, and (until recently) the Philippines, but it fails to account for other situations. The second is that countries with lower gross-national-product-per-capita produce more seminarians, who see vocations as a means for getting education and influence. But this theory also fails to account for some countries, especially in South America, where incomes are low but vocations have been chronically sparse.[13] Neither theory is compelling.

The effects of declining numbers of priests have been felt especially in Europe. For example, in France, over 22,000 parishes were without resident priests in 1982 and were being administered by a non-resident priest. Other parishes are entirely vacant. In such situations, Sunday "assemblies in the absence of a priest" are becoming common.[14] In Austria, where the number of priestless parishes tripled between 1950 and 1976, a study in one diocese found that being without a resident priest has a deleterious effect on the parishioners. Sunday attendance, Easter duty, and communion were all less frequent among parishioners in parishes without a resident priest, and the number of people leaving the church altogether was greater in priestless parishes.[15]

Differing Interpretations of the Problem

Social theorists have long taught that social facts or social trends do not define a "problem." The belief that a problem exists requires a definite viewpoint about the meaning of the facts. What are routinely called "social problems" on the surface turn out, upon analysis, to have more than one interpretation, and what to one group is a problem is seen by another as no problem at all.

In various settings I have listened to debates as to whether the shortage of priests is really a problem. Reasons are given back and forth on why it is or is not. It became clear that definite patterns exist in observers' views. For present purposes these would best be presented in terms of the interests of the groups most involved. We begin with popes, then move on to bishops, priests, and laity.

(1) Popes

Papal words about the shortage of vocations all state that it is a crucial problem of the Church. Pope John Paul II said in 1981:

> The problem of priestly vocations — and also of male and female religious — is, I will say so openly, the fundamental problem of the Church.[16]

In the same sermon he said,

> In spite of all the circumstances that are part of the spiritual
> crisis which exists in the whole of modern civilization, the Holy
> Spirit is constantly at work in souls. In fact, He is working even
> more intensely. And it is precisely from here that the favorable
> prospects with regard to vocations open up also to the Church
> of today, provided she seeks to be truly faithful to Christ;
> provided she sets unlimited hope in the power of His redemp-
> tion — and tries to do everything possible to "have the right" to
> this confidence.[17]

The shortage of vocations is linked to the "spiritual crisis which exists
in the whole of modern civilization," with the inference that the vocation
crisis is really a deeper spiritual crisis.

In a message on December 30, 1976, Pope Paul VI rhetorically
asked,

> If there is a crisis of vocations, is there not perhaps first of all a
> crisis of faith?[18]

Again the shortage of vocations is linked to a deeper crisis, this time a
crisis of faith. The assumption seems to be that a crisis of faith would
directly lead to a questioning of the institutional Church, whose total
being is a part of the faith. That is, creed and Church structures are in-
separable. The assumption is not supported by research on American
Catholicism in the 1970s and 1980s. Rather, persons interviewed about
the Church commonly make a distinction, and whenever they say unkind
things about the present institutional church they quickly add that their
faith in God and their relationship to Jesus Christ are strong. Especially
among younger, educated Catholics, the Gospel and the present-day
church are seen as distinct entities.

The research we have seen suggests that the vocation crisis is largely a matter of institutional policies. Today, at the same time that the numbers of seminarians and vocations are far down from two decades ago, other indicators of spiritual health can easily be cited. The Protestant seminaries are full, not empty, and among Catholics many indicators of spiritual life such as retreat programs, parish renewal programs, and youth volunteer programs are strong. The vocation crisis is not occurring because of any alleged rejection of the faith. The crisis is at the institutional level.

(2) Bishops

Reliable information on the views of bishops is difficult to get, partly because the American bishops have not voted on any incisive statements regarding the vocation crisis. Also there is much diversity among 350 bishops. I am forced to rely on reading, interviews, and experiences in various meetings, including those of a Vocations Task Force sponsored by a committee of bishops.[19]

Without doubt, most American bishops see the declining numbers of priests as a serious problem.[20] They look ahead and see that they will not have enough capable priests to be pastors of their parishes. Bishops spend a majority of their time and emotional energy on personnel and organizational problems in their dioceses, and they directly feel the effects of not having enough good pastors to cover the needs. Someone has said it's like being a basketball coach who has no one sitting on the bench. In addition there is the loathsome prospect that the decline in priests will possibly have a spiral effect — that is, since all research shows priests to be the most effective recruiters of future seminarians, with fewer priests available to relate to young men, the recruiting of future seminarians can only deteriorate further. Therefore, the message from the bishops to the vocation directors and priests is simple: get us more vocations!

A common question among bishops when they get together takes the form of "How many did you get this year?" or "Did you get any this year?" They monitor the number of seminarians with care. And money is not a problem, at least for many of the bishops. If more money could produce more seminarians, they would find it.

The prospect of replacing some of today's priests by religious sisters or lay ministers in tomorrow's church is not welcome to many of today's bishops, since they are concerned about institutional control. They feel responsible for everything that happens in the diocese and urgently want to avoid any scandal or organized dissent. Thus, they tend to feel more at ease when their "officer corps" is composed of persons directly responsible to them and no one else. Diocesan priests are preferred over religious priests. Bishops vary greatly in this respect, but the picture sketched here, by all reports, is true of the majority.

Whether the bishops tend to see the problem as spiritual, or institutional, or cultural, is impossible to say. My impression is that there is diversity of opinion and a good bit of open-mindedness on the question, making the bishops ready to listen to all sides of a vexing problem.[21]

(3) Priests

I have asked many people what impact the priest shortage has on the priests themselves, and the answers contain three main themes which sound convincing. First, the dominant effect of the shortage of vocations is discouragement. It makes priests wonder if the Catholic community believes in them, and if their work will continue into the future. Inevitably, a dedicated member of *any* profession will have self-doubts if no young persons are choosing to enter that profession.[22]

Second, there is a more practical impact, that the priesthood will be declining in numbers and today's priests will be faced with more work and fewer associates in the future. This translates into less freedom of action and the prospect of more diocesan pressure to devote oneself largely to the sacramental ministry — which only priests can perform. It also means less priestly clubbiness than in the past, with fewer priests per rectory and more one-priest parishes. Loneliness, already a major problem of priests, can only get worse.

Third, and paradoxically, there is a positive impact. With a shortage of priests each priest gains power over against his bishop and chancery. He is now more precious than before, because the bishop is unable to replace him with anyone else. His waiting time for a pastorate is shortened. He can now venture to refuse assignments he does not want, and he can even consider moving from one diocese to another. All of these new conditions represent gains in self-determination for him. These conditions seem to apply mostly to younger priests serving as assistants; to older priests who are pastors of their parishes they probably apply less, since pastors already have lots of autonomy over against the chancery, and if young priests can't be furnished for associates, they can find qualified laypersons.

We had an opportunity to test the first two impacts in an indirect way in our 1985 survey of American priests. That is, we were able to see if self-esteem of priests and overwork of priests increased or decreased from 1970 to 1985. We expected, based on earlier interviews, that self-esteem had decreased and overwork had increased, but to our surprise the data came out just the opposite. Self-esteem, work satisfaction, and morale all *increased* between 1970 and 1985, and the reported average work week *decreased* by an average of 3.6 hours. Feelings of being overworked and lonely, measured separately, remained at the same level as 1970. These findings do not disprove the judgments of our interviewees, reported above, that the shortage of priests creates self-doubts and overwork, but only that for whatever reason these changes have not occurred between 1970 and 1985. Perhaps the shortage of priests has not impacted very heavily on priests during this time, so its effect was small relative to other trends in priests' lives, or perhaps many priests are not in dioceses which are already feeling shortages. We believe that the negative impacts on priests as of 1985 should not be overstated; apparently they are not overwhelming.

In talking with priests I heard widely varying views about the priest shortage. Two diocesan priests told me explicitly that the shortage of priests will be a good thing for the church, forcing an accelerated laicization of parish leadership, which is needed. Another said that the shortage didn't matter, since a different kind of leadership is needed in the future, and merely replenishing the supply of priests in today's mold wouldn't be very helpful. A religious priest replied to my question about whether there is a problem of priest shortage by saying, "It depends on what you want to have happen. If you want an active, caring church, we do not need more priests — certainly not more like the ones we have now." A campus minister objected to the statement that the basic need today is better recruitment of vocations; he argued that deeper re-thinking of the priesthood is badly needed: "Are we going to repaint the Titanic and not worry about the icebergs?" A religious priest serving a parish said that the shortage is not a major problem: "We will find new ways of managing the parishes. It will stretch our imagination, but that may be very creative. More lay persons are interested in serving than ever before." A dean of a seminary said, "In the long run, I'm not sure that we have a shortage of priests. What we do have is a shortage of imagination. More of the same thing is wrong. Working to fill the clergy gap — that is not what we should be doing." He likened the church's problems to those at the dawn of the automobile age. The Church is looking for more blacksmiths when it should be training auto mechanics.

In sum, priests have a wide variety of opinions about the alleged shortage, and they can be expected to provide a good number of ideas for future policy innovations.

(4) Laity

Views of laity about the shortage of priests are difficult to know. I asked dozens of people to estimate what they are, and the most common guess was that most laity have no feelings at all.

But some laity do; three credible reasons were suggested to me why certain laity see the shortage as a problem to them. First, as the quantity of priests goes down, quality will inevitably go down too. Inept pastors will not be removed from parishes, even if everyone is of one mind that it would be better for the parish, since bishops have no replacements. Second, fewer priests mean that sacramental services would be less available, that is, fewer Masses, fewer visits to the sick, fewer marriages witnessed by priests, and so on. Third, even apart from sacramental services, priests would be less available in all areas of parish life. Parishioners love it when pastors attend group gatherings, committee meetings, and the like. It gives the occasions a sense of officialness and importance. Fewer priests mean that this would be less possible, and lay ministers serving as stand-ins would not convey the same feeling.

On the other hand, two reasons were suggested to me why certain laity might welcome the decline in priests. First, highly involved laity who help run parishes and aspire to do more would see the decline as an opportunity for themselves and other laity to become more influential; there would no longer be so many priests in charge. Second, laity who are dissatisfied with status quo parish life in other respects would see the declining number of priests as a possible opening for innovations and reforms. For example, laity who dislike traditional clerical control or who desire to change the church's policies toward women might gain hope from the fewer and fewer priests.

Past research has not probed the question of priest shortage enough for us to know how many laity have definite opinions and what those opinions are. We are left to learn what we can from the diverse voices heard today. As an example, David Grissmer, a lay Catholic who works for Rand Corporation and has a strong interest in church personnel questions, recently asked, "Does the church really hurt because of the shortage of priests, or is it a non-problem? I have not heard any rumblings from laity about the shortage of priests. And no lay groups are rising up saying that they don't get services of priests which they want, or saying that the shortage is hurting them."

Lay theologian Monika Hellwig, in a 1985 symposium, argued that the so-called shortage of priests is really a time for reconsidering the nature of the priesthood, the terms of ordination, and the question of who is eligible for ordination. The more educated laity in the post-Vatican II era, she said, are not much troubled by the decline in priests, but rather they welcome it as an occasion for critical reflection on the priesthood and ministry. Many educated Catholics think that seminaries are producing the wrong kind of priests — men too much attuned to an elite status in the church, not focused enough on the tasks facing it.

Eugene Kennedy of Loyola University, Chicago, sees no priest shortage because an unprecedented number of educated and committed laypersons are ready for ministry today:

It is dangerous to misread statistics and to think that, because there are fewer priests and religious, something has gone wrong in the American Church. This shift in numbers, instead, signals that something has been right with it. There may be fewer men and women entering seminaries and convents but there are more men and women than ever with a sense of vocation about their responsibility for gospel values in their lives. There is, in other words, a leadership level of lay Catholics already in place.[23]

Attitudes of Laity in the 1985 Surveys

Careful surveys provide more reliable estimates of lay attitudes than interviews and attendance at meetings. In 1985 we put some questions into the college student and adult surveys about the declining numbers of priests. First, we asked college students and adults: "Some people think there is a shortage of parish priests in America today. Have you experienced any shortage?" Of the campus ministry leaders, 37 percent said yes, and of the student random sample, 27 percent said yes. The rest said no or didn't know. Of the adults, 34 percent said yes. Clearly the majority of Catholics in 1985 had not personally experienced any shortage of parish priests. It is plausible that the lack of outcry from Catholic laity about the scarcity of priests is simply because most Catholics haven't experienced any scarcity.

In the student surveys we were able to put a second question to those who had experienced a shortage: "What was the thing you experienced?" The open-ended responses were categorized according to their main thrust. The main responses were (1) "Our parish has fewer priests than formerly" (24 percent of the leaders who responded, 26 percent of the random sample who responded); (2) "I know priests who need to cover more than one parish," or "I know a parish which was closed or forced to share a priest" (25 percent of the leaders, 16 percent of the random sample); (3) "Priests are overworked — thus too stressed" (7 percent of the leaders, 9 percent of the random sample); (4) "Priests are overworked — thus the number of Masses and programs is cut" (10 percent of the leaders, 5 percent of the random sample); (5) "Priests are overworked — thus they cannot have good relationships with people, or they are not available" (6 percent of the leaders, 3 percent of the random sample); (6) "Available priests are not capable or qualified" (3 percent of the leaders, 5 percent of the random sample); and (7) "I know old priest(s) who need to retire or who are no longer able" (7 percent of the leaders, 6 percent of the random sample). In the students' eyes, quantity and quality of priestly leadership are interrelated and priestly overwork is becoming a problem. The tone of the comments indicates that the scarcity of priests is felt as a loss, not a gain.

Prior to the 1985 surveys I was in some meetings in which speakers called for greater participation by laity and religious sisters in parish leadership; they said that for most laity this was more important than replenishing the supply of priests. To test the strength of this sentiment we wrote an item for the student and adult surveys. See Table 2. The question puts the alternatives squarely to the respondents, and in every survey the majority chose alternative B — restructuring parish leadership to include more deacons, sisters, and lay persons. This is a higher priority for laity than recruiting many more priests to overcome the

Table 2

Attitudes (in Percents)

	All adults	Adults: Age			College Students	
		39 or under	40–59	60 or older	Campus ministry leaders	Random sample
Here is an issue facing the Catholic Church. I will read two statements, A and B. Would you tell me which of the two comes closest to your opinion?						
A. For the good of the Church today we must first of all recruit many more priests to overcome the existing shortage in parishes.	32	25	36	45	18	19
B. For the good of the Church today we must first of all think of new ways to structure parish leadership, to include more deacons, sisters, and lay persons.	54	62	52	39	72	74
C. Cannot choose, or don't know.	14	14	12	16	11	7

Table 3

Attitudes on Reduction of Priestly Activities (Percents)

If a shortage of priests required a reduction of priestly activities, which of the following would you be willing to accept in your home parish? Circle one response after each.

	Adults			Campus Ministry Student Leaders		
	Very acceptable	Somewhat acceptable	Not at all acceptable	Very acceptable	Somewhat acceptable	Not at all acceptable
Reduce the number of Masses each weekend.	18	50	32	26	58	16
Reduce the number of Masses to less than once a week.	6	23	71	2	10	88
Baptisms performed only by deacons or lay officials of the Church.	22	35	42	13	47	41
Marriages performed only by deacons or lay officials of the Church.	14	24	61	6	23	71
Reduce the availability of the Sacrament of Penance and Reconciliation.	14	39	48	7	43	50
No priest available for visiting the sick.	6	19	75	4	24	72
No priest available for administering Last Rites for the dying.	4	12	85	1	9	89
No resident priest in the parish, but only a lay parish administrator and visiting priests.	7	32	60	8	38	54

shortage. The younger the layperson, the more intense the feeling about restructuring parish life and the less interest in recruiting more priests. In further analysis we found three other noteworthy patterns — (1) the more educated the layperson, the less interest in recruiting more priests, (2) the less regular the layperson is in Mass attendance, the less interest in recruiting priests, and (3) women are less interested in recruiting priests than men — among both adults and students.[24]

These findings took us by surprise. They indicate that the laity desire more participatory parish life, and achieving it is important to them — apparently even more important than acquiring more priests to bring back the conditions of the recent past. The lay attitudes do not deny a problem of priest shortage but merely tell us that laity see it as one problem among several, and certainly not the most preeminent one today. Restructuring parish leadership is more urgent.

We included an additional series of items in the adult survey and campus ministry leader survey, asking attitudes about possible reductions of priestly activities in the future. Table 3 has the exact form of the questions and the results.[25] The eight types of reduction of priestly activities are realistic, judging from the scenarios being developed by diocesan planners thinking about the worsening priest shortage. Will laity accept them?

The answer is no. The least acceptable prospect is "no priest available for administering Last Rites for the dying," deemed not at all acceptable to 85 percent of the laity. Second least acceptable is "no priest available for visiting the sick," not acceptable to 75 percent. Third least acceptable is "reduce the number of Masses to less than once a week," not acceptable to 71 percent. Attitudes of adult laity and college student leaders are similar in evaluating these possibilities. The most unacceptable situations have to do with access to the sacraments.

We looked further into these responses, breaking them down by age, sex, frequency of Mass attendance, and so on. The patterns in the breakdowns were weak and difficult to interpret, telling us that the feelings are broadly felt among Catholic laity and Catholic college students. We conclude that laity will not easily accept any great reduction in priestly services. They want the same access to the sacraments they are accustomed to now, and they will be unhappy if the access is reduced. (Some mitigation of lay reaction in such a circumstance could be achieved through plenty of advance warning and widespread education.)

An important research finding in this regard was reported in Chicago in 1985. The Archdiocese of Chicago has been doing long-range planning in a "Project 1990," and as a part of the project a team of researchers interviewed lay leaders in 23 parishes. The interviewers talked about "mega-trends" in society and in the church, then asked the lay leaders their views of the future. The results were quoted in *The Chicago Catholic*:

> "The message was quite clear," the report states. The leaders were saying, "We need and want full-time priests to serve us, whether they are celibate, male, or not. In short: There is no shortage of vocations to the priesthood, but only to the qualifications. . . which have been set." The report states that the desire to obtain married men and women to the priesthood was found in both the "liberal-minded" and "conservative-minded" parishes.[26]

The Chicago lay leaders were adamant about wanting priests to serve them, and this need was so urgent that it overrode current rules about eligibility for ordination. The newspaper account of the Chicago report continues to discuss differences in reactions to the shortage.

The report defined a liberal parish as a "parish with a history of clergy who have actively involved laity in co-responsibility for the parish life." A conservative parish is "one where the clergy continue to be in charge of parish life, where there is a sense that the parish belongs to the priests and not to the parishioners." Both types of parishes exist in the archdiocese. Faced with a clergy shortage, the two types responded differently. In a parish where laity have some sense of "ownership" of the parish, the report says, leaders responded by saying, "Let's start strategizing tonight!" In conservative parishes the response was more likely, "What will happen to us?"[27]

The research findings appear to be inconsistent. First the respondents to our 1985 surveys said they consider restructuring parish life to be more important than recruiting many more priests. Then they said that a reduction in access to the sacraments would be unacceptable, and the Chicago parish leaders agree. But this implies that they want adequate numbers of priests. Do they want more priests, or don't they? The only plausible conclusion appears to be that access to the sacraments is very important and restructuring parish life is also very important. Relative to these desires, feelings about more or fewer priests are somehow secondary.

Table 3 should lay to rest an argument I have sometimes heard, saying that American laity wouldn't mind a reduction in priestly services, since in other parts of the world, for example Latin America, the number of priests per 10,000 Catholics is much lower, yet the people there are happy. The argument is empirically wrong. American laity are accustomed to a certain level of priestly services and want the situation to continue.

Is There a Priest Shortage?

To sum up the argument to this point, the decline in priests results in some winners and some losers. The biggest losers are the bishops, since they lose their professional leadership corps and are faced with a decline in leadership quality. The priests themselves seem to be losers more than winners, but many priests have no feelings on the question. The laity are not yet affected very much, and most don't have any attitudes at all about the priest shortage. The main winners are those laity who want more participation in church ministry or who hope for changes in church structures.

Since the bishops are the biggest losers, we might expect them to put on the most pressure for recruiting more vocations. They will pass on a strong signal to vocation directors. Since priests have lukewarm feelings and laity have almost no feelings, priests and laity will not share the same feelings of concern, and vocation directors can be expected to complain that priests and laity are not helping them. They will say that they feel like "lone rangers" out to do a difficult job, getting no help. Exactly this is the situation in the middle 1980s.

One topic hasn't been discussed yet in this chapter, and that is: How many priests are needed for maximizing the total mission of the church? That is, if we begin by considering the total mission of the church rather than the interests of one group or another, do we conclude there is a shortage, or not? Robert Sherry analyzes this question from several viewpoints in a helpful recent article.[28] He argues that the mission of the church is vast and can use many more trained and committed full-time personnel than it has. I agree. I think the number of full-time personnel should be increased. The church should have as many and as good personnel as possible, so long as they can be supported financially, organizationally, and spiritually, and so long as they do not set themselves off as some sort of elite corps which discourages participation by all laity. I believe that the organizational problems can be handled, so I suggest, for starters, that the number of personnel be *doubled*. The church's total mission would be advanced.

Let us be clear about the concept "shortage." The limitations to full-time church personnel in reality are (a) the number of capable candidates available for the positions, (b) the dollars available to pay them,

Table 4

Comparable Data on Three Denominations

	Roman Catholic	Episco-palian	Lutheran Church in America
Members per Minister or Priest[a]	912	245	372
Contributions per Member[b] (not including school tuition)	$125 (est.)	$339	$205
Total Contributions per Minister or Priest	(unknown)	$83,000	$76,000

Sources: Yearbook of American and Canadian Churches, 1986 (1984 data); Official Catholic Directory, 1985 (1984 data).

[a] Membership is "inclusive membership" as reported in annual reports. For the Catholics it is "Catholic population" in the Directory. Numbers of ministers or priests include retired persons and those active in ministry but not in parishes. The Episcopalian figure was estimated by the Office of Professional Ministry of the Episcopal Church (11,317 in 1984).

[b] The Episcopalian and Lutheran figures are from the Yearbook, based on "inclusive membership." The Catholic figure comes from three research projects and is based on registered Catholics; it is more equivalent to the other figures than contributions per person of the Catholic population.

and (c) the organizational structure available to coordinate and support them. If any of these limits are reached, we can speak of a "shortage," either of candidates, dollars, or organization.

Comparisons with the Episcopal Church and the Lutheran Church in America will help clarify the argument. Look at the data in Table 4. In the Episcopal Church there are 245 laypersons per full-time priest, and in the Lutheran Church in America, the figure is 372 laypersons. Both denominations are proportionately much more staffed with clergy than the Roman Catholic Church, where the figure is 912. In both the Episcopal Church and the Lutheran Church in America there are abundant numbers of qualified seminarians, male and female, who would like to serve as full-time priests, and the organizational structures have been in place for years. Both denominations could undoubtedly carry out their overall mission more fully with more professional leaders, but they have financial limitations. The Episcopalian Church has more dollars per member in contributions, partly explaining why it has more clergy. But both denominations are operating at their financial limits.

The Catholic Church, by contrast, appears to have dollars and organizational support available for an increase in priests, but it lacks capable candidates for the priesthood. It has a candidate shortage. This is true even though the level of contributions is much lower. (The figure of $125 in Table 4 is an estimate, which we made in consultation with three experts on Catholic parishes. We are certain that the true figure is somewhere between $115 and $135.)[29]

We hoped to make some analysis of financial support available in the Catholic Church, but we were not able to do much because of lack of information. The bottom line of Table 4 demonstrates a possible line of analysis. In the Episcopal Church, one full-time minister is hired for every $83,000 in contributions, and in the Lutheran Church in America, one is hired for every $76,000 in contributions. These figures might help us estimate how many priests or full-time lay ministers could be hired in the Catholic Church if costs were roughly comparable. If we knew this, we could speak with more precision.

Several pieces of specific information are missing. First, there is no precise information on the costs of hiring Catholic priests. Good data can be assembled on salary levels, but the total cost of training, housing, paying, and pensioning priests has not been determined on any broad basis. From the information we have, the total cost seems similar to the costs of hiring Episcopalian or Lutheran ministers. Second, many Catholic parishes have an additional burden of supporting schools. The Notre Dame study of parishes found that in 1983, 45 percent of all parishes had a primary or secondary school, which was partly supported by parish contributions. But we lack data on the average amount of those contributions as a percentage of parish income. Third, although we know that registered Catholics contribute an average of $125 per year to the church, we lack the number of registered Catholics. Other researchers have estimated that the number is 50 percent to 80 percent of all Catholics. The Notre Dame researchers judged that one-third to one-fourth of all Catholics are not registered; this would put the percentage registered between two-thirds and three-fourths. But we also don't know the total number of Catholics, since methods of counting them differ. As a result, the bottom line of Table 4 has "unknown" in the Catholic column. But when we made initial estimates, we were led to guess that the figure is not greatly different from the Episcopal and Lutheran figures.

This is only a guess. If future research finds that it is true, we would conclude that the Catholic Church is now staffed more or less up to its financial limits, just like the other two denominations. Then we could not expect any noteworthy expansion of professional staff unless the laity contributed more money. We *could* still expect an expansion in lay ministers, as the number of priests decline and laity are hired to replace them — but not overall expansion. In such a situation some new options would warrant investigation, such as utilization of part-time priests whose main income comes from secular work; indeed, in the late 1980s several Protestant denominations are experimenting with the idea. But if our guess turns out to be false, or if laity are willing to contribute more money, the financial limitations would not loom large. Unfortunately we lack data.

What is interesting in this respect is that in the past two years all the Catholic experts I consulted agreed that "money is not the problem" in future Catholic parish leadership. In their view, the reasons why Catholic contributions are lower than Lutheran contributions — when the level of family income in the two denominations is roughly the same — are that Catholics have been less consistently challenged with giving as integral to their spiritual life, and parish finances have less consistent-

34 Future of Catholic Leadership

ly been explained to the laity by other laity. All observers agree that levels of giving can be raised in most parishes if the people are effectively served by the priests and staff, if laity are involved in parish decision-making, and if the meaning of giving is stated forthrightly. The experts (including a bishop) told me stories of how contributions in this or that parish they knew doubled within a year or two after an effective pastor came, replacing a less effective one.

Monsignor Joseph Champlin of Syracuse has been a leader in the development of parish giving. He has recommended challenging laity to tithe, that is, to give a tenth of their total income before taxes, dividing it between 5 percent to the parish and 5 percent to the world's poor through other channels. If people can't do this, they should set lower goals for themselves. He stresses that giving must be understood as a religious, not just an organizational, act. He has worked in several hundred parishes to date, and in the Diocese of Syracuse giving in the 100 or so parishes he has assisted has increased an average of over 40 percent. Monsignor Champlin stressed in an interview that there is more money available in the Catholic community than is being contributed now.[30]

Our analysis is not at all precise, but it does suggest that any sizeable increase in professional staff in the Catholic Church, clerical or lay, will depend on increased contributions. Meanwhile we can expect tensions with other people desiring their share of the available dollars, especially Catholic school administrators.

What remains to be discussed is whether the full-time personnel in the Catholic Church in the future should be priests or laypersons (including brothers or sisters). To answer this, the first consideration must be the number of priests needed to maintain satisfactory access of laity to the sacraments. Robert Sherry considers this question and reflects that the present-day concern over reduced access to the sacraments does not date back farther than ten years. So he proposes the laity-per-priest figure of 1975 (791 according to his calculations) as a minimum standard of priests needed.[31] By this standard the number needed in 1985 would be 66,101, contrasted to the actual number of 57,317 (based on membership figures in the *Official Catholic Directory*). That is, the shortage of priests in 1985 was about 8,800. In 1990 it will be about 13,000. These calculations seem reasonable and useful for understanding the needs of sacramental ministry.

We emerge with the conclusion that there is a shortage of priests of perhaps 8,800 today. But the goal of the church should not be merely to find the 8,800 priests; rather it should be to expand professional staff in ways which genuinely promote thc mission of the church — be the staff clerical or lay — until limits of candidates, dollars, or organizational support are hit. At present there is a shortage of priesthood candidates but no limit to the number of lay ministry candidates. Organizational structures are fairly well in place. Thus, the first limit looming ahead is dollars to pay the augmented staffs.

But there is still ambiguity in the analysis. Remember that levels of contributions in the future will in turn depend on quality of leadership in parishes. That is, effective leadership evokes enough financial support to provide more staff and even more effective leadership. It is the old story of the chicken and the egg. We will return to this topic later.

Options for Action

The remainder of this book has two themes. Chapters 2 and 3 analyze social change in America which puts pressure on the institutional church in various ways. Then Chapters 4, 5, 6, and 7 look more closely at eleven options for coping with the priest shortage. The options are of four types: reshape parish life or institutions to reduce the need for priests (discussed in Chapter 4), get more priests, using existing eligibility criteria (Chapter 5), get more priests by broadening the eligibility criteria (Chapter 6), and expand the diaconate and lay ministries (Chapter 7). Chapter 8 ventures some conclusions. We believe that the eleven options exhaust the possibilities for responding to the priest shortage, short of theological reformulations, and hence the basic issue facing the church is which one or ones to choose.

2

The Historical and Social Context

Like all institutions, religious institutions thrive only in certain social and cultural conditions. When the conditions are favorable, they grow, and their leaders take credit or attribute it to the Holy Spirit. When the conditions are unfavorable, the institutions weaken, and the leaders are troubled. Some blame themselves for poorer leadership than their forebears had provided a generation earlier, and others look for one or another approach to turn the corner and bring back the old glory days. Debates grow up about what went wrong. In such a situation most church leaders are helped by an analysis of underlying social trends which have been subtly helping or hurting them all along, but which are invisible from the midst of everyday life pressures.

A clear depiction of social trends influencing religious institutions helps everyone see present-day trends in a more realistic context. But often it leaves church leaders unsatisfied, since most social trends are too powerful to be influenced, and leaders eager for action feel frustrated in the face of them. Like it or not, churches cannot do much to change migration patterns, urbanization and suburbanization, methods of mate selection, or forms of recreation. The task of leadership is to carry out God's mission as well as possible within the givenness of the historical situation.

Who Are American Catholics?

We begin at the basic level of who American Catholics are, how they got here, and what their life circumstances are. The majority of Catholics in America arrived in two major waves of immigration. The first wave was the one most commonly described in history books — the European immigration which began in about the 1830s, peaked at the turn of the century, and ended in the middle 1920s when new immigration laws cut it off almost completely. Between 1820 and 1920, 33.6 million immigrants came to the U.S. The largest Catholic ethnic groups in this immigration were the Irish and German, who together made up about half of the total. Next largest in representation were the Italians and Polish.[1] The second wave is the one going on today. Since 1965, when American immigration quotas were abandoned, a new stream of immigrants began arriving, but now mostly from Latin America and Asia. They are coming from a different direction; today Los Angeles is the new Ellis Island. Someone has suggested that the Statue of Liberty be moved from New York to Los Angeles International Airport.

Most important for understanding today's Catholic community is the first wave of immigration — the European. It ended in the late 1920s, that is, 60 years ago. In 1977 Greeley reported on the immigrant generation of Catholics at that time:

We know that in 1974, 85 percent of American Catholics were born in this country, that 40 percent of them had at least one foreign-born parent, and that 80 percent had at least one foreign-born grandparent. One can then say that at the present time 15 percent of the American Catholic population is first generation, 25 percent is second generation, 40 percent is third generation, and 20 percent is fourth generation -- two-fifths of American Catholics are either immigrants or the children of immigrants.[2]

The vast majority of Catholics in the first immigration settled in the economic core of the nation — roughly a rectangle with corners at Boston, Baltimore, Milwaukee, and St. Louis. The southern border was approximately the Potomac and Ohio Rivers. This was the heartland of Catholicism in the late 19th and early 20th centuries, where 72 percent of all Catholics lived in 1916.[3] Most chose to live in cities, more on the average than Protestant Americans.

The second immigration, from 1965 to today, is less well-known and less researched. It began when the McCarran-Walter Immigration Act was amended to eliminate the national origins quota system, which until then had preserved the overwhelmingly European character of the nation. At once a large-scale immigration began from outside of Europe, and about a half-million arrived annually throughout the 1970s. In 1984, of the 544,000 legal immigrants, the largest numbers were from Mexico (57,000, or more than 10 percent), followed by the Philippines (42,000) and Viet Nam (37,000).[4] Almost all are Hispanic or Asian. Many of the new immigrants are undocumented; a 1983 research team estimated the number at 2 to 4 million, mostly Hispanic. Other estimates have varied from 3.5 million to 7 million.[5]

The second immigration is entering the U.S. from the West and Southwest. The main destination is California; 64 percent of the Asians and 35 percent of the Hispanics go there. Whereas the first Catholic immigration started in the North and East, the new immigration is starting in the West and Southwest.

According to the 1980 census, 14.6 million Americans are Hispanics. A 1984 survey estimated the figure at 17.6 million. Ninety percent of them live in cities and towns. An estimate for the year 2000, based on present trends, has predicted 30 to 35 million Hispanics in the nation.[6]

Given the economic problems and population pressures in Mexico and Central America, it is highly likely that immigration — legal or illegal — will continue in large volume. There is no end in sight to the new immigration from the south, and realistically nothing can stop it. New immigration laws, or border patrols, or even a Chinese wall along the Rio Grande cannot stop it. The pressures are too great. The numbers of Hispanics in the U.S. will double or triple or more. Already Los Angeles is over 50 percent Hispanic, and by 1990 Chicago will be over 50 percent Hispanic.

The percentage of Catholics in the new immigration is high. Among Hispanics about 95 percent are nominal Catholics when they arrive. But in the U.S., fundamentalist Protestant and Pentecostal groups vigorously evangelize them, and some are lost to the Catholic Church. Theologian Allan Figueroa Deck estimates that 10 percent to 25 percent of Hispanic Catholics are involved with a fundamentalist sect, and perhaps higher in Southern California.[7] A survey of Hispanics in metropolitan New York City found that 83.5 percent said they were Catholic, just under 10 percent said they were Protestant, and the rest had no religious preference.[8] The years ahead will see a vigorous competition for the religious loyalties of Hispanic immigrants.

Assimilation

In the European Catholic immigration, assimilation pressures were inevitable. Whereas some community leaders resisted American ways and tried to keep Old World culture intact, they could not hold back the strong opposite forces. Many leaders of the immigrant communities embraced American ideals such as free enterprise, democracy, religious freedom, education, and making money any legal way possible. Involvement in politics called for intergroup cooperation and ethnically balanced tickets. Intermarriage followed—first among groups from different provinces of each homeland (for example, between Germans from different areas in Germany), then between Catholic nationality groups. Higher education came within the reach of many within a generation or two, further immersing Catholics in mainstream American culture. The impact of the assimilation process was so far-reaching that it is basic to any understanding of American Catholicism in the 20th century.

Assimilation is a process which has occupied sociological theorists for decades. Arnold Rose, a student of American immigration, defined "assimilation" as:

> the adoption by a person or group of the culture of another social group to such a complete extent that the person or group no longer has any characteristics identifying him with his former culture and no longer has any particular loyalties to his former culture. Or, the process leading to this adoption.[9]

Assimilation is not only one-way; it can be two-way, as each group affects the other. But it normally is very unbalanced, with one group dominant. Assimilation can be prevented, if the subordinate group puts social or institutional barriers around itself. The barriers may be consciously constructed, or they may be unconscious. An example of conscious barriers is the set of community institutions erected by the Pennsylvania Amish to prevent assimilation of their people into the surrounding "English" culture. An example of unconscious barriers is the radical cultural disjunction between American culture and many Native American tribes.

It could have happened that Catholic immigrants to the U.S.A. would have developed barriers around themselves to prevent assimilation to the English-dominated, Protestant culture. But for the most part they did not. Except in the early decades after immigration, the dominant pattern of Catholic history in the U.S. has been one of assimilation.

The early decades were different. The institutional Catholic Church was a potent instrument for preventing assimilation, setting up defenses around the immigrant communities and providing the people with social and educational support. This is the meaning of the "siege mentality" interpretation of the ethnic church phase, which historians trace well into the 20th century. Bishops and priests erected walls, religiously and sometimes physically, between their people and the Protestants, lest the Catholic faith be lost. The Vatican helped mightily in this endeavor by its suspicion and even condemnation of much that Americans stood for. The "Syllabus of Errors" issued by Pope Pius IX in 1864 amounted to a frontal condemnation of religious freedom, separation of church and state, and democratic government. And in 1899, Pope Leo XIII issued the encyclical *Testem Benevolentiae*, further lambasting American culture and thought. In the "Modernist controversy" the Vatican demands for orthodoxy had the effect of holding back assimilation pressures in America for almost half a century.[10]

But the historical processes in American towns and cities were such that assimilation pressures could not be contained. Institutional Catholic resistance weakened in the 1940s and 1950s, then collapsed in the 1960s. The experiences of the Kennedy presidency, the papacy of John XXIII, and the Vatican Council decisively told American Catholics that they were fully American and that it was okay.

By the 1980s the assimilation of the first immigration of Catholics has moved quite far. Today Catholics partake fully in the societal network of institutions and corporations, they have intermarried with many non-Catholics, they feel almost entirely free from discriminatory behavior and prejudice, and they have few conflicts with other Americans.

Assimilation, in my opinion, should not been seen as either good or bad from a Christian ethics viewpoint. The New Testament severed Christianity from an identification with a particular culture ("There is neither Jew nor Greek," Gal. 3:28), thus de-emphasizing assimilation questions. Yet in the real world people have strong feelings about assimilation versus maintenance of tradition, with predictable outcomes. An experience of assimilation produces parties in the group undergoing the process, which battle each other over the specifics of assimilation — such as the use of one language or the other in worship, specific laws of ritual or purity, religious versus secular education, intermarriage with outsiders, and so on. Parties of this type have arisen in American Catholicism as well as in other immigrant religious groups.

I am arguing that assimilation, analyzed sociologically, helps us to understand very much in American Catholic history and also sensitizes us to the overall direction future events are likely to take. Decisions by bishops and councils will guide the institutional church in one way or another but always within the outer limits of what is socially and culturally possible. Some sensitivity to overall directions of social change will help us discern in a general way what will probably be viable or not viable in years ahead. Two well-informed Catholics told me within the last year that with regard to the future of the Catholic Church in America, all bets are off. Anything can happen. Both told me that the events since the 1950s were all unexpected, and even today no one knows what might happen. This way of thinking pays too much attention to the political process of decision-making and not enough to underlying social processes. We can do better. All bets are not off. We can

make general statements about the pressures on the hierarchy and the
directions in which future decisions, at some time or other, will have to
go. Eugene Kennedy states the argument well:

> The essential changes of the coming decade will not follow
> from agreements or documents signed and sealed by church of-
> ficials but from the already well-established attitudes and be-
> havior of the believing community. . . . The best predictions
> about tomorrow are based on what people are doing today.
> These are the only reliable mega-trends.[11]

Facilitators of Assimilation

I have said that in general any social policy or behavior which lowers
barriers between one's group and surrounding groups, and any policy or
behavior which promotes more intimate contact with those groups, will
facilitate assimilation. Examples can be cited in American Catholic life.
I will point to five.

First, adoption of a common language is very important, and this has
happened as virtually all ethnic groups in America, Catholic or non-
Catholic, have adopted English for popular discourse and often for worship. No important language enclaves remain in American Catholicism
except those resulting from the most recent immigration — mostly
Spanish.

Second, movement from ethnic urban neighborhoods to non-ethnic
suburbs in which Catholics live side by side with non-Catholics speeds
up assimilation. Suburbanization of Catholics has occurred in all
American Eastern and Midwestern cities. In the Mountain and Pacific
regions the history has been slightly different in that few ethnic Catholic
neighborhoods ever did exist. They are hardly to be found west of, say,
Omaha or Kansas City. We would therefore expect that assimilation
would be faster in the Mountain and Pacific regions than on the Eastern

seaboard, and all indications are that exactly this has happened. Everyone agrees that Eastern seaboard Catholicism is closer to European ways than Midwestern and Western Catholicism.

Third, intermarriage with non-Catholics is a strong force for assimilation. Today the intermarriage rate is between 40 percent and 45 percent, up about 6 or 8 percentage points since the 1950s.[12] That is, for every 100 Catholics getting married in the late 1980s, between 40 and 45 are marrying non-Catholics (usually Protestants).

Fourth, education of Catholic youth in non-Catholic high schools and colleges speeds assimilation. In the late 1980s, of every 100 Catholics in college, between 9 and 10 are in Catholic colleges.[13] Today the brightest Catholic youth seem to prefer non-Catholic colleges. Early in 1986 the National Merit Scholarship Corporation listed the 51 colleges who had attracted the most National Merit scholars in 1985 (a total of 6,021). None of the top 51 were Catholic institutions. Some other church-related institutions were in the list, such as Baylor, Southern Methodist, and Brigham Young, but no Catholic colleges.[14]

The fifth facilitator of assimilation is more difficult to discuss with any precision. It is consumption of American mass media, especially secular television and press. These media are overwhelmingly secular, though almost never consciously anti-Catholic or opposed to any other religious tradition. The secular media subtly produce a common culture which is religiously neutral and which of course contains few elements specific to Catholicism. Religious denominations are treated like rival brands in a religious marketplace.

The assimilation model is empirically testable, and it stands up well under test. From the model, the corollary follows that change will be faster among educated young adults than others in the community, since they are in closer contact with the surrounding culture; indeed, that has been the case for Catholics.[15] Secondly, it follows that change should be faster in geographical locations away from the immigrant ports of entry and first settlement; that is also the case. The main locus of innovation in Catholic church life today is the Midwest and West. Thirdly, it follows that the pace of change will vary, predictable from existing channels of communication or barriers to comnunication. That is also the case today, with assimilation greatest in the middle-class urban areas and least in ethnic enclaves and rural areas.

Four Questions About Assimilation

From the vantage point of the five facilitators outlined above, we can gain some perspective on four important questions about Catholicism which the assimilation model poses. First, can the process be slowed down if Catholic leaders decide to do so? It would not be easy. It cannot be slowed down by church pronouncements or by attempts to enforce rules of living which the people don't strongly agree with. But some limited impact could be made through Catholic university life and parish life. To realize the difficulty of slowing down assimilation, consider what it would take to get more Catholic students into Catholic colleges and universities. Or consider what it would take to reduce interfaith marriage; to do so one would have to alter the sociology of mate selection in the U.S.

Second, is the assimilation of American Catholics completed? Has it run its course or somehow come to a conclusion? A precise answer is impossible, but my impression is that the answer is no. There are still distinctive elements in American Catholic culture, such as a high level of denominational loyalty, a unique attitude toward clergy, and unique motivations regarding Mass attendance and devotions. And there is still a different attitude toward marriage of a Catholic with an Episcopalian from the attitude toward, for example, marriage of a Lutheran with an Episcopalian, or a Lutheran with a Methodist. Andrew Greeley agrees that assimilation is still in process, and it will continue:

The transformation from immigrant to professional upper-middle class for non-Hispanic Catholics has been achieved almost completely. . . All the indicators are that the pace and the scope of this transformation will continue and accelerate in the remaining years of the century.[16]

Third, can anything be learned about the future of Catholic institutions by looking at other religious groups? This question is often raised in discussions, and it is rich with implications. My guess is that American Catholics in the future will come to resemble other groups lying directly ahead on the assimilation path. These groups are the Lutherans and Episcopalians — mostly the Lutherans. The Episcopalians are theologically and liturgically similar but include strong elements of elitism less commonly found among Catholics. The Lutherans have less of this but they have a fundamentalist faction in the Missouri Synod. If we turn our attention away from the Episcopalian elites and the Missouri Synod fundamentalists, the idea becomes useful. Even today, German Catholics and German Lutherans in the American Midwest are almost indistinguishable culturally. In many respects, then, today's Episcopalians and Lutherans predict tomorrow's Catholics.

It follows that some future pressures on the Catholic Church can be discerned now by looking at the Episcopalian and Lutheran churches. This is true in principle, but concretely it remains an exercise in guesswork. The analyst must look for elements in Episcopalian and Lutheran church life which are not theologically specific to them (that is, which Catholics share) and which seem important and legitimate based on members' experiences in middle-class America. I would guess that three such elements are (a) a desire for total financial accountability of the church to members, at all levels, (b) a desire for lay participation in parish decision-making, including budget priorities and staff hiring, and (c) a desire for more sense of supportive community life in parishes or other faith groupings. These are guesses. Research could be carried out to test them empirically.

An important qualification needs to be made, and it can be introduced by the fourth question: Can we speak of a "Protestantization" of
American Catholicism? The term is frequently used. I agree that many
of the changes have been in the direction of Protestant religious life. But
the term "Protestantization" is misleading and should not be used. The
reason is that it implies too much control of American culture by the
Protestants. Perhaps it was apt a century ago, but not today, since today
the Protestant churches are also caught in pressures for change which
feel to Protestants as if they are coming from outside, and (to simplify a
bit) *are* coming from outside. Whereas once Protestant spokesmen were
to a great extent in control of developments in American culture, they
are no longer. W. Clark Roof and William McKinney speak of "dises-
tablishment" of mainstream Protestantism in a culture no longer
responding to it.[17] Social changes are just as bewildering to Protestant
church leaders as to Catholic leaders. So the pressures for Catholic assimilation today come from sources deeper and broader in American
culture than just Protestantism, and the term "Protestantization" misses
the point.

I have been arguing that social pressures are pushing the Catholic
Church in the general direction of the Protestant experience, even
though the source of the pressures is broader than the Protestant churches. The prospect of increasing resemblance to Protestant denominations is not an unmixed blessing. The problems besetting the mainline
Protestant churches in America today are deep enough to give pause to
anyone seeing his or her religious community headed in that direction.
Membership is down — especially among educated young adults,
theological identity is in a situation of drift, leaders are beset with feelings of malaise, and there is a prospect of becoming mere culture
religion.[18] I cannot go into the specifics here, but as a summary I can say
that whereas the main problems of American Catholicism in the 1980s
are institutional, not spiritual, the problems of mainline Protestantism
are spiritual, not institutional. American Catholicism needs organiza-

tional change to free the Spirit and energize the people, while mainline Protestantism needs to regain spiritual touch with its people. Organizational change in Catholicism would strengthen, not weaken, it.

Vatican II and After

The analysis presented here can provide some clarification about the effects of Vatican Council II, which met from 1962 to 1965. It was the most important historical event in modern Catholic history. The Council documents strongly affirmed open-style Catholicism, which most Americans liked, and the documents produced new spiritual energy in our country. English was approved in place of Latin in the Mass, the liturgy became more participative, rules about abstinence were changed, and congregational hymn-singing was greatly increased. The relation of church to state was clarified in the direction most American Catholics felt was right. Quasi-democratic structures appeared at all levels — parish, diocese, and national. The doctrine of the church shifted away from apostolic authority to emphasis on the "people of God."

The volume and speed of the innovations after the Council demonstrate that American Catholics were ready. They had been waiting for some time for a signal from Rome which allowed them to do what they inwardly felt should be done. The Council, that is, was not solely the cause of the developments after 1965, but it must be seen in the perspective of assimilation pressures. The most helpful model to explain these events is that of a dam across a river. Water slowly builds up creating more and more pressure, and when the floodgates are once opened, the water rushes out with vast stored-up energy. Then after a time the flow decreases as the water level subsides.[19] The Council had this character. Pope John XXIII wanted to open the windows of the church, as he put it, and hear the feelings and recommendations of Catholics everywhere.

The model of the river and the floodgate helpfully distinguishes underlying social pressures from the effects of institutional decisions. It can shed light on the current debate about the effects of the Council. One faction argues that the Council ruined the Church, and the other that it saved the Church from disaster a little later. The evidence seems to indicate that it had a modest impact on guiding the general direction of changes in the Church, but it does not explain the high level of spiritual energy and the rapidity of the changes. No one had to sell the Council teachings to the American laity; the teachings sold themselves.

The pace of change slowed after the middle 1970s, and a sort of normalcy returned, which, as we will see, has brought spiritual benefits and a new self-confidence. An important event took place on May 3, 1983, with the publication of the bishops' pastoral letter on war and peace. This was something new for American Catholics, and it was greeted by other Americans with genuine surprise. The bishops were addressing the most central moral issue of our age in a way which spoke to all earnest people, not just Catholics, and which pierced through layers of propaganda by government and special interests.   The document was the result of an exemplary process of consultations, hearings, and theological debate. The American Catholic leadership enjoyed two solid years of unprecedented positive publicity, and they were taken more seriously by all Americans than ever before. In 1985 and 1986 a similar process began toward formulating a pastoral letter on the American economy, another central moral issue of our age similarly beset with layer upon layer of propaganda.

Trends in the Catholic Community

I have said that the Catholic Community has been undergoing rapid change and that the change affects feelings about religion and the church. Here I will review several recent studies giving more detail. Table 5 compares Catholics, Protestants, and Jews on education and family income. It is based on nationwide polls between 1982 and 1984. At that time 14 percent of all Catholics 18 or older in the U.S. were college graduates, and Catholics had a median family income of about

Table 5
Educational and Income Levels, 1982-1984

	Percent College Graduates	Approximate Median Family Income
Roman Catholic Total	14	$20,500
Irish Catholic	26	25,000
German Catholic	16	20,400
Polish Catholic	11	22,900
Italian Catholic	12	22,900
Hispanic Catholic	5	13,200
Protestant Total	15	17,300
Methodist	18	18,300
Baptist	8	14,100
Lutheran	14	20,500
Episcopalian	44	25,300
Presbyterian	27	23,000
Jewish	44	31,000

Source: General Social Survey, 1982-84.

$20,500. They were about as well educated, on average, as Protestants and had somewhat higher income levels. But both Protestants and Catholics were far behind American Jews in education and income. Within the Protestant community the denominations most similar to Catholics were the Lutherans and Methodists.

Using earlier nationwide surveys, Andrew Greeley was able to look at historical trends in college-going by various religious and ethnic groups. He found that the Catholic propensity to go to college matched the Protestant rate already in the 1950s and 1960s (if Hispanic Catholics are not included). In the period of about 1965-75 the college-going rates of youth in various groups were: Protestant, 41 percent; Irish Catholic, 59 percent; Polish Catholic, 49 percent; German Catholic, 45 percent; Italian Catholic, 45 percent; Slavic Catholic, 42 percent; and French Catholic, 19 percent.[20]

Figure 6 depicts trends in fertility of Catholic and non-Catholic women, using "Total Marital Fertility Rate" as a measure. It is the number of births a married woman would have by the end of a specified number of years of marriage if she reproduces at the then current rate for women of each duration.[21] The baby boom of 1950-1960 was disproportionately a Catholic phenomenon, but more important here is the convergence between Catholic and non-Catholic fertility during the 1970s. The fertility rates for the latest period in the figure are only slightly over two births per woman.

Not only in births but also in birth control practices there has been convergence between Catholics and non-Catholics. Charles Westoff calculated the percentage of married Catholic women aged 18-39 who were conforming to Catholic Church teachings banning any use of contraceptive methods other than periodic continence. A dramatic change occurred between the early 1950s and the early 1970s; of the women married less than five years in the early 1950s, 80 percent were conforming to church teachings, but of their counterparts in the early 1970s, the figure was only 9.5 percent. Of the women married 5 to 9 years in the

Figure 7

Fertility of Catholic and Non-Catholic Women

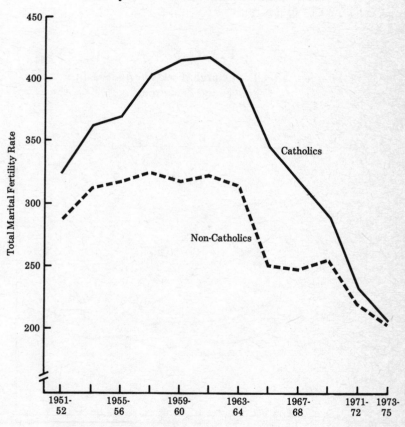

Source: Westoff (1979), p. 237.

early 1950s, 58 percent were conforming; in the early 1970s the conformity rate of their counterparts was only 4.5 percent. Westoff concludes:

The inescapable conclusion from this evidence is that Catholic contraceptive behavior has lost almost all of its distinctiveness; by 1980, there will be nothing to differentiate Catholics from non-Catholics in this area.[22]

Figure 8

Percent Attending Church Weekly by Age Strata, Catholics and Protestants

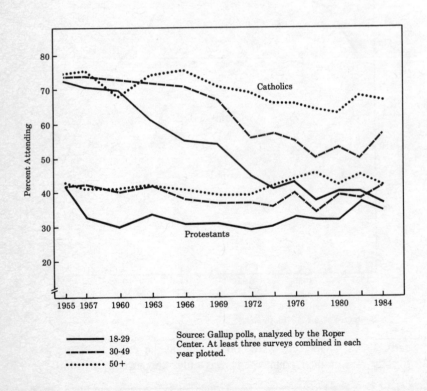

Source: Gallup polls, analyzed by the Roper Center. At least three surveys combined in each year plotted.

18-29
30-49
50+

The trends in church attendance are especially revealing of the patterns of assimilation. See Figure 8, where Gallup poll data on a question about church attendance within the past seven days is plotted. At the beginning of the time period (1955) the Catholics were attending church much more regularly than the Protestants, and in each community there was little variation in churchgoing rates by age. Then while the Protestant trends remained fairly constant (except for a decline among persons 29 or younger in the late 1950s), the Catholic trends depict the classic assimilation pattern — the younger people assimilate to the surrounding culture. That involved decreases in churchgoing until their rate reached the Protestant rate for their agemates, a convergence which took place sometime after 1980. Catholics aged 30-49 also converged toward the Protestant rate beginning in about 1970, but the convergence was only partial. Catholics 50 or older changed little during the whole period. The result is a much larger gap between young and old among Catholics than among Protestants, and a total convergence of young Catholics to young Protestant behavior levels.

Trends in Attitudes

Catholic attitudes on issues concerning sexuality and marriage became more liberal during the 1960s and early 1970s. Greeley reviewed trend data between 1963 and 1974 for Catholics in their twenties:

> One sees that the opposition to contraception fell from about half to about 4 percent; opposition to divorce from 41 percent to 11 percent; and opposition to premarital sex from 70 percent to 17 percent.[23]

Westoff and Bumpass studied changes in Catholic attitudes about sexuality from 1963 to 1973. In 1963, 29 percent of American Catholics agreed strongly that husband and wife may have sexual intercourse for pleasure alone; in 1973 the figure was 50 percent. Remarriage after divorce was approved by 52 percent in 1963 and by 73 percent in 1973. In 1963, 41 percent thought that "a family should have as many children as possible and God will provide for them;" in 1973 only 18 percent

agreed with that statement.[24] College student trend data indicates that
the greatest changes in Catholic attitudes on moral teachings were between the early 1960s and early 1970s; after about 1975 the changes
were small.[25]

Greeley concluded that ecclesiastical authority on moral questions
weakened after the issuing of *Humanae Vitae:*

> As humiliating as it may be to church leaders, it would seem
> that they have influence on their people only when their people
> decide to permit them to have such influence. The authority of
> the government apparently rests on the consent of the
> governed, not only in civil matters of the United States but also
> in Catholic ecclesiastical matters.[26]

Catholic-Protestant differences in child-rearing orientations have
disappeared. Alwin found that whereas Catholics in the 1950s stressed
obedience more and autonomy less than Protestants, by the 1970s the
Catholics had shifted so that their attitudes were the same as Protestants. Rising levels of education among Catholics were a major explanation for the shift.[27]

On feminist issues, Catholics in the early 1980s were a bit more
liberal than Protestants. Seventy-nine percent rejected the notion that a
woman's place is essentially in the home; among Protestants, 70 percent
rejected it, and among Jews, 89 percent rejected it. Thirty-one percent
agreed that women should leave politics to men; among Protestants 40
percent agreed, and among Jews it was 18 percent.[28] On repeated surveys between 1975 and 1984, Catholics supported the Equal Rights
Amendment more than Protestants.[29] Also, Catholics in the 1980s are
more likely to support the civil liberties of Communists, Socialists, and
homosexuals than are white Protestants.

Approval of interfaith marriage rose in all religious groups during the 1960s and 1970s. Between 1968 and 1983 the percentage of Americans who approved of marriage between Catholics and Protestants increased from 63 percent to 79 percent. In 1980 Catholics were more approving than were Protestants — 89 percent among Catholics, 74 percent among Protestants.[30]

On theological issues, Catholic attitudes changed in the 1960s and 1970s but not much since then. See Table 6, which shows trends between 1963 and 1985. Between 1974 and 1985 Catholics became less worried about the sinfulness of missing Mass, but on the other items the trends after 1974 were small. The biggest changes were between 1963

Table 6

Five Statements on Theology and Ecclesiology
(Percent Saying "Certainly True" or "Probably True")

	1963	1974	1985	Change 1963–74	Change 1974–85
It is a sin for a Catholic to miss weekly Mass obligation he or she easily could have attended.		69	58		−11
Under certain conditions, the Pope is infallible when he speaks on matters of faith and morals.		60	62		+2
God will punish the evil for all eternity.	73	52	53	−21	+1
Jesus directly handed over the leadership of His Church to Peter and the Popes.	86	71	68	−15	−3

Note: Changes of less than 6 percentage points are not significant and may result from random fluctuation in the samples.

and 1974; there was a 21-point drop in the belief that God will punish the evil for all eternity and a 15-point drop in the belief that Jesus directly handed over leadership of His Church to Peter and the Popes.

Gallup polls have periodically asked, "How important would you say religion is in your own life — very important, fairly important, or not very important?" The results since 1952 are shown in Figure 9. There was a decline between 1965 and 1978, with little change since then. The decline was greater among Catholics since 1952 than among Protestants, and the reason is unclear. Unlike the pattern in Figure 8, this cannot easily be interpreted in assimilation terms — though in the absence of age group trend data we cannot be very certain. It is curious that

Figure 9

Percent Saying Religion is Very Important in Their Lives

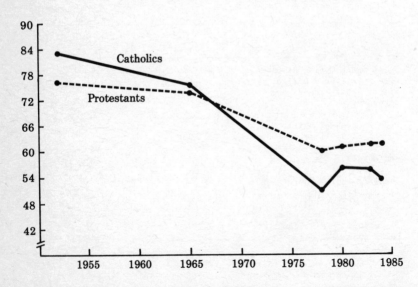

Source: *Emerging Trends,* November 1984, p. 5.

Protestants after 1965 reported that religion is less important in their lives, even though church attendance levels did not go down. It is also baffling why the Catholic line in Figure 9 should descend faster than the Protestant line. Greeley attributes the Catholic dropoff to the disillusionment many Catholics felt after *Humanae Vitae*, the papal encyclical condemning artificial birth control. Whether this is the actual reason is not clear.

In spite of the decline in feelings that religion is very important in their lives, Americans continue to have high confidence in the church as an institution. In periodic Gallup polls from 1973 to 1983, "Church or organized religion" consistently ranked first among ten institutions named, including the military, Congress, and the U.S. Supreme Court.[31] We cannot say that Americans are turning their backs on organized religion today.

To sum up, Catholics have converged with middle-class Protestants in many ways, and in some ways they have passed the Protestants. They are higher than Protestants in income, rates of college-going, support for civil liberties, and support for feminist positions. They are similar to Protestants on most questions surrounding sexuality and marriage. The life structures of today's Catholic laity are middle class, slightly in the liberal direction on many issues, and unabashedly American. Avery Dulles believes that the new laity will be more critical of all institutions, including the church, in the future:

> In an earlier day, when people were accustomed to being ruled by alien powers in every sphere of life, the institutionalism of the Church caused little difficulty. People took it for granted that they could have little control over their own lives and that someone would have to tell them what to believe and do. In a paternalistic society, a paternalistic Church was felt to be appropriate. In some respects it even offered relief from the tyranny of other institutions. But today, especially in the North Atlantic nations, people take a critical view of all institutions. If

a given institution seems well attuned to their needs and demands, people support it, but without implicit faith and ardent devotion.[32]

Parishes Today

In the late 1980s we have good information on the state of American parishes, since several research studies were done recently. A few of their findings are pertinent to issues of future leadership, and I will present them here.

The Parish Project, supported by the Bishops' Committee on the Parish from 1978 to 1982 and directed by Rev. Philip Murnion, carried out several studies, most important of which was a look at "effective parishes." They asked diocesan representatives to name two or three parishes in their dioceses which they considered very good, then they gathered extensive information on them and compared the "effective" parishes with all others in the nation. The effective parishes turned out to be of all sizes and located in all kinds of communities, similar to the overall profile of U.S. parishes. But they were unique in program and leadership. They had more programs than other parishes, especially in adult religious education, liturgy planning, and youth ministry. Compared with the overall average, they were three times more likely to have set up mini-parishes or small communities.

Leadership of the effective parishes tended to be open and participative in style. Compared with the overall average of parishes, they were more likely to have a team style of staff operation, more frequent staff meetings, more parish councils, more use of formal planning processes and leadership training, and more use of outside consultants. The effective parishes were more likely to use sisters in non-school ministries (49 percent compared with 33 percent in other parishes), deacons (50 percent versus 23 percent), and lay staff (54 percent versus 30 percent). The staffs reported that they were participative in style; two-thirds of the staffs said they were trying to operate as a team, and eight out of ten reported staff meetings at least every two or three weeks. They thought that their vitality was largely a result of the variety of programs which parishioners could participate in.[33]

In its final report, the Parish Project commented on changes in parish life in the last two decades. A major change, already noted, was the growing shortage of priests and the expansion of lay ministries and lay volunteers. A second change was a proliferation of small groups in parishes. They were prayer groups, scripture reflection groups, *comunidades de base* (largely among Hispanic Catholics), neighborhood groups, and other kinds. Typically the groups gathered similar persons together, and the participants engaged in some combination of reflection, study, discussion, and prayer. In the groups many people felt they could express themselves more intimately and trustingly, they could make connections between the religious tradition and their day-to-day situations, and they had personal support in their commitment of faith. The groups typically had lay leadership, which in itself developed lay ministers.[34]

The Notre Dame Survey of Parishes, done in 1982-84, provides us the best information on American parishes today. The survey was planned as an outgrowth of the Parish Project work. Questionnaires were sent to a careful sample of 1,900 parishes throughout the nation, and 58 percent responded. Thus the Notre Dame Survey data is on these 58 percent, undoubtedly more active than average. In a second phase, the research team carefully selected 36 parishes, representative of the total, for indepth study (Due to research difficulties, Hispanic parishes were excluded from this second phase, so the findings represent non-Hispanics only.) They sent questionnaires to the staffs of these 36 parishes and to a sample of all registered laypersons. Fifty-nine percent of the laity returned the questionnaires. Also members of the Notre Dame research team visited all 36 parishes. The result of all this work is a gold mine of information.[35]

The central theme in the Notre Dame findings was that a new kind of parish is emerging, befitting the new American Catholic. Leege states it forcefully:

> Catholics are found decreasingly in ethnic enclaves. The immigrant parish with its emphases on devotional pieties, parochial education for the children, passive liturgies, a plenitude of vocations, and hierarchical leadership is giving way to the post-Vatican II parish with biblically oriented adult education, participatory liturgies, a scarcity of priests and religious, and ministries and governance shared by the laity. When the Church began to view itself as the people of God following the Second Vatican Council, it found an American Catholic laity with many of the advantages of education and with middle-class attitudes that made it ready to assume responsibility.[36]

Today's parishes are large. Half have more than 2,300 members and half have less than that figure. Eighteen percent have fewer than 500 Catholics, and 16 percent have more than 5,000. About a third could be classified as urban, a quarter are suburban, and close to half are rural or small town. The average number of full-time priests per parish is 1.7. Three percent of the parishes have no full-time priest; more than half have one full-time priest; 25 percent have two full-time priests; and about 20 percent have three or more full-time priests.[37] About 25 percent have permanent deacons. One-third have sisters in parish ministry, not counting the sisters serving in schools. And about 30 percent have laypersons serving in professional pastoral positions.

Today's parishes have many volunteers who give countless hours of work. They carry out major responsibilities in ministries of nurture, mercy, liturgy, and governance. A majority are women. When the Notre Dame researchers counted up all the persons who fill positions of responsibility in parishes besides pastors, they found that 83 percent of the leaders are lay, and most of them are volunteers.

An estimated 76 percent of the parishes have a parish council. But the importance of the council varies widely, and often it is not the most important component of the leadership network. Other strategies have been developed — congregational assemblies, elected executive committees, special boards, and so on. Today's laypersons wish to have a say in parish governance:

> Regardless of the structure of governance, our studies clearly show that laypersons expect to participate in it. No parishes are in deeper trouble, based on measures of identification and loyalty, than those where lay involvement in formal liturgical roles and in parish governance is suppressed. It is not that laity want to dominate. They simply want to be heard and to be affirmed as responsible members of a community.[38]

About 85 percent of the registered parishioners said that their parish satisfies their religious needs, while only 45 percent feel that it meets their social needs. The suburban parish was rated by its parishioners as least likely to meet social needs. But from other data it appears that suburban Catholics typically want little more out of the church than a satisfying religious life; they conduct their social life elsewhere. It is quite the opposite in the small towns where parishioners place heavy social demands on their parishes.

Fifty percent are reasonably content with the homilies, though only 25 percent seem genuinely impressed or moved by them. Two-thirds are satisfied with the liturgy. In some respects the parish programs were seen as not meeting people's needs. The parishioners stressed practical needs in their lives:

> In fact, there is a decidedly this-worldly rather than otherworldly cast to the programmatic priorities of core Catholics. For example, not only would they like their parishes to offer more effective service when marriages are in trouble, but they

would also like to get better help on some of the things that make marriages go on the rocks — alcoholism and substance abuse, economic problems, and so on.[39]

When asked to rank the traits they most value in a pastor, parishioners named sensitivity to the needs of others by a wide margin over holiness, learning, good preaching skills, good organizing skills, or anything else. They seem to want a pastor who understands them, who consults them as responsible contributors to parish life, and who respects them.

Thomas Sweetser, S.J., has been working as a parish researcher and consultant for over fifteen years. In 1983 he published his observations on changes in parish life.[40] He said that we are seeing a shift from an authoritarian approach in parish leadership to a facilitating approach. Instead of telling people what to do, parish leaders provide occasions for people to come together to share their visions and plan their parish life. Parishes which have made the transition seem to have greater loyalty from laity. Also there has been a growth in small groups and communities in parishes, usually for worship and sharing. The need arises because of the underlying changes in community life. In the past the ethnic parishes of the American Catholic survived because they touched the need for belonging and for personal involvement. The ethnic communities created a sense of community due to commonalities in language, customs, and fears of the new world. But today the suburban parishes do not enjoy these ready-made community ties and must find new ways of uniting people. Large suburban parishes feel impersonal to many persons, and new ways must be found to tie people together. In Sweetser's experience, the new bonds will be along lines of common interests and shared concerns.

There is a trend toward greater emphasis on adult spiritual development. People hunger for a deeper relationship with their Lord, and they want to know how to include the Lord in their relationships with their spouses, children, and friends. Therefore programs of adult spirituality are becoming popular, as are parish renewal programs such as Christ Renews His Parish and RENEW. There are trends toward greater lay participation, more involvement of women, and more long-range parish planning. [41]

My own research in 1980 produced considerable information on how Catholic laypersons feel about parish life. In a nationwide study we asked around 600 persons what the direction of the Catholic Church should be in the years ahead. The topic was also discussed at some length in 36 in-depth interviews. Some of the interviewees were caught unprepared by the question and took a few minutes to assemble their thoughts, but the majority had definite thoughts to share. Three themes in their recommendations related to parish life.

First, Catholic laity want personal and accessible priests. Many asked that the priests get out more with their parishioners, try to understand the problems in people's lives, and avoid aloofness. Persons in parishes with such priests praised them, and other persons whose parishes did not seem to have such priests complained. Everyone appreciated priests who are human and approachable.

Second, many hoped for warmer, more personal parishes. We heard a number of complaints, especially from people in large and impersonal parishes, that it was hard to relate to the parish. People often asked for more fellowship and more diverse opportunities to become involved. The size of the parish was not mentioned as much as its climate, but generally, smaller-than-average parishes were preferred.

Third, people called for more support for family living. This included religious education, adult education, and family-oriented programs.

These viewpoints were voiced thoughtfully, and we took them seriously. They represent a sort of "laity agenda" for the future of parish life. They are couched in practical, down-to-earth terms and demonstrate the practical level on which most people view their spiritual and religious needs.[42]

In the 1985 surveys we were able to include two sets of questions about parish life in the nationwide survey of Catholic adults. First look at Table 7. It gives the results when we asked the respondents if eight

Table 7

Attitudes of Catholic Adults, 1985, on Whether Eight Suggestions Would Help or Hurt the Church

	39 or under		40–59		60 or older	
	Help	Hurt	Help	Hurt	Help	Hurt
Creation of more small groups in parishes to encourage face-to-face relationships.	83	3	79	4	66	4
More frequent informal relationships between priests and laity.	82	3	87	2	76	4
More influential roles for women in parishes.	80	5	81	5	51	21
Greater lay participation in decision-making in parishes.	77	6	80	9	74	7
Greater stress on obedience to priestly authority among the laity.	33	22	38	31	42	14
Allow parishes to help choose the priests who come to serve them.	55	21	58	23	47	29
Allow priests to live where they wish, not just in rectories.	38	24	34	42	23	51
More recruitment of older men into the priesthood.	57	9	74	9	63	13

suggestions for parish life would help the Church, hurt the Church, or not have any effect one way or the other. We introduced the series of suggestions with this sentence: "There have been many suggestions for possible changes in the Catholic Church in America to help it become more truly what it should be and carry out its mission more effectively. I am going to read a list of them." (The total list is shown in Appendix B, Table B-2.) Table 7 gives only the eight suggestions most pertinent to parish life, and it gives only the percent saying "Help the Church" or "Hurt the Church." The first two ideas relate to the desire for more personal parishes and more accessible priests. Both are strongly endorsed, especially by young adults. The votes are almost unanimous. The third and fourth ideas have to do with lay participation in leadership, and they are also strongly endorsed. The fifth idea, that of giving more stress to obedience to priestly authority, received mixed reactions, but more positive than negative.

The last three ideas in the table have to do with priestly leadership. The idea of allowing parishes to help choose their priests (6th in the table) received considerable support but by no means total. The idea of allowing priests to live where they wish got mixed reactions, with much opposition from older laity. Finally, the idea of recruiting older men into the priesthood got very strong support.

Here again we see the desire for more personal parishes, more personal and approachable priests, more opportunities for lay leadership, and in general a greater sense of community in parish life. One could expect that the attitudes of laity toward future parish leadership would be formed to a great extent by how they aided or impeded realization of these goals.

Table 8 shows the results of four more questions about priests in the 1985 survey of laity. All four were asked earlier, so trends are visible in the responses. The first two items ask for ratings of priests on their ability to understand people's practical problems and on their sermons. Whereas the ratings become more negative between 1952 and 1974,

Table 8

Attitudes of Catholic Adults About Priests, 1952 to 1985

	1952	1965	1974	1985
How would you rate the priests in your parish on their ability to understand your practical problems--would you say they are very understanding, fairly understanding, or not very understanding? Very understanding.	72	62	42	50
Do you think the sermons of the priests in your parish, in general, are excellent, good, fair, or poor? Excellent.	43	30	20	29

	1963	1974	1985	Change 1963-74	Change 1974-85
In general, would you say you approve or disapprove of the way the priests in your parish are handling their job? Approve.		81	88		+7
Most priests don't expect the lay members to be leaders, just followers. Agree strongly or somewhat.	46	44	39	-2	-5

from 1974 to 1985 they reversed and became more positive again. The third item asks for a rating on how priests are doing their job in general, and the rating in 1985 was more positive than in 1974. The last item has a mild change away from earlier criticism that priests don't expect laypersons to be leaders; apparently priests were perceived as more open to laypersons in 1985 than earlier. In short, all the trends since 1974 are in the direction of more positive attitudes toward priests and more appreciation of their leadership.

3

Staffing Problems in Other American Institutions

The last chapter argued that American Catholicism is in the midst of an assimilation process. Here in Chapter 3 I will focus not on assimilation but on changes in the total American culture. When the culture changes, everyone feels its effects. The most pertinent topic is how cultural changes affect institutions in their efforts to recruit and retain the best possible leadership personnel. All institutions face this problem, and all face agonizing decisions about whether their traditional policies are the best ones.

Taking a brief look at changes in other American institutions may be interesting to Catholic leaders, if only to see how others are coping. The most relevant institutions to look at are (a) certain of the Protestant denominations, (b) the military, and (c) corporations. At numerous places in this book I have discussed Protestant institutional life. In the present chapter I will look only at the military and at corporations.[1]

The closest institutional analogy to the Catholic Church with respect to professional leadership is the military. Both the American military and the Catholic Church have a two-class system — either officers or enlisted persons, and clergy or laity. (I will use the word "officer corps" for both, referring to clergy in the case of the church.) Both institutions are totally dependent on their officer corps for maintenance and effectiveness. Both must attract the officers voluntarily from the population (except for the military in a time of national emergency) through inducements and rewards, and both must attract sufficient numbers of a certain quality and retain them over a period of years. Both provide prolonged periods of indoctrination and re-socialization in military academies or seminaries, encouraging the trainees to embrace the values, beliefs, and ideals of the organization. In both, members pledge service to a "higher good," even at great personal sacrifice. Service in both organizations tends to separate the officers from the societal mainstream and to produce a distinctive subculture which makes up their total way of life. In return for service, both organizations provide their officers a version of cradle-to-grave benefits in which one is provided for in all circumstances — sickness and health, active service and retirement. And in death, one's service is honored and memorialized by current organization members as having been rendered to the greater glory of God and/or Country.

Both organizations traditionally had monopolies over the services they offered to their constituents — defense and security, or justification and salvation. (This situation is less true with respect to the Catholic Church today, in nations with religious freedom.)[2] Both are quite free from short-term evaluations utilizing yardsticks such as profit, return on investment, or percentage of votes won.

U.S. Navy, 1970-1986

We begin with the U.S. Navy, the clearest case of organizational self-analysis to improve recruitment and retention of high-quality officers. In 1970 Admiral Elmo R. Zumwalt, Jr. was appointed to be Chief of Naval Operations in the midst of a crisis of recruitment and retention. The problem existed at all levels. In that year re-enlistment rates had dropped to their lowest levels since 1955. Barely 31 percent of servicemen of all ranks and branches signed up for a second term, and in the Navy the figure was only 10 percent.[3] Initial recruitment was not a serious problem at that time, since the draft was still in effect (until 1973). But personnel turnover threatened the fighting capacity of the Navy. Admiral Zumwalt believed that innovative action was needed. He set up "retention study groups" in which about a dozen officers from a particular part of the Navy would be called to Washington for a week. Each group would spend four or five days reaching a consensus about the living and working conditions which made the Navy difficult or disagreeable, then forming recommendations which were delivered to Zumwalt in person. The first study group was of junior aviation officers, and others were from various Navy communities as diverse as destroyer and mine force officers, black officers, women officers, submarine officers, and ROTC midshipmen. As a direct result of the recommendations of these groups, major changes in personnel practices were implemented.

Zumwalt came to believe that four kinds of changes would make service in the Navy more attractive and satisfying. One would be to re-examine the regulations and practices dealing with personal behavior (dress, grooming, and so on) to bring them closer to the customs and tastes of the 1970s. Second would be to develop operational schedules, job rotation systems, and home-port facilities that would reduce the long separations from families — always the greatest obstacle to officer retention. Third would be to provide bright young men and women with more responsibility early in their careers and thus to increase their job satisfaction. Fourth would be to start ridding the Navy of its persistent discrimination against minorities and women. He pursued all four objectives.

To improve communications directly with all naval personnel, Zumwalt started a series of special messages which came to be known as "Z-Grams." During his four years he issued 120 of them, which went to all naval personnel on sea and land. They established various personnel programs, including a Human Resource Management program (which I will describe below), an Action Line telephone which could be used by any member of a ship or base to communicate directly with his or her commanding officer, Equal Opportunity programs, a Drug Exemption and Rehabilitation Program, a Career Counseling Program, and guidelines concerning alcohol abuse and alcoholism by naval personnel.

One Z-Gram in particular, number 57, created considerable controversy. It was entitled "Demeaning and Abrasive Regulations, Elimination Of," and it became famous as the "Mickey Mouse" or "Chicken _____" Z-Gram. In the picturesque words of Admiral Zumwalt:

Mickey Mouse or Chicken _____ Regs — as they are called just as often — is a term that covers, for one thing, those self-serving regulations and practices by which some commanders attempt to give an appearance of efficiency or smartness but which in fact make no contribution to either of those desirable conditions. Hastily painting over rust spots the day before inspection is that kind of Mickey Mouse, and so is making a sailor change out of dungarees into liberty uniform before going to the Commissary for a candy bar. For another thing, the term covers those niggling, or even deliberately harrassing, regulations and practices that don't even purport to affect efficiency or smartness, but seem to derive from an institutional notion that everyone below the rank of commander, say, is immature. Requiring a person going home on leave to prove he or she had the money for a round-trip ticket is that kind of

Mickey Mouse, and so is refusing to provide parking spaces on
naval stations for motorcycles on the ground that motorcycles
(unlike nuclear submarines or guided missile frigates or
helicopters) are too dangerous for sailors to ride.[4]

He went on:

Demeaning and abrasive regulations have, in my judgment,
done at least as much to depress retention rates as have extended family separations and low salaries.[5]

Z-48 established a new office in the Bureau of Naval Personnel for
implementing the changes announced in the Z-Grams. Zumwalt assigned as director one of the Navy's front-running young Rear Admirals
— who was later promoted to Chief of Naval Personnel. This did not go
unnoticed by the troops. Zumwalt believed that if an organization truly
wishes to make a change, it must visibly and highly reward those who accept the risk and lead the change movement. Otherwise officers will
often select the safe course and not participate in anything controversial
— and organizational change is inevitably controversial.

While later Chiefs of Naval Operations have modified some of the
changes implemented by Admiral Zumwalt, many of his programs have
survived and have been incorporated into the institutional structure of
the Navy as if they had always been there. Here are three examples.

First, the Human Resources Management Support System was instituted to find means of raising morale and retention. Its specific objectives included "improved personnel stability through the retention of
top quality personnel;" "improved communications at all levels in the
chain of command;" "improved image of the Navy as a professional organization which recognizes individual contribution and desire for
respect by Navy personnel and the Navy's desire for recognition of the
unique contributions provided by personnel of all grades, races, creeds,
and national origin;" "greater career satisfaction, leading to increased

recruitment, retention of capable and dedicated individuals, and development of a stable force of career personnel within the Navy;" and "identification and reduction of conditions and opportunities leading to drug and alcohol abuse, and willing acceptance of successfully recovered personnel upon return to duty."[6]

Second, Organizational Effectiveness Centers have been established at various locations where there is a large concentration of fleet or shore units. The task of these centers is to provide any commanding officer who requests it, organizational consultancy services to diagnose problem areas and assist in devising solutions. The title "Organizational Consultant" was not in the Navy's nomenclature until the reforms of the Zumwalt years.

Third, the Leadership and Management Education and Training Program was originated in 1973-75, designed to provide Navy personnel with professional competence in leadership and management. Since 1981 this instruction has been presented to officers and petty officers at all levels. Today training sites are located in 12 centers in the U.S. and overseas. Their curriculum includes goal-setting, management control, use of influence, team-building, development of subordinates, advising, counseling, and conceptualization. This program has had an impact on the Navy's officer retention problems.

Since 1980 any officer who resigns his or her commission at the end of the initial time of service has been asked to complete a questionnaire giving the reasons for leaving. The results, cumulative to 1985, are shown in Table 9. The most common reason cited was separation from family, a condition intrinsic to seagoing. The second most common reason was "too much crisis management," referring to work experiences in which people had to work long hours to overcome crises which should have been foreseen. The third, fourth, fifth, sixth, and seventh all had to do with lack of autonomy, lack of self-determination, suppression of initiative, and lack of recognition for accomplishments — in sum, over-regimentation and excessive detailed authority. The eighth reason,

Table 9
Results of Officer Separation Questionnaire, U.S. Navy

Rank	Reason
1	Too much family separation
2	Too much crisis management
3	Unable to sufficiently plan and control my career
4	Suppressed initiative, creativity, or professional stimulation
5	Insufficient leadership qualities of seniors
6	Lack of recognition for accomplishment, or lack of respect
7	Poor utilization of abilities, skills, or education
8	Possible erosion of benefits
9	Problems with assignments
10	Geographic instability and transient nature of Navy life

Source: Report of Navy Military Personnel Command, Washington, DC (based on 2538 cases).

"possible erosion of benefits," refers to expected changes in rules which would reduce pay or pension, and the ninth, "problems with assignments," has to do with the process of making individual assignments, which is sometimes seen as too arbitrary and unfair. These feelings signal the kinds of organizational shifts needed to improve commitment by today's naval officers.

Twelve years have passed since Admiral Zumwalt was replaced as Chief of Naval Operations. Most of his innovations have remained in place, but not all. The retention rate for officers rose markedly from 1970 to 1974, but we cannot be certain that the Zumwalt innovations are entirely responsible, since the Vietnam War and the draft both came to an end during these years. Very likely the innovations had some effect.

As might be imagined, Zumwalt quickly became controversial, and already in 1970 some top admirals thought he was going too far in changing traditional rules. Admiral John Hyland asked, "How far can we permit absolute freedom of speech, deportment and dress, and still hang on to the indispensible element of discipline?" Military historian S. L. A. Marshall said, "Once you deviate from the sanctity of an order, you're in trouble. And we're right on the ragged edge of reducing discipline to the point of danger."[7]

The rate of officer retention in the Navy dropped again in the late 1970s, and by 1980 the situation was grave. Recent years have seen more initiatives to improve work satisfaction and reduce alienation. The Zumwalt innovations were apparently inadequate to solve the retention problem for the long run.

U.S. Air Force, 1979-1986

In 1979, officer retention rates in the Air Force were at an all-time low. For pilots in the crucial 6-11-year group (crucial because those who stay in usually do so until retirement) it was only 26 percent. In 1979 an Officer Retention Branch was begun, and in 1980 the first

Worldwide Officer Retention Symposium was held, an event which has been repeated annually. In the symposia several initiatives were developed and set in motion.

An early initiative was to survey all officers who leave. The survey results indicated that the greatest job-related dissatisfactions came from too little geographic stability, inadequate quality of leaders, inadequate opportunity for creativity, and lack of recognition. Written-in comments mentioned poor leadership, an inadequate officer evaluation system, and bureaucratic "filling in squares."[8] The questionnaire data helps the Officer Retention Branch identify "career irritants," and these, according to Major Greg Seidenberger, Chief of the Branch, constitute the main area of the branch's work.

There are also many other factors in officer retention, but most of them are external to the Air Force and hence out of their control — such as the state of the economy for finding alternative employment, the number of pilots needed by civilian airlines, and the like. The Air Force calls these "pull" factors, since they pull officers away. The internal factors are "push" factors, which push the people out.

One "push" factor is the difficulty of family life on military bases. In 1982 the Air Force began Family Support Centers on all the large bases. These offered financial counseling, job placement for spouses, assistance with family crises induced by residential moves, help with househunting off base, and so on. Recent research found that bases with Family Support Centers have higher rates of officer retention than the others, and Major Seidenberger believes that the Centers have some effect.[9]

In 1984 the Officer Retention Branch instituted a toll-free line which any officer may use at any time to discuss opportunities, decisions, or gripes. Callers need not identify themselves, and most do not. But the counselors compile the content of the calls and file monthly reports with higher command. The toll-free line gets about 10 to 15 calls a week, and the Branch tries to offer as much accurate information and helpful advice as possible. It is advertised in the *CareerOfficer* newspaper.

The most recent initiative, begun in 1986, was a change in the assignment process. Each officer in the Air Force up for re-assignment fills out a standard form giving his or her preferences (commonly called a "dream sheet"), and in the past someone matched up positions with available personnel. Officers often griped, alleging that the decisions were made by someone throwing darts at a dart board or by a random-number computer. Beginning in 1986, the commander of each unit has become involved in the decision-making. He or she is given a bloc of openings, and he or she is asked to comment on which of the officers would be the best fits. The commander is encouraged to talk with the officers about the opportunities and even to make suggestions to them. The process is still in the test stage, but it is probably an improvement, because now the officers feel that someone is on their side, and a personal judgment is involved — not just a throw of darts. Commanders are also asked to show personal attention to the officers and to urge them to remain in the Air Force. In the words of one officer, "I would have stayed in if someone had asked me."

Major Seidenberger said that good leadership aids retention. Leaders who were actively involved with their men and "present with them" called forth higher rates of retention. The best leaders are those who use "M.B.W.A.," a phrase from the business world: Management By Walking Around.

In both the Navy and the Air Force, unit commanders are responsible for maximizing the retention rate of their units. In the Navy, but not the Air Force, each commanding officer is evaluated in this regard along with other criteria such as unit administration, rates of discipline and desertion, unlawful activity, and maintenance of equipment. The Officer Retention Branch of the Air Force wishes that Air Force officers would also be evaluated partly on their retention rates, but this has not happened. The Branch personnel argue that retention difficulties in any organization can be ameliorated only if the officials directly responsible for the units are held accountable.

The retention rate in 1986 was as high as 56 percent, but no one knows if the new policies are responsible. Probably the slowdown in commercial airlines is just as important. There seems to have been an increase in patriotism in the past few years, according to interviews done, and this probably has helped.[10] In any case, retention efforts are continuing.

American Corporations

The analogy between American corporations and the Catholic Church is partly weak and partly strong. The weakest elements are four in number. First, corporations, unlike the Church, have measurable outcomes which are monitored annually or more often, almost like scores in a ballgame. Everyone can see how well each corporation is doing. Second, there are many competing corporations, not at all like a monopoly, and each must engage in ongoing experimentation and innovation to keep its share of the market. (The Catholic Church traditionally was a monopoly, but it is not today; yet many basic decisions presume a monopoly.) Third, commitment to a particular organization is weaker in the corporate world, and managerial-level employees move from one to another easily. There is little family-feeling in the leadership group, and no long-term commitments are made either by corporations or by employees to be loyal to each other. Fourth, there is much less of a distinct subculture in each corporate organization and less isolation of the corporate managerial class from outside society.

The elements of the analogy strong enough to warrant our attention have to do with the mentality of managerial-level workers in recent years and the new approaches taken by corporations to attract, motivate, and retain them. Business schools have been studying successes and failures of corporations in handling management personnel in the past two decades, and a series of books published since 1980 have expressed a consensus about what works best in America today.[11] This consensus about "new management theory" has elements of ideology in it, so we should not see it as scientifically proven, like Newton's laws, but merely the state of the art in the middle 1980s. It can be taken as proven only in the sense that certain front-running American corporations have become highly successful with the policies of the new theory, and others are following along to save their skins. It remains possible, of course, that the new theory will turn out to be a mutant of the special conditions of the 1970s and 1980s without more permanent validity. But more likely, it tells us something about deeper trends in the culture.

Two Models of Authority

Several writers begin by contrasting the traditional model with the modern model of authority in corporations.

Traditional management practices in American corporations were based on force and domination, and they arose during the heyday of industrialization, about 1890 to 1920. These practices are characterized by: (a) The paternal model. It is assumed that the superordinate persons act as "substitute parents" for the subordinates, since junior personnel are not able to determine what is in their best interest or what courses of action are best. (b) A hierarchical style. The incentives and penalties inherent in direct chains of command serve to control the behavior of subordinates. (c) Priority concern for efficiency and short-term goal accomplishment. Human resources are seen as instrumental for short-term organizational goals. (d) Use of one style of leadership to fit all circumstances, and use of uniform procedures in all units. (e) Minimal level of technology. Work is seen as essentially composed of simple, repetitive tasks, and senior staff can perform all the tasks assigned to juniors. Senior staff are assumed to be better educated, more capable, and more self-directed than junior staff.

The modern model of authority grew up recently due to new experiences in the workplace. It has several features: (a) The fraternal model. Managers and workers are assumed to be essentially equal, like siblings, and all organizational life emphasizes this equality. (b) Variable styles of leadership. The style in any situation is best selected by the person directly in charge, and he or she is empowered to decide and then carry it out. (c) Concern for equity and justice in the treatment of all personnel. Openness, fairness, and morality are needed to achieve long-term efficiency and commitment. (d) Integration of the needs of the individual with the needs of the organization. The fit between individual interests and organizational interests must be maximized, and when this is impossible the top managers must discuss openly how some personal interests need to be subordinated to those of the organization. (e) Complex technology. Managers cannot learn and perform all the tasks which junior staff can do, so they must forge high levels of trust and honesty with subordinates. Educational and aptitude differences between senior and junior personnel are assumed to be small and likely to diminish further in the future.

Today's Junior Executives

As industry becomes more technical, education levels rise, and cultural assumptions shift, corporations must re-evaluate their policies toward junior executives and skilled workers. Today's junior executives have a greater desire than ever to exercise their decision-making skills in tasks and projects over which they have some control. They consider themselves too qualified to be saddled with mindlessly repetitive or routine jobs. They are easily frustrated by superiors who impose excessive rules and limits on them, especially if the superiors reveal an inherent lack of trust in subordinates. The new workers resist and resent being manipulated or handled. Boring supervision, boring organizational pep talks, and boring bureaucracies lower young executives' performance and cause them to start looking for employment opportunities elsewhere.

Today's junior executives expect more individual rights than ever before. Bosses may feel anxious about this, but the evidence seems to show that most of the anxiety is unnecessary. Well-educated, thoughtful, and intelligent people are fully aware of the need for the integration of organizational and personal needs; all but a few understand that the nature of organizational endeavor has ever been so. The few who do not appreciate this fact must be corrected, but the others merely need to be trusted by higher-ups. Robert Kelley speaks of the demise of past assumptions:

> Workers have willingly offered themselves complete with their personal and family lives to the organization. Like children, they have allowed the organization to determine what is best for them and how they should best be used. They expected no power and that is precisely what they got. Such childlike passivity is fading fast. The divine right of kings or managers no longer exists.[12]

The job of managers is harder today than in the past. To get the best performance out of their staffs they need to be creative, flexible, and more trusting of their organizational subordinates than ever before. Their honesty must be unimpeachable. "Games people play with people" have no place. Their personal security and self-confidence must be high, for defensiveness or inappropriate exercise of power kills organizational spirit. Bosses must be strong facilitators of the growth and success of juniors. They are dealing with more highly trained and self-starting people than ever before. They need to replace authoritarian management with a networking, collegial style.

Corporate Innovations

A few examples of the new management style's elements may be helpful. These are all taken from vigorously growing firms.

Merck and Company, Inc. is the largest prescription drug manufacturer in the United States, employing 16,000, and it has one of the most sophisticated Human Resource Departments (formerly called Personnel Departments) in American business. The department takes regular employee surveys to find out what Merck people are thinking and it compares those results with similar surveys taken at other companies.

In the 1983 survey, 80 percent of Merck employees said they would choose the company again as a place of work (this compared with 60 percent in the nation), and 59 percent said they feel they have been treated with respect as individuals (the national norm was 43 percent). Merck's communications efforts are superb. The newsletters, newspapers, magazines, and booklets issued to employees show an openness in discussion of the company's business, and they portray employees in straightforward human terms. The tone is intelligent communication without phoniness or condescension.[13]

Kollmorgen Corporation makes sophisticated electro-optical instruments, with 4,500 employees. The plant has recently adopted a system that institutionalizes Kollmorgen's philosophy of employees as partners. It is called the "reverse review." In addition to the normal annual performance review that all assembly-line workers receive from their supervisors, employees also get to evaluate their supervisors. Kollmorgen sees the supervisors as partners, but merely with a different role. Each month managers and employees hold "people meetings" to discuss the state of the business and give employees the opportunity to talk about any issues that concern them. Employees report that they are given a feeling that they count, that they mean something.[14]

H. B. Fuller Company is one of the world's largest makers of adhesives and sealants. It has 1,650 employees. The chairman of the company makes himself available once a year to everyone in the company through what is called the "President's Hot-Line." Anybody can call him on that day on a special toll-free number to complain about their supervisors, make suggestions for improving the products, or talk about anything else on their minds. He usually gets 40 or 50 calls on that day.[15] Similarly, Eastman Kodak Company has a suggestion plan with financial awards. It gives prizes averaging $1.65 million annually to the 9,000 people who turn in ideas.[16]

Control Data Corporation makes and services computers, with 47,000 on its payroll. Employees can avail themselves of one of the largest numbers of employee programs in the country, including EAR and Peer Review. EAR (Employee Advisory Resource) is a 24-hour counseling service for employees or their families. EAR counselors can be telephoned for advice about either personal problems (alcohol, drug, marital, health, or financial) or work-related difficulties. Peer Review is a collegial grievance procedure. If an employee cannot resolve a complaint with his or her supervisor or that person's boss, the employee can contact EAR, and it will assign a representative to try to resolve the dispute. If that does not work a review board is set up, consisting of an EAR representative, two employees at the same level in the company, and one company executive. The peers and executive are selected by random drawing. The board votes on the case and submits its findings to a company vice-president for a final decision.[17]

These examples show the philosophy and direction of personnel innovations which are proving successful in today's workplace. All of them emphasize collegiality, not hierarchy; ownership, not subordination; trust, not control. Their value in the context of this book is not as policy suggestions but as indicators of social change helping church leaders to take the pulse of educated young adult America. The examples let us see how social change is affecting other institutions and how the institutions are re-examining policies to stay viable.

Research on work satisfaction of priests confirms that the general principles for enhancing morale of management personnel in other organizations apply to priests as well. Studies have shown that priests' morale is enhanced by greater autonomy in their work, greater participation in institutional decision-making at several levels, and feelings of being supported and cared for by others.[18]

Part II:
Options for Action

4

Type A Options:
Reduce the Need For Priests

At the conclusion of Chapter 1, I outlined eleven options for action to help the Church carry out its mission in the face of the shortage of priests. They naturally fall into four types:

Type A: Reduce the Need for Priests

1. Combine or restructure parishes, or re-educate Catholics to have lowered expectations of priestly services.

Type B: Get More Priests, with Existing Eligibility Criteria

2. Reassign or redistribute existing priests to get better utilization for parish leadership.

3. Get more parish priests from religious orders.

86

4. Get priests from foreign nations.

5. Recruit more seminarians.

Type C: Get More Priests, with Broadened Eligibility Criteria

6. Ordain married as well as celibate men.

7. Ordain women.

8. Institute a term of service for the priesthood, or institute an honorable discharge.

9. Utilize some resigned priests as sacramental ministers.

Type D: Expand the Diaconate and Lay Ministries

10. Expand and develop the permanent diaconate.

11. Expand and develop lay ministries.

Part II of the book investigates these eleven options. Chapter 4 looks at Type A options, Chapter 5 looks at Type B, Chapter 6 looks at Type C, and Chapter 7 looks at Type D. My purpose is to provide factual information about each, not to advocate one or another.

We need to be clear about the nature of the problem: It is the shortage of priestly services for American Catholics. Policy options which are interesting but do not solve the problem will not be discussed here except as they indirectly help. For example, some people advocate using resigned priests who are currently married as paid lay ministers in parishes. This is not relevant except as it might increase the quality and quantity of candidates for lay ministry positions — but since good candidates are already in abundant supply, the idea will not occupy us. Another example is the idea of opening up the permanent diaconate to women. This may be advisable from many points of view, but it will not occupy our attention here, since there is no scarcity of candidates for the diaconate, and opening it to women would hardly affect the availability of priestly services even indirectly.

To portray the available options as eleven in number is somewhat arbitrary. I have done so for sake of convenience. Actually there are more than eleven, and I had to group them together to arrive at the current list. That is, several options could be divided further if we wanted to make the list longer; these subtypes will be visible as we proceed.

In addition there are two options which I have heard discussed at meetings or seen in print, yet which are not covered by the eleven. I have deliberately left them out, and I should explain why. First is the idea of having part-time priests, men who work full-time or nearly so in secular occupations and fulfill priestly functions on the side. This idea is basic to the worker-priest movement in Europe, and it is proposed in the U.S.A. for various reasons. But how will it help with the shortage of priestly services? It won't help us recruit more seminarians or slow down the rate of priestly resignations. Men who quit the priesthood rarely say they liked the status but disliked the full-time priestly work. On the contrary, the main deterrents to recruiting new vocations and the main sources of resignations are celibacy and loneliness. In various Protestant denominations the idea of part-time ministers is being pursued as a way of supplying ministers to small congregations who cannot afford a full-time minister and who are not easily yoked with a neighboring congregation in a combined charge. But the problem in Catholicism is people, not dollars, and the option is not pertinent.

Second is a change in the theology of sacraments so that, for example, deacons could be empowered to celebrate all the sacraments. This option would definitely increase the availability of priestly services. But it is a change going to the core of the doctrine of sacraments, and it is not discussed here because we are not looking at anything entailing important theological changes.

Let us proceed with Type A options. They do not seek to produce more priestly services but rather to reduce the demand for them or help parishes cope with the available supply. These options are appropriate if (a) it is decided that more priestly services are not needed, or (b) in spite of all efforts, no increase can be obtained. For many dioceses today situation (b) is realistic, and they are planning ahead.

Case Studies of Diocesan Projections and Plans

I will explore Type A options by telling the stories of three dioceses making plans for how they will cope with the shortage of priests. Many other diocesan stories could be recounted, since planning is being done in numerous places; these three were selected because they are diverse and well documented. My stories cannot relate the full richness of what is happening in these dioceses, since the present topic is limited in scope.

Archdiocese of Baltimore

In 1981 the Archdiocese of Baltimore saw that it would have fewer priests in the future, yet more Catholics to serve and more pastoral demands. It set up a long-range planning process called "Project 83" under direction of the Department of Personnel.

The process was one of consultation with all diocesan groups concerning upcoming shortages of priests. The researchers found that net losses of diocesan priests were averaging about 5 a year (out of 301 priests in all in 1981). The median age of diocesan priests had risen four years between 1976 and 1981. The ratio of priests per 1,000 parishioners was higher in the inner city and rural areas than in the suburbs.

After numerous consultations, eleven proposals were made and passed on to the Archbishop:

1. Since people have strong feelings about closing parishes, there will be no parishes closed.

2. In the next three years, 9 associate pastor positions will be eliminated. The procedure for selecting the parishes to be cut will entail making three lists: first, a list by the Placement Committee based on its best judgment; second, a list based on the laity-to-priest ratio in all parishes; and third, a list based on the level of sacramental activity in each parish. Parishes with a low laity-to-priest ratio and low sacramental activity would be first in line for cuts. Before any final decision, the Archbishop and Vicars will consult with the local people involved.

3. No more than one new parish per year will be established for the next three years.

4. The total number of priests in Central Services will be reduced by at least two in the next three years, based on interviews with all now in Central Services. All decisions must be approved by the Priests' Council and the Clergy Personnel Board.

5. The Clergy Personnel Board will recommend at least three priests to return to parish ministry from specialized ministry in the next three years. Each priest in specialized ministries will be interviewed before any decisions are made (about 40 to 45 in all). There will be a general freeze on assignment of priests to specialized ministries with exceptions made only in unusual cases of specialized training or distinctive talent.

6. There will be no more than three priests on extended educational leave at any one time.

7. In the next five years there will be no reduction in the number of parishes staffed by religious, and possibly the number will increase.

8. Efforts to promote vocations will be increased.

9. A census of lay ministers will be done, including information on their jobs and qualifications, and consultations will begin to identify other ministries in parishes which lay ministers could fulfill.

10. An archdiocesan-wide educational program will be set up telling about the shortage of clergy and the utilization of new lay ministries.

11. A process of consultation will be started in the parishes where actual clergy reduction will take place to investigate other resources available for maintaining pastoral service.[1]

These recommendations were accepted by the Archbishop, and the processes were set in motion. Meanwhile the reduction in priests continued, and within two years there were $11\frac{1}{2}$ more reductions in priest positions — 9 from multiple-priest parishes, 2 from special ministries, and one-half from Central Services. Also in 1983 a discussion began about a reduction of Masses in all parishes of the archdiocese, to lighten the load on priests.

In late 1982 the Archbishop named a Task Force on One-Priest Parishes, since they represented a difficult problem given the shortage of priests and the strong feelings about closing parishes, and removing full-time pastors. The task force found 56 one-priest parishes in the archdiocese. They varied widely in size, but most were under 1,500 persons. Almost all had lay pastoral associates or DREs. They were of all types, including small rural parishes, small urban parishes and growing suburban parishes. The task force looked at their growth or decline trends, their lay age distributions, and the length of service of their pastors. They made overall projections about available priests in the future; the best guess was a reduction of 42 diocesan priests in the coming ten years.

There were lengthy deliberations about staffing parishes with lay pastoral associates. Task force members agreed that small parishes are generally desirable, since they lend themselves more than large ones to the creation of community feelings. They affirmed that the celebration of Eucharist is at the heart of the parish community, and that the person who presides at Eucharist should also be the one who presides over community life and integrates the gifts of the members of the community. But removing a resident pastor from a parish community prevents this unity of roles, and it also intervenes in the inherent right of a parish community to have reasonable access to the Eucharist and other sacraments. The task force even criticized church policies which are reducing the numbers of priests available, such as the restriction of ordination to celibate men.

But recommendations were needed, and the task force came to its conclusions. Since more reductions in priests are inevitable, it recommended that one-priest parishes should not be exempted from future reductions in priestly positions; parishes first to lose resident pastors will be those which are small in size, close to neighboring parishes, and possessing a high potential for collaboration with neighboring parishes. But no parishes will be closed; parishes without a full-time resident pastor will have lay leadership. All changes in ministerial leadership will be done only after full collegial consultation. "Reaching decisions about reduction of clergy staff in parishes will elicit strong resistance if it is not done collegially."[2]

The most recent planning effort was done by an Advisory Panel on Parish Life appointed by the Archbishop in early 1985. It was charged especially to look further into the problem of priestless parishes in the future. The task force was dubious about the viability of priestless parishes, since the leadership functions in them could not be united in a single person: "We need to maintain the constant value. . . of uniting the sacramental leadership with the moderating function."[3] Also it called for more priests in the future:

> The Church must secure sufficient numbers of pastors with the qualities needed for moderating. This involves looking seriously at the possibility of ordaining women and married persons. The key question is the right of the Church to be served by competent leaders in sufficient numbers.[4]

For the immediate future it recommended that the archdiocese recognize a new role, "pastoral leader," which could be carried out by a layperson in a parish where no priest is available. As of early 1986 the archdiocese had 54 one-priest parishes (about one-third of the total), and inevitably some will lose their resident priests before long. The task force recommended making an experiment. Nine parishes would be selected for a period of at least two years, during which six will share a pastor with another parish and three will have a full-time lay, religious, or deacon administrator who has the responsibility for the moderating leadership, with a part-time priest supplying liturgical ministry. The nine will be selected after visitations by Vicar Bishops and consultations with parish leaders. They will be publicly recognized as an experiment for the entire archdiocese.

The experiment will be set up in the fall of 1986. The archdiocesan leadership is moving cautiously, since feelings about the new venture are mixed.[5]

Archdiocese of Cincinnati

The Archdiocese of Cincinnati is now engaged in a planning process which is far-reaching and destined to be a guide to others. In March 1983 the Archbishop appointed a committee to carry out planning for a future with fewer priests and religious. The committee was composed of eight diocesan leaders and a full-time project manager, a man who had taken early retirement from personnel work with Proctor and Gamble. They designed a planning process called "For the Harvest." First they gathered information on the current number of priests and reasonable future projections.

In 1985 the archdiocese had 339 diocesan priests, and in the year 2000 the number will probably be 190 or 200. (The archdiocese has 257 parishes.) In short, there will be massive reductions in numbers of priests available. The planning committee proposed some guidelines for future parish staffing, which were publicized throughout the diocese. For example:

By 1990, the Archdiocese may not be able to provide a full-time resident priest to a community of less than 700 registered Catholics (which translates into approximately 350 Sunday Mass attendance). Nor will the Archdiocese be able to provide an associate pastor to a community of less than 4,000 registered Catholics (or 2,000 Sunday Mass attendance). Likewise, when parishes are in close proximity, the Archdiocese may not be able to provide a full-time resident priest to both parishes.

The Personnel Office should try to raise the percentage of priests serving in the parishes from the present 70 percent to 75 percent. [6]

The planning committee then worked with diocesan leadership in forging a two-year planning process which would be mandated in all parishes. It in effect asked parish leadership to set out *their own* plans for the future within a few specified guidelines. All parishes were required to participate, and a sequence of regional meetings, training sessions, educational campaigns, and consultations was planned.

The guidelines were explicitly stated in all the materials. First, the planning is for the long haul, not just for *ad hoc* solutions here and there to the shortage of priests. It should be thorough and totally consultative, so that it will be driven by the true feelings of pastors and laity in all the parishes. Second, this is not a program for closing parishes. No residential parishes will be closed. Third, parishes must be realistic about future availability of priests and about future financial costs. Fourth, no ideal parish organization or style of ministry is being advanced, but two guiding principles are required: a parish should strive to be both ministerially complete and financially solvent. By "ministerially complete" is meant that it offers the total range of functions, including worship, catechesis and education, pastoral care, outreach, and administration. By "financially solvent" is meant that it supports its own ministry, meets diocesan obligations, pays just and fair salaries, and maintains its physical plant. Fifth (and most interesting), if any parish cannot be ministerially complete and financially solvent, it should enter into discussion with other parishes in considering "cluster" arrangements. Clusters of parishes should begin planning for ways to work together to combine financial resources or coordinate programs to serve everyone in the cluster.

The Cincinnati plan therefore requires long-range planning discussions by all parishes and initiates discussions of cluster parishes, and then it stops there. The rest is up to the local parishes, led by a combination of pastors and lay leaders. The Archbishop sent everyone a strong signal: get ready for changes, since priests and religious are no longer available in the way they once were. There is no more business-as-usual.

The process was designed to have two phases. First, the planning committees were to have several meetings in which they spelled out the "desired outcomes" in the ministries of their parishes. The focus was to be on *ministry* rather than on questions of personnel or roles. Form was to follow function. For this task, nine months was allowed. Second, after review of the outcomes by the diocesan planning committee, the second phase was to be devoted to defining strategies. At this point cluster discussions were to be introduced, and deanery leaders took the initiative to suggest clusters, made up of 5 or 6 contiguous parishes.

Since virtually all of the parishes had no experience at all in cluster cooperation, this was something entirely new whose outcome was unknown to the planners. Everyone realized that the second phase would be awkward. As Rev. Robert Schmitz, coordinator of the process, put it:

> It would be a serious mistake to underestimate the difficulty we may face adjusting to new ministerial models. One need only recall the debates concerning communion railings to forecast the difficulty we face.[7]

As of summer 1986, the first phase is completed, and the general directions of parish planning are known. Father Schmitz said that local parishes are frequently interested in more ministry and more paid lay staff, and they are inclined to take money away from school budgets to achieve it. They tend to ask that school financing become more autonomous from parish financing, with its own separate fund-raising. Already there are trends in this direction — each of the high schools in the archdiocese has its own paid fund-raiser, and the school office is exploring the possibility that each deanery or region might profit from having its own fund-raiser. Thus, the local parishes suggested that the way to pay for future ministries will be to separate school and parish budgets more than in the past and pay for the schools independent of parish budgets. This is a development which was not anticipated. The planning committee is greatly encouraged by the energy and initiative shown by the parish planners. Without doubt the number of lay ministers in the archdiocese will double in the next few years. The grass-roots planning process seemed to have a revitalizing effect on many parishes.[8] Whether cluster projects will succeed remains to be seen.

Meanwhile the priest shortage worsens. A letter went out from the archbishop to all parishes saying that from now on any parish with weekend Mass attendance of less than 1,800 (that is, 3,600 registered Catholics) will lose its associates when their terms expire.

Archdiocese of Portland, Oregon

Like many others, the Archdiocese of Portland, Oregon is faced with a dwindling number of priests. In 1984 a study day brought together the bishops, the members of the Priests' Personnel Board, the staff of the Office of Ministry, and selected pastors to begin deliberations about the future. A researcher presented projections of future availability of priests. In 1984 there were 130 diocesan priests, and the most realistic projections were for 112 in 1990 and 87 in 2000. In 1984 there were 97 parishes, but in 1990 there will be about 102 and in 2000 about 110, if new parishes are split off from today's "megaparishes" in growing areas as they have been in the past. Clearly there will be a major priest shortage. Even if there were no new parishes established by the year 2000, still there would be at least 20, and maybe 40, parishes without resident ordained pastors.[9]

Some decisions were made at the study day. One was that the Archbishop should never close a parish merely because there is no priest pastor available. On the contrary, new parishes should be *opened* in coming years as needs and conditions warrant. Everyone agreed that smaller parishes are preferable, since they have more growth potential and offer people more opportunities to take responsibility for the church — opportunities the laity accept eagerly.

Another decision was to begin appointing lay pastors. One small-town parish was entrusted to a lay pastor to be selected by the parishioners, who would work under the supervision of a nearby priest. Not many months later the person was selected — a Franciscan sister, Eunice Hittner, OSF, who assumed all the duties of pastor. Twice a month the supervisor (called the "Priest Moderator") comes from another town to celebrate Eucharist, and on the other Sundays Sister Eunice moderates at a Communion service. From the beginning, Sister Eunice has met monthly with the Priest Moderator and diocesan staff for guidance. This venture was intended not just as a stop-gap solution to the clergy shortage, but as a form of church renewal with the hope that it would cause people to think of the church not as "it" or "they" but as "we." Indications are that community spirit in the parish has been renewed.

A second study day in the archdiocese took place in October 1985. It resulted in three more decisions. First, a second parish was entrusted to lay leadership. This time a different structure was used, a parish ministry team composed of parish members appointed by the Archbishop. The team in turn selected one of its members, Joan Dotter, a long-time active parish member, to be coordinator. Twice a month a priest from Portland comes to celebrate Eucharist, and on the other Sundays Joan celebrates a Communion service. She administers all parish affairs and is paid a salary. Each week she consults with the Priest Moderator.

A second decision from the study day was to initiate a parish-based planning process that would lead to a comprehensive plan for ministry in the archdiocese in the year 2000. A central concern is personnel practices in parishes without resident priests. The optimal structures for leading these parishes needs to be worked out through experimentation. The planning process presumes that the best planners are those on the local scene, not those in the central office.

A third decision was to explore a new concept, the "pastoral zone." The idea derives from the necessity in the future of a Priest Moderator in a small town or rural area to supervise several outlying parishes which have no ordained pastors. This pattern appears inevitable. But the concept could also apply in urban areas where church life would be enhanced by a similar decentralization of large parishes. Thus, instead of a single gigantic parish in a suburban area, several smaller worship communities could develop under the leadership of lay parish ministers. They would be supervised by a Priest Moderator who would be responsible for the zone. It is probable that smaller worship communities will be able to develop a richer sense of community than is possible in a large parish. But the details of planning must be left to the local people:

As we plan for pastoral zones or clusters of parishes, it is essential that we know the nature of local allegiances — where people identify themselves as community members, where they shop, where they send children to school. It is important, too, to know the past history of a parish as well as its distinctive character and mission in the present. All of this is information that only people on the local scene have.[10]

The archdiocese is planning to install more lay pastors in the future, at the rate of about two or three a year. In 15 years it expects to have about 30 parishes without resident priests. Meanwhile some of the parishioners in the first two lay-led parishes are asking why their pastors couldn't be ordained, since they are ministering well.[11]

Option 1: Combine or restructure parishes, or re-educate Catholics to have lowered expectations of priestly services

If there is no prospect of getting more priests, the church must be somehow remodelled so that it can carry on with the priests available. Several steps could be taken. One would be to close small parishes and amalgamate all Catholics into larger ones. This is analogous to the policy in American public schools several decades ago when country schools were closed and children were bused to centralized schools. It would reduce the number of parishes and the demand for priestly services.

Virtually all American Catholics oppose the idea. People are committed to their parishes and react with great indignation if the parishes are threatened. As we saw in Baltimore, Cincinnati, and Portland, all planning processes came quickly to the conclusion that no parishes will be closed.

There are other arguments against the idea besides the feelings of
parishioners who love their parishes. All observers agree that smaller
parishes are spiritually and organizationally better, since they facilitate
more feelings of community, more networks of friends reaching out to
each other, more involvement by everyone. One bishop suggested to me
that the ideal size of a parish would be about 300 families. Thomas
Sweetser reports the same from his work with parishes:

> People experience many large, impersonal, highly-structured
> organizations in their daily lives and do not want the parish to
> be like that. People need the support and friendship of others
> they know personally if they are going to remain active mem-
> bers of the parish. The ethnic parishes of the American
> Catholic past survived because they touched this need for
> belonging and for personal involvement. This sense of belong-
> ing must be recaptured and nurtured in the parishes of the
> 1980s.[12]

Surveys in the Archdioceses of Boston and Omaha found that smaller
parishes have higher percentages attending Mass. For example, in
Omaha in 1981, very small parishes (averaging 160 families) had 68 percent attendance; small parishes (400 families) had 60 percent attendance; but very large parishes (1,600 families) averaged 46 percent
attendance. [13] Parishes which are very large often experience spon-
taneous formation of smaller worshiping and sharing groups within
them, since people desire face-to-face groups with others having common interests.

If parishes should not be closed, we must plan for the other alternative, that of an increasing number of parishes. A realistic assumption
would be that the total number should grow, since new housing developments will continually call for the establishment of new parishes in ur-
banized areas. How can they be administered with a dwindling number
of priests? This question is often raised today and leads naturally to an
analysis of two kinds of situations. The first is the "priestless parish,"

where no resident priest is available at all. The second is the parish where resident priests are still available, but where the laity-to-priest ratio rises so high that priestly leadership loses effectiveness. These two situations are different enough that they need to be discussed separately; the most obvious solution to the first (the priestless parish) involves some sort of resident lay leadership in collaboration with a travelling priest who visits periodically and provides supervision, and the most obvious solution to the second (the understaffed parish) involves use of trained lay ministers. Of the two, the first is the most important to scrutinize carefully since it carries the most weighty implications, as we will demonstrate. We will turn our attention to it here, and leave the second situation to chapter seven, when we look at lay ministers.

The problem of priestless parishes exists in numerous countries, and some lessons can be learned from experiences there. In Africa the number of available priests in many areas is very low, and most religious services are led by lay leaders — without the Eucharist. Parishes with 20,000 members and 50 to 100 widely dispersed rural "outstations" are not uncommon.[14] In this situation Catholics need to be taught that weekly Eucharist is not necessary, since in reality it is not available. Worship services are led by catechists, not priests, and the emphasis is on celebration of the Word rather than the Eucharist. Under these conditions the sacramental identity of the Catholic faith is often lost sight of, and the Catholic Church is seen by the people as similar to the Protestant missions — which also stress preaching rather than the sacraments. Raymond Hickey reflects on this:

> A Eucharist-less Catholic community will in time become a non-Eucharist community and scarcely distinguishable from the many Protestant churches which flourish in Africa. . . . A sacrificial priesthood and regular celebration of the Eucharist can be expected to become more and more irrelevant to a Christian community which has managed for long periods without them.[15]

Hickey's observation is a serious one. The option of re-educating American Catholics away from weekly Eucharist should not be accepted without understanding its consequences. Not only does it fly in the face of decades of catechesis but it also endangers the sacramental nature of the church.

A variation on this would be to put emphasis on the value of Communion services, which do not require priestly celebrants, as a substitute for the Eucharist. If Catholics came to accept this teaching, many of the worship services (as an estimate, more than half) could be in the form of Communion, led by deacons or lay ministers. This appears to be a viable option. It may have an important long-term implication, if Catholics in the future come to regard the Eucharist-versus-Communion distinction as not really important. Then people who are effectively ministered to by lay leaders celebrating Communion services in their parishes could come to the attitude that they are doing very well without priests, thank you, and anyway the visiting priest is really only a bother. Another question could be expected to arise in this context, as to whether the clergy-versus-laity distinction is really important. This possible scenario needs investigation, but at present we can only make speculations.

The idea of appointing lay pastors to staff parishes which are served by visiting priests providing Eucharist every few weeks is already being widely tried in American dioceses. As we saw above, Portland has two experiments underway, and Baltimore is about to start nine experiments. Scores of others have been started in the Midwest and West. Has anything been learned?

Parishes with Lay Pastors

Dioceses faced with diminishing numbers of priests often have rather small, scattered parishes in small towns and rural areas which are the first to be deprived of full-time resident priests. It is always a shock to the people when the bishop tells them he cannot send a priest. Then the bishop and the people are faced with a decision about what to do. If another parish nearby has a full-time resident priest who can travel to the parish each weekend for Eucharist, a likely solution is to assign the priest to two parishes. This has the disadvantage that no one is available at the parish during the week to carry out pastoral work or to be responsible for the buildings.

If there is no full-time priest nearby who can come each weekend, another option is to appoint a lay pastor for the parish, under the supervision of a priest not far away who can visit once or twice a month for Eucharist. The bishop selects the lay pastor, who often turns out to be a religious sister, and she celebrates Communion services or services of the Word whenever the priest does not come. During the week she is active in pastoral calling, committee chores, and administration of the parish. Sister Eunice in Portland exemplifies this option.

Another possibility is that the bishop appoints a council of parishioners to administer the parish under the supervision of a diocesan priest. The council selects a person to be the lay pastor, often from within the parish itself. The appointee is usually obliged to carry out a training program within a few months or a year, and he or she must work under the guidance of the supervising priest. Joan Dotter in Portland is an example.

A variation on this is sometimes found, in which a non-ordained person functions as a member of a pastoral team responsible for several parishes in different communities. One of the team is a priest who celebrates Eucharist in the various parishes, but the others are each responsible for one of the parishes and reside there.

The number of parishes with lay pastors is growing each year, but we do not know how many there are. All we have is data on how many American parishes have no resident priest pastor — a larger number. The Notre Dame parish survey found that 4.5 percent of all parishes in 1982 had no resident priest pastor.[16] Suzanne Elsesser made a study and found that there were 977 parishes without resident priest pastors in 1985 — 5.2 percent of the total.[17] Of these possibly one or two or three hundred have lay pastors in some arrangement or other.

An impressive study of lay pastors was done in 1985 by Peter Gilmour of Loyola University, Chicago, in his Doctor of Ministry thesis.[18] Gilmour visited about a dozen non-ordained persons pastoring Catholic parishes in five midwestern dioceses. He visited the churches, interviewed the lay pastors at length, talked with parishioners, and took part in liturgies and social events. All of the lay pastors were women religious with some years of prior experience in leadership. All of the parishes were small, located in towns or villages.

The typical pattern was that the sisters were acting as pastors in these rural parishes, with visiting priests coming weekly or bi-weekly for Sunday Eucharist and other sacraments. The sisters seemed to enjoy breaking new ground in ministry and in church life, as they slowly defined their roles and priorities for the parishes. The parishioners came to appreciate and love the sisters after initial periods of puzzlement or even hostility (hostility if they saw the appointment of the sisters as a signal that the parish would soon be closed entirely). Some of the lay pastors were obviously effective spiritual leaders who related well and were able to build up church life better than it had been in anyone's memory. Gilmour emerged from his travels impressed by what he saw.

Of course the use of religious sisters as lay pastors is an innovation and an experiment. There are problems of definition and policy. People commented that there is not even an agreed-upon name for the job. The common designations are "lay pastor," "pastoral administrator," and "parish administrator" — and people don't know how to relate to lay pastors in some situations.[19] Many parishioners appreciated the sisters but would prefer having a resident priest if that were possible. Gilmour reflected on his data and concluded that the outcome of the experiment is unknown, largely because having lay pastors sets in motion other changes whose effect is still unclear. He concluded that what he saw is probably not a permanent structure for ministry but more likely a transitional phenomenon which will in time lead to something else. To illustrate, he described three kinds of problems.

First is the difficulty, widely discussed today, of the separation of liturgical leadership from enabling leadership. The lay pastors live full-time in the town, visit the people, take part in their picnics and ice cream socials and church dinners, and call forth their gifts in parish life. Inevitably the sisters carry out pastoral counseling and preparation for sacraments but of course they cannot perform the sacraments. A visiting priest must do that — a person whom the parishioners don't know very well. The psychological impact is to reduce the people's understanding of a sacrament to a kind of magic divorced from the human relationships which led up to it. In the words of one of the sisters interviewed by Gilmour:

> I have had people who will come to me who are scared to death of a confessional. I had a woman who was very concerned a-bout something in her past life that she confided in me, and the way she wanted this handled was that she wanted me to tell the priest first what she was going to tell him. And then he does the absolution, you see, in order to make it a ritually correct sacrament.

> The last marriage we validated, he had not even met the couple and had no idea who they were. They were standing in the back of church, and he said, "Now which ones am I marrying?" I said, "The one in purple and the guy in the brown jacket." And he said, "Well, what's their names? Write their names down."[20]

There were other dramatic examples in anointing the sick or confessions, where the laypeople loved and confided in the sister but not in the visiting priest. The situations were spiritually jarring.

Second is a feeling among several lay pastors that they are hindered in their ministry by church tradition and law. One sister told of how she found the attitudes of other priests and even bishops galling when she was publicly identified as an assistant to the visiting priest, and not a pastor and leader in her own right. She explained that she is carrying out virtually all of the pastoral functions in the parish, not the visiting priest. Yet many people (including some parishioners) define her as in a supporting role. Another sister complained that other priests did not respect her and even avoided — for a few months — inviting her to deanery meetings. Fortunately attitudes changed with time.

Third is the experience of the priests who are cast in a circuit-riding role. They have no opportunity to forge strong personal bonds with the people in the parish and sometimes feel like permanent outsiders. Someone said they were "pop dispensers." Gilmour talked about the issue with several of the visiting priests and to his surprise found that they did not have strong feelings. They seemed to get satisfaction from their tasks. So apparently the problem was not felt to be bad.

Gilmour's conclusion that the lay pastor arrangement in its present form is temporary, not permanent, is intriguing and to me convincing. There are other pressures for change also. The decline in available priests has not come to an end, so more lay pastors will have to be appointed in years ahead. The lay pastor arrangement will come to be experienced as routine. Also the women's movement in America is still largely an urban phenomenon now, but eventually it will permeate rural culture too. What all this will lead to is unknown, but we may expect grassroots pressure to upgrade the status of lay pastors.

Parishes With Understaffed Priests

As we said earlier, the second kind of situation caused by the priest shortage is a parish still having a resident priest or priests but with an unwieldy laity-to-priest ratio. The most obvious step is the appointment of lay ministers, but several other steps are possible and should be mentioned here. A parish could institute communal celebration of the sacraments of anointing and baptism, so as to avoid too much burden on the priests. Already many seriously ill or elderly persons are now anointed before death is foreseen, thus eliminating the need for last-minute deathbed visits by busy priests. Also parishioners could be told that marriages and baptisms would no longer be celebrated by priests but only by deacons. Both of these measures would be somewhat unpopular with American laity, as we saw in Chapter 1, Table 3. Our 1985 poll found, for example, that 85 percent of American Catholics would find it "not at all acceptable" if no priest were available for administering Last Rites for the dying. Were this situation to occur anyway, the most reasonable expectation would be alienation from church leadership or even rebellions by individuals or groups against hierarchical authority. At the very least, laity need to be warned ahead of time when reductions in priestly services are coming.

In sum, the option of educating Catholics to have lowered expectations of priestly services, with or without a resident priest in the parish, is viable in many situations. It should be exercised with some caution, however, because of probable changes in the experiences of laity which endanger not only church teachings about the sacraments but also feelings of loyalty.

5

Type B Options: Get More Priests, With Existing Eligibility Criteria

Option 2: Reassign or redistribute existing priests to get better utilization for parish leadership

The topic of reassigning or redistributing priests is being widely discussed. It takes four forms. The first is raised by globally-conscious Catholics who argue that by global standards the United States does not have a shortage of priests; on the contrary, it has an oversupply. Thus for the sake of global equity a large number of American priests should be sent to those nations with an undersupply. Most frequently Latin America is mentioned as a region in dire need. I agree with this argument but consider it too visionary to discuss here, except in the sense that American Catholics should expand their overseas missions considerably. The idea of exporting large numbers of American priests to help priest-poor nations asks too much of American Catholics who feel a pinch at home. It is not politically feasible.

The second form concerns redistribution within the United States. It argues that priests from dioceses which are priest-rich should be re--allocated to dioceses which are priest-poor. Several observers told me that the Eastern cities are priest-rich and should be sending priests to the South or Southwest, which are priest-poor. To check, I looked at the 1986 *Official Catholic Directory* to compare the laity-per-priest ratios in all the dioceses in the nation. The situation turned out somewhat different than I had been told. In the official data the laity-per-priest ratio (including both diocesan and religious priests) was 921. In the ten largest dioceses (Los Angeles, Chicago, Boston, New York, Detroit, Brooklyn, Philadelphia, Newark, Rockville Centre, and Pittsburgh), the figure was 1,075 — showing that they have a poorer ratio than average. A few of the large cities had a much worse laity-per-priest ratio. Los Angeles had 1,892, Rockville Centre had 1,852, and Detroit had 1,452. Of the ten largest dioceses, only New York and Boston could be called priest-rich (745 and 783, respectively).

The five states in the U.S. with the most adequate supply of priests are Arkansas, District of Columbia, Alabama, Mississippi, and Alaska. Except for the District of Columbia (a special case due to its colleges and offices), all are in areas far from the older heartland of Catholicism, and all have rather small Catholic populations. The five states with the least adequate supply of priests are Nevada, Hawaii, Texas, California, and Michigan. Except for Michigan all are in the West or Southwest. As a general conclusion, the Southwest is the region with the worst laity-per-priest ratio.

We should not forget that parishes vary widely in size, and this complicates the discussion of the priest shortage. The average size of parishes is much larger in urban centers than in rural areas. Most talk today is about priestless parishes, and they most often occur in dioceses having the greatest number of small and scattered parishes, usually in rural areas. But if we focus on quality of ministry, and if we use the laity-to-priest ratio as an indicator of quality (the lower the ratio the better the ministry) then the large urban centers have lower quality ministry. The reason is simply that urban parishes are much larger. The national average of persons per parish in the U.S. was 2,700 in 1986, but in the Archdiocese of New York it was 4,400; in Brooklyn, 6,400; in Chicago, 5,300; and in Los Angeles, 9,300. By contrast, in Arkansas they averaged 675; in South Dakota, 682; in Alaska, 797; in Mississippi, 813; and in South Carolina, 873. The priest shortage needs to be assessed using both indicators — the number of priestless parishes and the laity-to-priest ratio.

Apart from the question of precision, the option of redistributing priests within the United States is a potential method to ease critical shortages in one place or another. But the problem is that no bishops feel that they have any surplus priests to offer. To make the system a reality, an incentive system will need to be devised so that priest-rich bishops will be induced to send a few to priest-poor areas. The option strikes me as maybe workable in a few special conditions, but not workable in general and not hopeful for dealing with the enormity of the priest shortage.

The third form of the argument talks about redistributing priests within dioceses. It takes note of the many priests working in chancery offices, social ministries, schools, and agencies and asserts that non-ordained people could do many of the jobs just as well. If this could be done, the priests could be re-allocated to parish work. In our 1985 survey of priests we asked them what their current position was, and the results are shown in Table 10.   It shows that 22 percent of diocesan priests and 58 percent of religious priests are working outside of parishes. A portion of these diocesan priests could probably be asked to devote themselves partly or fully to parish work. For example, in the Archdiocese of Baltimore's planning project called "Project 83," it was explicitly stated that diocesan priests would be gradually moved out of

Table 10

**Current Position of Non-Retired Diocesan and Religious
Priests, 1985 (Percents)**

	Diocesan Priests	Religious Priests
Full-time diocesan administration	6	3
Pastor with special work outside the parish	12	7
Pastor without special work outside the parish	37	14
Full-time associate pastor	22	15
Associate pastor with special work outside the parish	7	5
Educational apostolate	5	15
Hospital chaplaincy	4	7
Prison chaplaincy	1	1
Social service apostolate	1	1
Other	5	31

central administration and specialized ministries into parish work. Specifically, "The total number of priests in Central Services will be reduced by at least two over the next three years," and "The Clergy Personnel Board will identify and recommend at least three priests who could return to parish ministry from specialized ministry in the next three years."[1] Also a general freeze on all assignments to specialized ministries was recommended.

In the Archdiocese of New York, Archbishop O'Connor formulated a similar plan to move priests from administration into parish work. He said he wanted to move as many as possible of the 38 priests working in administration to parishes, replacing them with lay people, nuns, and deacons. Within four months, he said in an interview, eight of the priests would be moved out and replaced by lay people, nuns, and deacons, and in the months following more would go. "The parishes are hurting," he explained. "That's where the action is."[2]

Would priests be willing to shift their work in the direction of more sacramental ministry? To find out, we asked in the 1985 survey, "In the future if you would be asked to restrict your work to sacramental and liturgical duties, would you be satisfied or dissatisfied?" (Note that the question does not ask specifically about parish work but about one portion of parish work.) The results are in Table 11. To our surprise, the responses of the diocesan and religious priests were not much different;

Table 11

**Reaction If Asked in the Future to Restrict Work
to Sacramental and Liturgical Duties (Percents)**

	All Diocesan Priests	All Religious Priests
Very satisfied	13	22
Somewhat satisfied	21	16
Neither satisfied nor dissatisfied	7	9
Somewhat dissatisfied	24	20
Very dissatisfied	31	31
I don't know	4	3

55 percent of the diocesan priests and 51 percent of the religious priests would be dissatisfied, but 34 percent of the diocesan and 38 percent of the religious would be satisfied. The rest had no strong feelings. In further analysis we found that the younger the priest, the more dissatisfied he would be (64 percent among those 35 or younger, compared with 34 percent among those 66 or older).

In general, priests have mixed feelings about this question. But what about the priests not serving in parishes at the present time? They are the ones who would have to make a change. Their responses are summarized in Table 12. The first line of the table shows that priests work-

Table 12

Percent Satisfied or Dissatisfied If Asked in the Future to Restrict Work to Sacramental and Liturgical Duties

	Percent Very or Somewhat Satisfied	Percent Very or Somewhat Dissatisfied
Full-time diocesan administration	44	47
Pastor with special work outside the parish	25	64
Pastor without special work outside the parish	40	49
Associate pastor with special work outside the parish	28	67
Full-time associate pastor	29	57
Educational apostolate	34	58
Hospital chaplaincy, prison chaplaincy, social service apostolate, or other	35	54

ing full-time in diocesan offices would be more willing than average to shift their work to sacramental and liturgical duties only; only 47 percent would be dissatisfied. By contrast, those serving in the educational apostolate, chaplaincy, social service apostolate, or other position would be less willing; 54 percent to 58 percent would be dissatisfied (last two lines in the table). The priests most unwilling to restrict their work to sacramental and liturgical duties are those in both parish work and outside work. Apparently they like the mix of duties they presently have.

The issue is not only willingness to shift to sacramental and liturgical duties in parishes, but also effectiveness in this role. Priests are needed who are not only willing to shift their jobs but also capable in the new jobs. Information on this question is unavailable, but my impression is that many older priests who have not served parishes for some years would be rather ineffective as parish leaders.

One implication of the idea of redistributing priests within dioceses is that it leads to less freedom of action for priests but more opportunities for laypersons, sisters, and deacons, since the latter groups will find additional opportunities in non-parish positions being opened up. Diocesan administration will move toward more lay control and less clerical control.

The option of redistributing priests within dioceses is feasible and indeed is underway in many places. An increase in priestly services can be achieved. We have seen that 22 percent of diocesan priests are employed outside of parishes and about 40 percent of them would be satisfied with a change to mostly sacramental and liturgical duties. That adds up to about 9 percent of all diocesan priests which could conceivably be re-assigned. If bishops made strong appeals or put on pressure, the figure would rise higher. Also a number of diocesan priests now part-time in parish work could be assigned to it full-time, for an additional gain in sacramental leadership. As a rough estimate, this option would seem able to increase priestly services by 10 percent to 15 percent from the diocesan priesthood.

The fourth form of the argument about redistributing priests is somewhat different, but the logic is still the same. It says that many parish priests are spending large amounts of time and energy doing tasks which are non-religious and non-liturgical. If they had assistants or helpers to do these tasks the priests could devote themselves more fully to sacramental and liturgical ministry, and as a result more priestly services would become available to the parishioners. Then one priest could perform more marriages and baptisms and could celebrate Eucharist more often than at present. This topic can be more effectively discussed alongside lay ministries (in Chapter 7) than here, and we will take it up later. We mention it here merely for sake of completeness.

Option 3: Get more parish priests from religious orders

As we saw in Tables 10 and 11, 58 percent of religious priests today are working outside of parishes, and 35 percent to 45 percent of them would be satisfied if they had to devote themselves solely to sacramental and liturgical ministries. This amounts to 20 percent or 25 percent of religious priests open to carrying out sacramental duties. In the United States in 1985, 39 percent of all priests were religious priests, and if a portion of them could be recruited to parish work it would increase priestly services available.

It is difficult to speak on this topic with any certainty, since the idea of getting more parish priests from religious orders depends on the attitudes of the orders. They have their own priest shortages; indeed, religious orders have been less successful in the last two decades than dioceses in attracting new seminarians. They have their own institutional obligations, their own special ministries, their basic identities as servants of Jesus Christ in dozens of specialized ways. Why should they abandon these commitments in favor of more involvement in parishes? How many could be attracted to take responsibility for parishes? It is difficult to know.

There are arguments against this option. One is not widely voiced, yet it is often present, and that is the caution among bishops of assigning parishes to religious orders, which are only indirectly under their control. Another is described by Rev. Philip Murnion:

> There is a tendency in some parts of the country to invite religious orders to take responsibility for more parishes. This trend needs to be monitored. For while religious orders have in the past, do now, and will in the future make an important contribution to parish life — in some areas they are its mainstay — parish work is neither the particular apostolate nor the priority of many orders. This creates a temptation to staff parishes with men who simply do not fit the order's own primary ministry.[3]

The question of quality of leadership in order-run parishes compared with diocesan-run parishes is continually debated, and one doesn't know what to believe. I can only add that in a time of dwindling supplies of priests, quality of personnel will inexorably be sacrificed in the pressures of finding *someone* to staff the parishes. The choice may be between not-well-qualified diocesan priests and not-well-qualified religious priests.

As a rough guess, the quantity of priestly services in parishes could be increased by 10 percent or 20 percent through asking more religious orders to take over parishes. Beyond that, it would seem to require either pressure from bishops or some form of incentive to the orders. The topic is so under-researched that I find myself dealing with mere guesses.

Option 4: Get priests from foreign nations

The United States has always imported priests. During the highpoint of the European immigration at about the turn of the century, many hundreds of priests came to the U.S. along with their people. American bishops desperately needed them and pleaded with the bishops of Ireland, Germany, Poland, and elsewhere to send priests to America.

Today the European immigration is virtually over, but the Asian and Hispanic immigrations are in full motion. Can priests be gotten now from Asia and Latin America? Or can more priests be gotten from Europe to ease the shortage?

Let us consider Europe first. In the early 20th century the principal source of overseas priests was Ireland. American bishops sent agents to Ireland each year to recruit seminarians and priests. Several from the southern states were especially active in doing this, so today hundreds of foreign-born Irish (affectionately known as "FBIs") are serving in dioceses in Florida, Alabama, Mississippi, and elsewhere throughout the South. The Irish bishops approved, since they had more seminary graduates than they could place, and they were happy to send their young men into the American mission fields.

But the Irish supply has almost dried up. During the 1970s, vocations dropped in Ireland just like everywhere else, and many young priests resigned, so by the end of the decade the Irish bishops no longer welcomed Americans coming over to recruit their young men. But the traffic was not stopped completely, and in the middle 1980s several bishops have been sending agents to Ireland in search of priests. As we saw in Chapter 1, Ireland today is the most priest-rich nation in the world, and it still has a few to spare. An Irish expert estimated the flow of priests to America at about 15 or 20 a year, and he said that this rate could be expected to continue or even increase a bit.[4] Irish priests are unique in that they speak English and can acculturate easily, so they are available to serve multi-ethnic American parishes. By contrast, all other foreign priests were recruited mainly to serve their own ethnic groups.

Hundreds of priests were gotten from Poland, and even in the 1980s a few are coming in to serve Polish ethnic churches or recent immigrants from Poland. The present flow is about 8 priests or seminarians a year. Some priests were also recruited from Portugal, a total of about 50 in recent years. The situation is different with regard to the new Asian and Hispanic immigration, which is bringing 400,000

Catholics to the U.S. each year. Many immigrant priests are coming with them. Today our country has about 300 Filipino priests, 200 to 300 Indian priests, about 250 Vietnamese priests, and about 40 Korean priests. Virtually all serve parishes in the immigrant communities. Latin America, by contrast, has produced almost none, not even Mexico.[5]

Within the last five years the bishop conferences of the various nations have made agreements regarding the flow of priests to the United States. Formal agreements have been signed with the bishop conferences of Mexico, Philippines, and Poland, stating that any priest wanting to come to the U.S. needs the permission of both bishop conferences, and he must serve his own ethnic group in the U.S., not any other parishes. The bishop conferences want to restrain third world priests from coming to the U.S. in search of better living standards.

The reason for the hesitancy in recruiting non-European priests is the problem of acculturation. The priests get culture shock, and so do the American parishioners. For example, in the Diocese of Rockville Centre, which has been a leader in using third-world priests, the policy has been changed. No longer is the diocese interested in incardinating foreign priests, since those who came during the last ten years have serious problems with the English language, and they lack knowledge of our culture. As Monsignor James Kelly, Personnel Director, put it, "We get too much flak from our people, who can't understand them."[6] Rockville Center has incardinated 17 priests from English-speaking nations and 25 from non-English-speaking nations within the past ten years, and at the present time they have 46 other foreign priests serving in various temporary assignments. Even though the diocese faces a severe priest shortage, it will not be incardinating more from non-English-speaking nations. Rather, the new policy will be to put more emphasis on training lay ministers.

All our informants agreed that getting priests from foreign nations is not a solution to the priest shortage. It is useful only for serving immigrant communities, and since immigration will continue, recruiting priests from these nations will need to continue. But otherwise few foreign priests are available who can be effective in American parishes.

Option 5: Recruit more seminarians

This option is different from all the others in that it has been everyone's favorite for years. It is the "of course" solution to the priest shortage. For many people today it seems to be the only visible option, judging from the meetings on vocations I have attended in which this was the sole option being considered.

But it has not been working. Seminary enrollments continue to sag, in spite of the time, money, and energy poured into vocation work in the last decade (see Appendix B, Table E-1). This changes everything. The number of seminarians today falls far short of what is needed to maintain the current supply of priests. Thoughtful people are asking, why? What are we doing wrong? Can we improve vocations recruiting so as to produce enough seminarians to supply the church's needs? If not, what other options do we have?

Already I have outlined some of the conclusions I think flow from the research already done on vocations. These conclusions are not infallible, but they seem to be the most reasonable lessons to be drawn for guiding practical action. Most important: the shortage of vocations is not a temporary thing which is self-correcting or a short-term low point in a cyclical pattern. It is a long-term situation with no end in sight. No large increases in the number of seminarians can be expected, even if recruitment efforts are expanded and improved. Therefore this option should not be pursued alone, to the exclusion of others.

Numerous studies have investigated how to go about recruiting seminarians for best results.[7] The most extensive was done in 1979 and published in a 1981 book written by Fee, Greeley, McCready, and Sullivan.[8]

These researchers surveyed young Catholic men and women age 14 to 29 nationwide, asking them about various topics including their interest or disinterest in vocations. They found 23 persons out of 1,243 (2 percent) to be already in a vocation, in training, or at least seriously interested. More men than women were in a vocation or interested. In comparing these 23 with the others, the research team found that the 23 had received much more encouragement for vocations from other persons. Thirty-two percent had received encouragement from their mothers (versus 9 percent of all others), 32 percent had received encouragement from religious (versus 12 percent of all others), and 26 percent had received it from friends (versus 3 percent of all others). The authors summed up: "In general, the dominant influences seem to come from those already in the religious life and from one's mother."[9] Also the persons interested in vocations had more history of regular Mass attendance themselves (and by their parents), of daily prayer, and (among the men) of experience as an altar boy. There was a slight tendency for those interested in vocations to have had more years of Catholic schooling and attendance at Catholic colleges.

The survey asked those young persons not interested in vocations why not, and the results are summarized in Table 13. The table has two columns to distinguish respondents who had at least thought about a vocation, but not really seriously, from those who had never thought about it. The main problem for respondents in both columns was "Not allowed to marry," the second most important was "My faith in the church's teachings is not deep enough," and the third most important was "Lifelong commitment." An important finding was that 30 percent of those who had never thought about a vocation said a very important reason was that "I don't know enough about being a priest, a nun, or a brother to be interested in the religious life."

The research team constructed a series of statistical models to test if celibacy was the main deterrent to vocations or not. They found that celibacy alone is not as potent a deterrent as the total package of attitudes shown in Table 13, but that the total package of attitudes is the

Table 13

**Reasons Why Youth 14-29 Were Not Interested in a Vocation
(Percent Saying Each Reason Is "Very Important")**

	Those Who Have Thought About a Vocation But Not Really Seriously	Those Who Never Thought About a Vocation
Not allowed to marry	51	55
Poor pay	5	14
Lifelong commitment	33	41
Lack of privacy	20	28
Uninteresting work	5	19
Too many rules and regulations	27	37
Poor professional standards	5	12
Undemocratic church structure	19	23
My faith in the church's teachings is not deep enough	47	52
I met some priests or religious who were unattractive human beings	6	6
I think that many priests and religious are lonely, especially in old age	14	14
I don't know enough about being a priest, a nun, or a brother to be interested in the religious life	18	30
The religious life does not seem to be a challenging enough career	7	21

Source: Adapted from Fee, et al. (1981), p. 140.

#1 deterrent. Second most important was the encouragement factor.
The researchers distinguished the early part of the vocation discernment process from the later part of actually training and persevering,
and they judged that encouragement and "warm images of God" are
more important than deterring attitudes in the early part, whereas the
celibacy issue seems more important later.[10]

The 1985 College Student Survey

In 1984 we proposed doing a new survey somewhat similar to the
1979 nationwide survey, but targeted to a more specific sample and asking different questions. We decided on surveying an identifiable group
which is a source of many vocations — undergraduate college students.
The survey was done in 1985 in 33 colleges. (For details, see Appendix
A.) At each college we asked the Catholic campus minister to name the
undergraduates who formed the leadership group responsible for carrying out ministry programs, and we surveyed them by mail questionnaire.
Second, we drew a random sample of undergraduate Catholics and
tried to reach them for a phone interview, to provide a comparison
group. Most of the students were 19 to 21 years old.

The basic question about the students' interest in a vocation is shown
in Table 14. Note that 16 percent of the men campus ministry leaders
and 5 percent of the women leaders are now training for a vocation or
seriously considering a vocation. To check on the seriousness of these
persons' interest we asked if they are in training now or at least have
talked to someone about their interest. The percent saying yes is shown
at the bottom of the table, and this represents a more realistic estimate
of the level of interest in vocations — 13 percent of the men and 4 percent of the women leaders, and less than 1 percent of the random
sample.

The percentage of the random sample interested in a vocation may
sound low, but in relation to the level of interest in the total Catholic
population it is high. Remember that the production of priests in the
American Catholic community is very low. Statistically it takes 10,000

Table 14

Number of College Students Considering a Vocation (Percents)

	Campus Ministry Leaders		Random Sample	
	Men	Women	Men	Women
Which of the following best expresses your attitude toward a religious vocation, that is, becoming a priest, brother, or sister?				
I am at present training for the religious life, or I am seriously considering it but have not begun training.	16	5	1	½
I began training for a religious vocation but later decided that the religious life is not for me.	1	0	1	1
I have seriously considered a religious vocation but decided against it before entering a seminary or convent.	21	14	8	5
The thought of becoming a priest, brother, or sister has entered my mind, but I have never really seriously considered it.	55	59	46	50
I have never considered a religious vocation, that is, becoming a priest, brother, or sister.	7	22	45	44
(For those presently training for the religious life or seriously considering it:)				
Persons in training now or who have talked to someone about their interest (percent of total sample)	13	4	1	½

Catholics an average of six years to produce just one ordained priest. This is far less than 1 percent of the boys born per year. Based on data from the U.S. Bureau of the Census, a community of 10,000 persons would have over 75 male babies per year, or over 450 in six years. The percent of Catholic boys who become priests is therefore less than one-fourth of 1 percent.

Table 15, Part A

Attitudes of College Students Not Interested in a Vocation
(Percents)

	Campus Ministry Leaders		Random Sample	
	Men	Women	Men	Women
(For those not presently training for the religious life or seriously considering it:)				
People decide against becoming a priest, brother, or sister for various reasons. Below are ten reasons people sometimes give. How important is each to you? (Percent saying "Very Important")				
Too many rules and regulations.	10	11	17	19
Not allowed to marry.	70	74	61	66
Church structures are too undemocratic.	9	13	18	9
These vocations are not held in high esteem.	4	3	9	4
A life-long commitment is required.	29	35	55	45
People in these vocations are often lonely.	24	26	27	26
A lack of privacy.	7	16	13	17
Church structures are too dominated by men.	9	26	11	25
The role of priest, brother, or sister is too unclear today.	6	12	13	13
I don't know enough about the life to be interested in it.	10	11	20	19

The percentage of the campus ministry leaders interested is higher than we expected. It shows that campus ministry groups are indeed an identifiable source of future vocations.

Table 15, Part B

Attitudes of College Students Not Interested in a Vocation (Percents)

(For those not presently training for the religious life or seriously considering it:)

Some persons are seriously interested in serving the Church in a way different than being a priest, brother, or sister. Below are some opportunities existing now or under discussion. After each, circle one number to indicate if you would be seriously interested or not. (Percent "Yes")

	Campus Ministry Leaders		Random Sample	
	Men	Women	Men	Women
(for males only:)				
Would you be seriously interested in becoming an ordained priest if celibacy were not required? Yes.	35	–	12	–
Would you be seriously interested in becoming an ordained priest if priests could have an honorable discharge, if desired, after 10 or 15 years of service? Yes.	11	–	16	–
(for females only:)				
Would you be seriously interested in becoming an ordained priest, if women could be ordained? Yes.	–	15	–	4

Everyone not seriously interested in a vocation was asked a series of questions, which are shown in Table 15. First we asked them to rate the importance of ten widely-heard reasons why people decide against a religious vocation. The ten were gathered from the 1979 research and other credible sources. The table shows the percentage saying that each was "very important." Note that "Not allowed to marry" is clearly the main deterrent. Second most important (especially in the random sample) is "A life-long commitment is required." Several other arguments about the vocation shortage one sometimes hears turned out not to be very important. For example, the argument that unclarity about the priest's role today hinders vocations is not very strong, judging from its apparent lack of importance among these students. And the argument that feminist objections to the male-dominated leadership in the Catholic church has hindered vocations is only moderately strong.

The bottom part of Table 15 gives responses to three hypothetical questions we put to the respondents. The questions are on topics important to the church, but they have a weakness in that they are only in the realm of the hypothetical, not the actual. If celibacy were not required, 35 percent of the male campus ministry leaders would be seriously interested in the priesthood, and 12 percent of the random sample. If an honorable discharge were available, 11 percent of the male campus ministry leaders and 16 percent of the random sample would be seriously interested. These figures should be treated with some reservations due to the unreality of the questions and, in the case of the random sample, the lack of time to reflect in the midst of a phone interview. But the campus ministry leaders had time to think about these issues while filling out mail questionnaires, and they probably had discussed the topics in the past. As a rough estimate, the number of young Catholic men who would be seriously interested in the priesthood under conditions of optional celibacy would increase fourfold or more from the present level.

The availability of an honorable discharge would, in effect, reduce the deterrent impact of the life-long commitment (which was the second strongest reason among the students for not choosing a religious vocation). It had a positive effect on the level of interest in the priesthood, especially among the random sample men. Among the campus ministry leaders the effect was smaller than the effect of optional celibacy. Nevertheless, in real-world terms the availability of an honorable discharge would have a definite impact on the number of young men interested in a vocation.

The last item in Table 15 asks women students if they would be seriously interested in becoming an ordained priest if women could be ordained. Fifteen percent of the women campus ministry leaders and 4 percent of the random sample women said yes. This change in discipline would have a large impact on women's vocations. The extent to which it would strengthen the vowed sisterhood is unknown, but the number of women interested in some form of vocation would increase — as a rough estimate, it would more than double.

The survey of campus ministry leaders included a series of questions about who had encouraged them or discouraged them concerning vocations. For the men the greatest encouragement had come from priests and from their mothers; the greatest discouragement had come from their friends. For women the greatest encouragement had come from religious sisters and from their mothers, and the greatest discouragement had come from their friends. The level of encouragement was lower, overall, for women than for men.

The survey of campus ministry leaders also included twelve questions about ecclesiological issues, thus allowing us to look more closely at the men who are seriously interested in a vocation compared with other men and with the women. Do they hold distinct opinions about the church? (A comparable study of the women interested in a vocation could not be made, since the number in the survey is too small — only 14 cases.) The table showing the results is in Appendix B, Table B-5; it includes additional information also, which we will discuss below.

The findings can be summarized easily: the men interested in a vocation are more conservative than the other students on many issues. They favor, more than other students, having the church insist on strict standards of doctrinal beliefs among members. They favor emphasizing a way of life for Catholics which stresses distinctiveness from prevailing American lifestyle, more than other student men or women. They favor recruiting many more priests to overcome the existing shortage more than other men and women students, who tend to stress restructuring parish leadership to include more deacons, sisters, and lay persons. They believe, more than other students, that the fact that leadership in the Catholic Church is held by celibate men is a strength, not a weakness. They are less interested than other students in having the church put more emphasis on aiding poor and hungry human beings, as opposed to putting more emphasis on counseling or spiritual guidance of members. They are less in favor of having women priests in the future. And they are less in favor of re-thinking the church's teachings on birth control and divorce. In short they are institutionally conservative relative to the other students, and the distance between their views and the views of the women is sometimes great.[11]

The survey results also allow us to look at the men who would be seriously interested in the priesthood if celibacy were optional and at the women who would be seriously interested in the priesthood if women could be ordained. This level of analysis is a "thought experiment" in that it tries to make conclusions based on thinking about hypothetical situations. Also the survey lacks any test of the seriousness of the students' interest in the priesthood under the hypothetical conditions. The data in the appendix, Table B-5, depict how the prospective non-celibate and women priests differ in attitudes from the other men and women. Here we will summarize.

Turning to the men first, we find that the non-celibate priests would no longer be very distinct from the rest of the men campus ministry leaders.[12]

Among the women the pattern is different. If women could be ordained as priests, those seriously interested would be different from the other women student leaders on six issues. They would (1) insist less than others on strict standards of doctrinal beliefs, (2) put less emphasis on clergy-laity status differences in the future, (3) see the church's male celibate leadership as more of a weakness (as opposed to a strength), (4) more strongly favor the ordination of married men, (5) more favor the bishops' taking public stands on some political issues, and (6) more favor re-thinking church teachings on birth control and divorce. In short, they would be more institutionally innovative than the other women. And the same pattern holds if we compare two hypothetical future groups, non-celibate men priests and women priests. The women would be more institutionally innovative. For example, they would more strongly desire re-thinking the church's teachings on birth control and divorce (67 percent versus 37 percent for the men).

Factors Causing Interest in Vocations

What are the factors which cause some college students to be interested in vocations? Using the campus ministry leader data we were able to measure which experiences in their past had influenced some to be interested. See Table 16. It shows product-moment correlations which indicate the strength of association between each factor and whether or not the men were seriously interested in vocations (13 percent were, 87 percent were not). A correlation of 0 indicates no association at all between the factor and whether or not the men were interested in vocations. Correlations of + .35 or +. 40 are strong, and correlations weaker than ± .15 are too weak for any practical importance. For that reason none weaker than ± .15 are shown. Twelve other predictors were tested, but the correlations came out too weak. They included age, race, college class, mother's and father's Mass attendance, past experience in volunteer church service, Catholic or public high school, and several attitudinal items. The "Church Institutional Factors" and "Ecclesiological Attitudes" in the table cannot be seen as definite factors causing interest in vocations, since they were measured after the student had ac-

Table 16

Relationships Between Four Sets of Factors and Interest in Vocations Among Campus Ministry Men Leaders

	Corre-lation*
Background Factors	
Ethnicity (German, Austrian, Dutch, Swiss, Irish = 2; others = 1)	.15[a]
Type of Elementary School (Catholic = 3; mixed = 2; non-Catholic = 1)	.16[b]
Encouragement From Others	
From mother	.26
From father	.32
From brother, sister, or relative	.32
From friends	.19
From Vocation Director	.48
From pastor	.20
From other priest	.35
From campus minister	.27
From Catholic school teacher	.22
From religious sister or religious brother	.38
Church Institutional Factors	
Church requires high standards of training for many ministries	.15[c]
Church has males in all top positions of leadership	.28[d]
Church usually pays lower salaries than secular organizations	.15[e]
Ecclesiological Attitudes	
The Church should rethink its teachings on birth control and divorce	-.17[f]

*All correlations are significant beyond .05. N = 237-248.

Explanations:
[a]German, Austrian, Dutch, Swiss, and Irish have higher interest.
[b]Those who attended Catholic elementary schools have higher interest.
[c]Those encouraged by high standards have higher interest.
[d]Those encouraged by exclusive male leadership have higher interest.
[e]Those not discouraged by lower salaries have higher interest.
[f]Those favoring re-thinking Church teachings have lower interest.

quired his interest in a vocation, hence may have been influenced by that decision. All we can claim from our data is that the attitude is *associated with* (for whatever reason) interest in a vocation.

The main finding in Table 16 is the very strong impact of encouragement from other people. Just as Fee and her associates found in 1981, again we found that personal encouragement is a foremost factor in promoting vocations. The most important for the students in our survey were encouragement by vocation directors, religious sisters or brothers, priests, and fathers and relatives. Unlike the earlier survey, this one found that fathers had slightly more impact than mothers.

The rest of Table 16 merely shows that other factors are less important than personal encouragement. This agrees with all other research. There are wide-ranging discussions today about how more vocations might be attracted — maybe through media campaigns, maybe through incentives to pastors, maybe through parish-based encouragement groups, and so on. The research shows that personal relationships and modelling by exemplary priests are the most effective means. Direct encouragement by priests and religious also have demonstrated effect. By contrast, media campaigns and advertising have little impact.[13] My experience with vocation directors indicates that they are very much aware of what methods work, and they are trying hard; thus I doubt if any great increase in vocations could be achieved through different methods or better training of vocation directors.

I agree, in sum, that personal encouragement is central to promoting more vocations. Whereas the earlier researchers were able to estimate the relative importance of personal encouragement and the deterrent power of attitudes about the priesthood (mainly the celibacy question), our survey was not designed to do that, and we cannot check out their conclusions. Our impression is that among college students the celibacy issue is very strong, since we saw that if the celibacy rule was changed the number of men interested in the priesthood would increase greatly. Whether an improvement in the encouragement factor would have such a marked impact is unclear. All we can say is that the two principal determinants of interest in vocations remain the "big two" emphasized by Fee and her associates — the encouragement factor and the deterrence of celibacy. A change in either one would affect the number of men entering seminary.

Trends in Encouragement to the Priesthood by Lay Persons

All research agrees that encouragement from other people is a major influence causing some young men to be interested in the priesthood. If this is true, it follows that any trends in the amount of encouragement given young men in the Catholic community would probably influence future trends in the number of young men entering seminary. Similarly, it is pertinent to know if the esteem of priests in the eyes of Catholic laity has risen or fallen, since this would probably affect the amount of encouragement they give to young men.

Table 17

Trends in Attitudes About Vocations

	1963	1974	1985	Change 1963–74	Change 1974–85
If a son of yours chose to become a priest, tell me whether you would feel very pleased, somewhat pleased, somewhat disappointed, or very disappointed. Very pleased.	67	50	55	-17	+5
Becoming a priest is not a good vocation for young people any more. Agree strongly or somewhat.		16	16		0
It would make me somewhat unhappy if a daughter of mine became a nun. Agree strongly or some-what.	17	21	25	+4	+4

We designed and commissioned a survey of Catholic adults in 1985 to gather trend data on these topics, since such data would give some indication about future trends in numbers of vocations. We repeated a series of questions used in surveys in 1963 and 1974 in order to get trend information. The results are shown in Table 17.

The first item in the table is the most important. It is a direct measure of overall encouragement or discouragement in the Catholic community for having sons become priests. It has been asked in three nationwide polls of Catholic adults 18 or older — in 1963, 1974, and 1985. The table shows that the level of encouragement dropped rather sharply from 1963 to 1974, but it rose slightly from 1974 to 1985. The 5-point increase to 1985 is barely enough that we can be confident it is a genuine shift in attitude and not just sampling fluctuation in the survey data. Probably there has been *some* rise, because most other indicators of satisfaction with the church rose from 1974 to 1985.

The second item is on a similar topic, but it is stated in the negative direction — saying that the priesthood is not a good vocation. Only 16 percent agreed in 1974, and again in 1985 16 percent agreed.

The third item is on women's vocations, and again it is stated in the negative direction. From 1963 to 1974 there was a mild decrease in encouragement of daughters to enter religious communities, and from 1974 to 1985 there was another slight decrease. The trends are so slight that some may be due to measurement error, but between 1963 and 1985 there was at least *some* decrease.

Figure 10 portrays breakdowns on the item about a son becoming a priest. The lines portray subgroups of the sample. At the top of the figure the breakdown by age shows that all age groups except those 51 and older have similar attitudes. Persons 51 and older are much more encouraging than others to their sons. (The line does not extend back to 1963, since the 1963 sample did not include respondents over age 57.) The breakdown in the middle of the figure is by number of children, of

Figure 10

Breakdowns, in Percentages

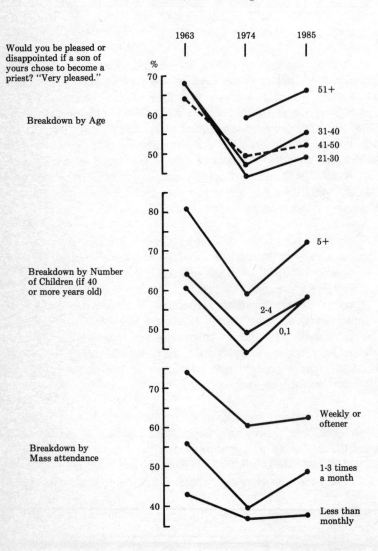

Would you be pleased or disappointed if a son of yours chose to become a priest? "Very pleased."

Breakdown by Age

Breakdown by Number of Children (if 40 or more years old)

Breakdown by Mass attendance

persons 40 or more years old. It supports the widely heard theory that parents with large families are more encouraging of a son to enter the priesthood than are other parents, supposedly because they will have a son "to spare" and not needed to carry on the lineage. The breakdown at the bottom demonstrates that parental Mass attendance has consistently been a strong predictor of encouragement to the priesthood. Two other breakdowns are important, but they are not shown. Women were more encouraging of sons than were men in all three surveys; for example, in 1985, 58 percent of the women would be "very pleased" if their son became a priest, versus 52 percent for the men. Also the amount of education predicted the amount of encouragement given to sons in 1974 and 1985, but not in 1963; persons with college degrees were less encouraging in 1974 and 1985. For example, in 1985, 48 percent of those with college degrees would be "very pleased," versus 57 percent of the others.

In sum, the greatest encouragement to sons concerning the priesthood comes from older parents without college education who have large families and attend Mass weekly. As education increases and family size decreases in the Catholic community one could expect a long-term weakening of encouragement of sons to become priests. But of course short-term shifts occur, responding to the changes in the religious and social climate, and the shift from 1974 to 1985 was in the direction of *more* encouragement of sons to the priesthood.

Has there been any discernible shift in the amount of esteem accorded to priests by lay Catholics? In Chapter 2, Table 8, we saw that the answer is yes. The various ratings of priests made by Catholic adults since 1952 indicate diminishing esteem between 1952 and 1974, then an increase from 1974 to 1985 — but not nearly to the 1952 level. The improved ratings of priests seem to agree with the increased happiness with having a son become a priest in 1985.

All the measures of attitudes among Catholic lay people concerning priests are moving in the positive direction since 1974, and they would seem to predict an increase, not a further decrease, in vocations in coming years. Let us turn to trends in priests' attitudes about vocations.

Trends in Encouragement by Priests

An important reason for carrying out the 1985 survey of priests was to procure trend data on two topics — priestly encouragement of young men into the priesthood, and priestly morale. The first is important for helping project future trends in seminarians, and the second is almost as important because it affects priestly encouragement. It is often said that "happy priests beget priests," and all research agrees. Hence we wondered if priestly morale has risen or fallen in recent years.

We repeated the landmark 1970 survey of American priests, which included good measures on these topics. The main measure is shown in Table 18. The table has four columns, not two, since in each survey the priests were asked to report their present attitude and also their attitude "4 or 5 years ago." The first response in the table is a good measure of priestly encouragement to young men; it increased a good bit from 1970 to 1985; whereas 30 percent said in 1970 that they actively encouraged young men, in 1985 48 percent said so. This is a rather great increase over 15 years. In 1970 the priests reported that their attitudes were different 4 or 5 years earlier — 60 percent said that 4 or 5 years ago they had actively encouraged young men. The events of the early post-Vatican years 1965-1970 had very demoralizing effects on the priests, and very likely the social climate of the late 1960s in the United States added to the bewilderment. By contrast, the change from the level of encouragement 4 to 5 years before 1985 and 1985 was small and should not be overemphasized.

To sum up: The level of encouragement of young men by priests was highest in 1965-66, then dropped sharply to 1970, then rose again to the 1980-85 period. As noted earlier, the years of most priestly resignations were 1967 to 1973, and probably these were also the years when

Table 18

Attitudes Toward Recruiting For the Priesthood and Religious Life
Today and 4-5 Years Ago (Percents)

	1970 Survey		1985 Survey	
	Today	4-5 Years Ago	Today	4-5 Years Ago
I actively encourage men to enter the seminary or novitiate, since I see the priesthood as a very rewarding vocation.	30	60	48	53
I encourage men but advise them about the uncertainties surrounding the role of the priest today.	29	15	27	21
I neither discourage nor encourage men, but allow them to make up their own minds.	36	22	22	22
Regardless of their personal qualities, I tend to discourage men from entering now and advise them to wait until the future is more certain.	2	1	1	2
Other	3	2	3	2
Total	100	100	101	100

priests were least inclined to actively encourage young men toward the priesthood. After that, resignations dropped off and encouragement of young men rose again. Also, in both 1970 and 1985, younger priests were less inclined to recruit seminarians than were older priests.

The priest survey had a number of measures of morale, and scores on all rose between 1970 and 1985. This surprised us, since most persons we had interviewed spoke of morale problems in the priesthood. But all the morale measures were up: A work satisfaction scale, which could vary from 1 to 52, rose an average of 1.8, a modest increase (the standard deviation in 1985 was 9.08). A question asked, "To what extent do you feel you are utilizing your important skills and abilities in your present assignment?" and the percentage saying "a great deal" or "fairly much" rose from 71 percent to 78 percent. A scale of psychological well-being measuring various aspects of happiness versus depression found an increase of 0.4, which is a moderate increase considering the 1985 standard deviation of 1.89. A direct question asked, "Taking things all together, how would you say things are these days — would you say you're very happy, pretty happy, or not too happy?" and the percentage saying "very happy" rose from 28 percent in 1970 to 39 percent in 1985. On the various measures, older priests gained more over fifteen years than younger priests.

Why has morale increased? The survey produces no direct explanation, so we are left with no more than speculation. One possibility is that the years around 1970 were particularly stressful due to the changes after Vatican II and the social unrest of America in the sixties, so that 1985 is a relatively calmer period. Another is that priests have made gains in self-determination in the past fifteen years, especially with regard to work assignments and chances for participation in diocesan decision-making. The changes possibly improved overall morale. Yet another is that the most unhappy priests in 1970 have resigned in the following years, thus raising the average morale scores for the priesthood. This no doubt had some effect, since we know that between 12.5 percent and 13.5 percent of all diocesan priests and between 15 percent and 17 percent of all religious priests active in 1970 resigned in the ensuing decade.[14] Also we know that the 1985 priests included fewer restless men than in 1970; in 1970, 12 percent said that they would probably resign from the priesthood or were uncertain about their future, and in 1985 this figure dropped to 7 percent.

The trend data we gathered, then, agrees in showing more encouragement to the priesthood from laity and priests than was the case 10 or 15 years ago. The most reasonable expectation, based on these findings, is an increase in the number of young men entering seminary in the years ahead. How big an increase? Is it likely to be enough to solve, or at least ease, the priest shortage? We cannot know, and all we can do is make some guesses.

Robert Sherry, as noted earlier, has calculated the number of priests needed in the year 2000 by using a laity-to-priest ratio of 791, which he considers adequate for sacramental ministries.[15] He comes up with the need for 73,242 priests in 2000, a figure which is probably on the low side, given reasonable expectations about Catholic immigration. He estimates that an increase of 904 priests per year over the present number (in 1985) would be needed to provide this number of priests by 2000. The increase of 904 is *after* replacing those who die or resign each year. How many die or resign? Schoenherr found that deaths in the late 1970s averaged almost 2 percent of the total priesthood annually, and we have seen that resignations have recently averaged about 0.5 percent. These add up to approximately 1,300 priests a year — a figure which agrees with Vatican reports as of 1983. (Retirements are not included in the figures, since Sherry's target numbers include a certain percentage of retired priests.) Thus we arrive at an estimate of 2,200 ordinations a year (904 + 1,300) needed to overcome the American priest shortage by the year 2000. By contrast, the actual number of ordinations in recent years is about 780 to 830 a year.[16] Taking 815 as an estimate, we see that the seminaries are currently operating at about two-thirds replacement level (815 divided by 1,300), that is, for every three priests leaving the priesthood or dying, two are being added. We also see that to overcome the priest shortage as we have defined it, an enormous increase in seminarians would be needed. The number of ordinations would have to jump from 815 to 2,209 annually.

This is not possible. We expect a possible increase in seminarians, but nothing like this. An initial guess might be an increase of 5 percent to 15 percent in the next decade, not more. And this is only a guess. Ordinations cannot be increased enough to solve the priest shortage by the year 2000 or even to maintain the number of priests at its 1985 level. The problem is too great. Even if encouragement levels could be raised, and even if vocation directors would find more effective ways of attracting men to the priesthood, it will not be enough. Vocation work needs to be supported, but at the same time *other options* need to be invoked too.

Comment on Two Topics:
The Mothers' Revenge, and Older Priests

In recent years one theory advanced for the shortage of men's vocations was called "the mothers' revenge." It held that Catholic women today are angry at the institutional church for the way it treats women, and therefore they are not enthusiastic about encouraging their sons to the priesthood.[17] Since past research has consistently shown the importance of mothers' encouragement of their sons, the theory is plausible. Certainly mothers would have a strong influence.

The theory can be tested in the recent research, and when we looked at the pertinent data we had to conclude that it is false. In three surveys — in 1963, 1974, and 1985 — Catholic women would be *more* pleased than Catholic men if a son of theirs became a priest. Also Catholic women in 1965, 1974, and 1985 rated the sermons of their priests higher than did Catholic men. On no relevant survey question did Catholic women come out more angry than men. Only among Catholic college women did we find evidence that their anger is higher than among men of the same age. We conclude that some Catholic women are no doubt angry, but a mother's revenge cannot be held to account for the downward trend in vocations to the priesthood.

Lastly, I would like to comment on the current debate about whether it is wise or unwise to encourage vocations among older men. A great increase in older seminarians has taken place in the past decade. A 1984 survey of Catholic seminarians in theology found that 30 percent were over 30 years old, and 4 percent were over 50 years old.[18] The principal reason for the increase in older men seems to be that the seminaries became more accepting of older candidates during the late 1970s and early 1980s.

In discussing this shift to older seminarians with other people, I have found strong feelings pro and con. Opponents of the shift argue that the older seminary students generally have lower academic abilities and less capacity for parish leadership. They point out that seminaries began accepting older men in large numbers only in the last six years, largely out of financial necessity, whereas in earlier years the seminaries rejected them in order to maintain academic and professional standards. Dioceses have reportedly had mixed experiences with the older priests, since they turned out to be more rigid, more authoritarian, and more oriented to the status of priesthood (as opposed to its ministry) than other priests. For example, Chicago has made an upper age limit of 40 for men entering theology.

The proponents of older seminarians deny these allegations as unproven and point out that in modern society career changes at all ages are common, so there is nothing suspicious about a man's desire to begin seminary in his thirties or forties. Until the last century or so, Catholic seminaries were open to men of all ages, and they should properly be open to all. The older men, on average, are more psychologically mature and wise about the ways of the world than young seminarians, and they are more committed to persevering through seminary to ordination. It is granted that some older men who present themselves for seminary training are unfit, but this is true of all ages, and proper screening will identify them without prejudice to others their age.[19]

Two recent studies of Catholic seminarians have produced new information pertinent to the debate. In 1984 a nationwide survey of seminarians in theology looked to see if the attitudes of seminarians of various ages were different.[20] It found that the older seminarians are more certain about their vocational decision and have fewer doubts about whether they want to become priests. Also the older seminarians are slightly more open to greater participation in church life by deacons and parish councils. But on all other attitudes tested, there was no difference between young and old. Except on this one topic, attitudes of younger and older seminarians were indistinguishable. The survey, however, gathered no information on the academic abilities of the students.

The second study, by Raymond Potvin, looked in more depth at a sample of seminarians in 1985. Again it found few differences between seminarians under 30 and those 30 or older. The older men were not more rigid or more authoritarian.[21] It did find that the older seminarians reported fewer symptoms of psychological distress and higher feelings of happiness and that the older men were slightly more traditional in theological attitudes. On attitudes about the priesthood as such the older and younger seminarians were indistinguishable. Potvin concluded that the study found no data supporting the charges against older seminarians. In his view, admittance of older men to seminaries is a viable policy in face of the decline in vocations.[22]

We conclude that the allegations against older seminarians are not supported by research, and we do not see why older men should not be welcomed by seminaries, subject to normal screening procedures, just like anyone else. Although no one has data on their academic capacities, we do not find that a telling consideration — partly because high academic standards can hardly be maintained anyway in a situation of shortage as crucial as we have today, partly because effectiveness in many priestly roles does not depend directly on academic qualifications.

6

Type C Options: Get More
Priests, With Broadened
Eligibility Criteria

If there is a need for more priests but more cannot be found using present-day eligibility requirements, maybe the requirements should be broadened. This chapter looks at four options: ordaining married men, ordaining women, instituting a definite term of service or an honorable discharge for priests, and re-instating resigned priests.[1] All four of these involve theological issues of varying degrees of seriousness; all four are unacceptable to the Vatican at this time. Yet they are being widely discussed by American Catholics, and some are even being recommended by diocesan planning units. We saw in Chapter 4 that planning committees in both Chicago and Baltimore suggested adoption of one or more of these options.

During 1985 we were able to assess the feelings of Catholic adults, college students, and priests concerning all four options. See Table 19. As the table shows, there is considerable support for some of the options. The three groups (adults, students, and priests) agree remarkably well on their views of the four options, especially on the first two. Also we see that one option is clearly preferred over the others — ordination of married men.

Table 19

Summary of Attitudes of Three Groups (Percents)

	Adults	Student Campus Ministry Leaders	Priests
Percent agreeing strongly or somewhat:			
It would be a good thing if married men were allowed to be ordained as priests.	63	51	63
It would be a good thing if women were allowed to be ordained as priests.	47	49	38
Percent saying it would help the Church:			
Allow priests to resign their priesthood with an honorable discharge, if they wish, after 10 or 15 years of service.	48	27	27
Invite ex-priests who are currently married to become active parish priests again.	48	31	40

Option 6: Ordain married men

This option needs close examination because of its important effects. As we have seen, the celibacy requirement is the single most important deterrent to new vocations to the priesthood, and if it were removed the flow of men into seminaries would increase greatly, maybe fourfold. Therefore this option provides a solution to the shortage of priests. As we said earlier, if celibacy were optional, probably the number of Catholic priests would increase over a period of years until it hit a financial limit, that is, until as many priests were in service as the Catholic community could financially support.

The option has fairly strong attitudinal support. As Table 19 shows, 63 percent of all Catholic adults and 63 percent of the priests support it. Younger adults support it more than older adults, and highly educated adults more than the less educated. Younger priests support it more than older ones, with an age gradient similar to that of laity. People who attend Mass regularly support it *less* than occasional attenders or non-attenders.

Detailed data on trends in these attitudes is not available. All we know is that attitudes of priests on this question were the same in 1970 and 1985, and that attitudes of laity regarding marriage of priests after ordination became 6 percentage points less favorable between 1974 and 1985.

Three points of clarification are needed at the outset to prevent confusion. First, the current discussion on married priests usually concerns only diocesan priests. People often argue that the charisms of religious orders should be preserved unaltered, or at least that such matters are the business of the orders themselves. We agree. Our sole concern here is the diocesan priesthood.

Second, there is a necessary distinction between allowing priests to marry after ordination and allowing already-married men to enter seminary and later be ordained as priests. The distinction is not as trivial as it may look at first, since attitudes regarding the two topics are not the same, and since important implications for priests are involved. In 1985 we found that Catholic adults are more in favor of ordaining already-married men (63 percent) than are in favor of allowing priests to marry (51 percent). Apparently the notion of letting ordained priests marry is more offensive.

But in practice the two need to be considered together, since allowing married men into seminary to prepare for ordination without allowing existing priests to marry would be seen as unfair and would arouse resentment. So the gradualist approach of taking the most acceptable step first would appear to be impossible.

Although the majority of priests themselves favor ordination for married men, this does not mean that they themselves desire to marry. In the 1985 survey, only 15 percent of all priests would definitely or probably marry if celibacy became optional. The issue is more pertinent with regard to attracting future vocations than with regard to retaining priests in service.

Third, we need to be more specific about our earlier statement that "the number of priests would increase until it hit a financial limit." How much of an increase would that be? How many priests could be supported? Regrettably this is one of the least understood topics in the whole area of church leadership. We lack reliable information on what the costs of leadership in the church are now, how much it costs the institution to hire a priest, how much seminary education costs, and so on. Also although we know the level of financial contributions in the Catholic Church, we have little idea of its potential under different leadership conditions. The current level, as we saw in Chapter 1, is low relative to the Protestant denominations, yet all responsible observers are convinced that Catholics would contribute more if they believed fully in church leadership, programs, and goals. As stated before, all experts have told us that "money is not the problem."

We can do no more than make a few general statements. Let us take a possible scenario. If in the next ten years, (a) Catholic contributions per-person would increase enough to maintain purchasing power (given inflation) and in addition grow by 25 percent, and (b) the cost of training and maintaining married Catholic priests would be similar to that for married Lutheran ministers, we could envision financial support for an increase in priests or other professionals by 20 percent or 30 percent over the 1985 personnel levels.[2] This is a rough guess, since there are many imponderables. For example, would the quality of leadership rise if there was a married priesthood? The most reasonable assumption would be yes, if only for the reason that seminaries and dioceses could be much more selective than today. For another example, will there be changes in the methods of financing Catholic schools? It is interesting that in the Archdiocese of Cincinnati, lay-led parish planning committees tended to desire greater separation of parish finances from school finances, partly to provide for better parish ministry. These optimistic hints are behind my use of a 25 percent increase in contributions in the hypothetical scenario.

This exercise is intended to make only one point: even if the flow of young men into seminaries would increase twofold, threefold, or fourfold, the church could not use them all, for funds are limited. So the screening process would be intensified, quality would rise, and the increase of priests would not go beyond 20 percent to 30 percent over the 1985 level, or about 70,000 to 75,000 priests. Alternatively, a portion of this number could be composed of professional lay ministers.

Possible Problems of Ordaining Married Men

The most obvious reasons for ordaining married men are to increase the quantity and quality of new vocations. But there are problems associated with the idea, and some research exists which clarifies the problems. Archbishop Daniel Pilarczyk outlined the main problems as he sees them:

> Changing the church's policy of ordaining only celibates to priesthood could bring with it as many problems as it proposes to solve. These problems include those of financial support, of mobility, of numbers, of marriage strain and divorce, of tension

between married and celibate priests. What effects would come
from the necessary sense of loss which parishioners would feel
as they learn that the priest is no longer "theirs" in the same
way he was before? What implications about the church's
teaching on human sexuality, about matrimony, and, indeed, a-
bout the nature of priesthood itself lie hidden in such a
change?[3]

This is a helpful checklist of the issues. They fall under seven headings:
(1) The greater expense of providing for a married clergy. (2) The
decreased mobility of married priests. (3) The number of candidates.
(4) Marital strain, divorce, and subsequent scandal among the flock. (5)
Tension between married and celibate priests. (6) Reduced availability
of married priests due to conflicting demands of family and parish. (7)
Adverse effects on the church's teaching on sexuality, matrimony, and
priesthood.

Some information is available on these topics, since Protestant denominations have been faced with them and have researched them. The
Episcopal Church is especially pertinent for us, since it is theologically
similar to the Roman Catholic Church and it has both married and celibate priests. We will proceed issue by issue.

(1) The greater expense of providing for a married clergy

As we stated above, the question of clergy costs is agonizingly unclear today, and yet one hears a wide array of alleged "facts" being
cited. A few clarifying points can be gotten from the practices of Protestant denominations. First, whether a clergyperson is married or single is
unrelated to his or her salary. The most it might affect salary is by influencing lay financial committees when they are discussing amounts of
salary increases from one year to the next. But when clergy are hired,
the salary offered is independent of the family situation of the candidate. Second, the only realistic measure of the expense to the institution
of having a clergyperson is the total package of salary and allowances.
This includes cash salary, payments for retirement and insurance, social

security payments, housing allowance or free use of a parsonage, travel allowance, continuing education allowance, book allowance, and any other allowances. Comparison of cash salaries alone, either from diocese to diocese or from denomination to denomination, is misleading and should never be made. Any figures used in research should be carefully specified as to what they include and exclude. For example, the Pension Fund of the Episcopal Church in 1983 reported a median salary in 1982 (this includes cash salary, housing, and utilities) of $22,576.[4] But the cost to the institution is higher by at least $5,000, possibly more. A cross-denominational Protestant study in 1982 defined "salary" as including cash salary, insurance, medical surgical coverage, housing, and utilities, and it found an average of $23,680 for the Episcopal Church and $22,400 for the Lutheran Church in America.[5] The only study of total costs of Catholic priests known to us was done in the Diocese of Richmond in 1976, and it found a total cost to the parish and diocese of $13,700 per priest, which would be $25,000 in 1985 dollars.[6] Episcopalian and Lutheran officials have recently told us that total cost packages for clergy are now over $30,000 in each denomination. We lack reliable cross-denominational data for evaluating the assumption that a married priesthood would cost more than a celibate priesthood. The problem is further complicated by the Catholic practice of paying for most or all of a priest's seminary costs — something not done by most Protestant churches.

In the absence of reliable data we can only report what leading financial experts today believe to be the case. They may be in error. But the best guess is that the total cost to the institutions of having celibate Catholic priests is not much different from having married Protestant ministers. If anything, the Protestant costs are a bit higher.

We may note here that most Protestant ministers have working spouses, and in the Episcopal Church it is as high as 90 percent. Also most Protestant ministers prefer to live away from the church building for the sake of privacy and "getting away from" the job. They prefer to own their own homes rather than live in rectories — if the denomination

gives them a choice. (This is mostly for financial reasons.) So if the
Catholic Church adopted optional celibacy for priests, it could be expected that the present on-site rectories would be used less and less for
housing priests.

(2) The decreased mobility of married priests

Without doubt, married clergy are less movable than celibate clergy.
The assignment and deployment system is slower and more difficult to
handle. Married ministers are less willing to move frequently and less
willing to do so on short notice.

Some insight into the problem can be gotten from the United
Methodist Church, which has a clergy deployment system similar to that
of the Catholic Church, yet whose ministers are almost entirely married.
Twenty years ago United Methodist ministers were often moved on
rather short notice by their bishops and district superintendents, but
recently the process has been altered in response to new circumstances.
Since more clergy spouses are working today than in decades past, there
is a need for more lead time before a move from one parish to another,
to help the spouse terminate one job and seek another. Also the
women's movement within the United Methodist church has lobbied
successfully for more attention to family concerns in the process of
moving ministers, so that today there is a mandatory process of consultation with the minister and a committee of both the church being served
and committees of churches where the minister might be going. A third
factor which has changed the deployment process is the oversupply of
ministers in recent decades, which further complicates the process.

The fact that ministers are married undoubtedly makes the system
more cumbersome. It reduces the flexibility available to the bishops and
district superintendents, and it in effect reduces the power of the officials in making appointments. Dr. Jackson Carroll, a leading Methodist
researcher, doubts if these complications have an adverse effect on the
total mission of the denomination. The United Methodist Church has
had to adjust to the new societal demands put on its deployment system,

and the result has been a slowing of the process, but without overall damage. Until recent years the typical pastorate was 4 to 5 years, and today it is a bit longer. For separate reasons there are leading voices in the denomination calling for longer pastorates as a general policy, since they seem to fit the modern circumstances better.[8]

(3) The number of candidates

This issue is not clearly spelled out in Archbishop Pilarczyk's paper, but in personal correspondence he has clarified it. He is concerned that ordaining married men would cause a reduction in the number of celibate candidates, since celibates would begin asking why they should be celibate if the Church no longer seems to value it.[9]

The best information on this topic comes from the Episcopal Church and the Orthodox Church in America. In both, secular priests may be either married or celibate, but in recent decades the vast majority have been married. This is both because the priests prefer marriage for themselves and, in the Orthodox Church in America, because the laity prefer married priests. (In the Episcopal Church there is no clear preference by the laity.) We may reasonably expect that the Catholic situation would be the same. The number of celibate candidates would decline, but the number of married candidates would be so large that the church could not use them all due to financial limitations.

It seems that the problem of "numbers" is really an issue of whether married priests would be as suitable as celibate priests. Pilarczyk mentioned two problems in this regard, the availability of married priests to their people and the financial cost. Both are discussed in this chapter.

(4) Marital strain, divorce, and subsequent scandal among the flock

With a married clergy, marital strain and divorce are inevitable. Divorce among mainline Protestant clergy has risen in recent years, but the rate is still well below the national average. A recent study of six denominations found that 14 percent of all clergy have experienced divorce. Some of the divorces could have been prior to their ordination, but probably not many.[10] In the total American population, about 38 percent of all first marriages end in divorce.

Until recent years, divorce of a minister was considered so scandalous to Protestants that the minister commonly left his parish and sometimes even the ministry. But this has shifted in the past decade, so that divorce does not require relocation. Now the experience is still disruptive and seen as regrettable by the minister, the congregation, and the judicatory, but divorced ministers are able to continue their work.[11] Congregations who are hiring new ministers find divorced persons somewhat less acceptable than married persons.[12]

Denominations are beginning to work in the area of divorce prevention through counseling clergy couples and minimizing external stress on the marriages. The stresses peculiar to clergy couples are lack of time alone together, lack of privacy, confusion about the role of "minister's wife," and the expectation that ministers' families are exemplary for display to the community. These conditions are not easily alleviated, though some assistance is gotten through improved clarification of role expectations of wives during the processes of placement and calling. Wives who see their main role as that of wife and mother in supporting the husband's ministry have been found to be the most satisfied, though others who see themselves as "associate pastors" are also satisfied. The most dissatisfied are those who do not share their husbands' commitment to the ministry or feel a role for themselves in the church.[13]

It seems, then, that whereas celibate clergy have problems of loneliness, married clergy have problems of managing marriage and family life. The 1985 survey of Catholic priests found that 14 percent find celibacy to be "a great problem personally." How this compares with the percentage of married clergy in, for example, the Episcopal Church who find marriage and family to be a great problem we do not know. Possibly a good system would be one letting each priest choose celibacy or marriage.

(5) Tension between married and celibate priests

With two kinds of diocesan priests instead of one, tensions could arise, and it is worthwhile to think about the forms they might take. We need to be clear that we are envisioning a seminary-trained married priesthood, not, as is being discussed in Africa and Asia today, a policy of ordaining married catechists who are functioning effectively as local leaders but who lack seminary training. The "African" proposal would explicitly produce a two-class system of diocesan priests, with celibate seminary-trained priests the superior class.[14] The most realistic option for the United States, given the many available and potential seminary-trained people, would be a fully trained one-class diocesan priesthood with optional celibacy.

Tensions between priests are inevitable, and they occur now, usually between old and young, or pre-Vatican II types and post-Vatican II types, or along other lines of cleavage. We are only concerned here with tensions which might arise between married and celibate diocesan priests. One possibility would be that bishops would remain exclusively celibate, as in the Orthodox churches, so that celibate diocesan priests would be eligible for elevation to the episcopate but married would not. In 1960 Fichter asked American priests in a survey whether, if celibacy became optional, promotion to the episcopate should be limited to celibates. Fifty-five percent of those who desired a celibate clergy said yes, and even 25 percent of those favoring optional celibacy said yes.[15]

The experiences of the Orthodox Church are not directly applicable here, since almost all secular Orthodox priests are married, and even though celibate secular priests are eligible for elevation to the office of bishop, it happens so seldom that no one thinks about it as a realistic possibility. Bishops are almost always chosen from among monks, and commonly a process of grooming future bishops begins early with promising young monks. So no tension is introduced among secular priests by the possibility that some could be bishops and not others.[16] This is in contrast to the present-day Catholic system, in which bishops are usually chosen from among secular priests. If the Catholic Church adopted a policy of allowing married men to become secular priests but requiring bishops to be celibate, the same system could be expected in the course of time as the Orthodox now have — the majority of secular priests would be married, and most bishops would be selected from the religious priests. In the meanwhile, for two or three decades there could well be tensions between married and celibate priests in this regard.

Another possible tension might arise if American Catholic laity came to resemble Protestant laity in preferring married clergy. In that case the celibates would feel discriminated against by the laity. We carried out a series of interviews investigating the current Protestant scene regarding the commonly discussed preference for married ministers and found a more complex situation than expected.[17] It is true in most Protestant denominations that laity prefer married men ministers over single men ministers; as regards women ministers there seems to be little or no preference. The preference for married men is stronger when considering younger candidates for positions than when considering older men; one denominational official said that the married-preference extends only to persons in their 50s.

The reasons for preferring married men are threefold, according to the officials we interviewed. First is a general feeling that married ministers are easier to relate to; they are regular people like everyone else, so parishioners can feel more natural around them. If they have families, the families provide additional means for relating to them and vice versa. They probably understand married people and parents better than single men. Second is a concern that unmarried men might be risky, either because of possible homosexuality or because they might be a source of sex scandal. People suspect that a single man might have a wandering eye. For this reason a single man candidating for a position needs to be forthright about his single status in order to put fears to rest; otherwise he is not likely to be offered the position. Third is a feeling that a married minister with a suitable wife would be preferable, since the wife would contribute to her husband's ministry and to church life.

Two well-informed Episcopalian churchmen said that the preference for married men priests occurs in the Episcopal Church only in suburban family-oriented parishes. Otherwise there is no clear preference. Celibate Episcopal priests have no undue difficulty in securing placements. Even as regards personal counseling, Episcopalians pay attention to the capabilities of individual priests, not their marital state. These churchmen guessed that the Catholic situation would come to resemble the present Episcopal attitude if Catholics adopted optional celibacy.

(6) Reduced availability of priests due to conflicting demands of family and parish

A common argument for a celibate priesthood is that celibacy frees the priest from family responsibilities, making him more available to minister to his parishioners. Opinions differ on whether or not this turns out to be true in America today. Those who believe it is not true argue that a priest's spouse is often an asset to his ministry, not a competitor or distraction, and that even celibate priests feel a need to "get away" from work for their own spiritual well-being. Research on the topic is sparse.

Several major studies have been made of Protestant clergy wives. One found that clergy wives put in an average of 10 to 33 hours per week of unpaid leadership, secretarial, and hospitality work.[18] A survey of clergy wives in 1964 found that the majority saw themselves as being very involved in their husband's ministry as "background supporters," and 20 percent shared directly in ministry, often feeling themselves personally called to ministry.[19] As more and more clergy wives enter the work force outside the home, the level of support they offer to their husbands' ministries will diminish, but still the expectation of most Protestant church members is that the minister's wife will be an important figure in the life of the church.

Studies of Protestant ministers show that they work far more than a 40-hour week, despite being married. (Our 1985 survey of Catholic priests found that their work weeks averaged 48.8 hours.) While in some cases the ministers put their work first, to the detriment of their marriages, most seem to strike a balance between ministerial commitments and family commitments.[20] They are not available at all times to their parishioners. Comparable data on how available celibate priests are should be gathered, to see if there is a difference.

Rev. Roy Oswald, a Lutheran expert on clergy problems who has worked with clergy of all denominations, said that in his experience the level of availability between married priests and celibate priests is about the same. The idea that married clergy are not as available to their people due to their split commitments is not true in middle class America today. The reason is that celibate priests need to get away too, and they cannot devote all their times and energy to their ministry.

Some information is available from two instances of married Episcopalian priests being accepted as priests in the Catholic Church. One case was in Australia in 1969, when three Episcopal priests were accepted as Catholic priests and served parishes. A researcher later questioned parishioners about their experiences with celibate versus married priests. A few of the parishioners said they felt a loss and preferred celibate over married priests, but most were happy with the married priests. They had felt strong reservations at first, they said, but they changed their minds after having been served by a married priest for a while. They had feared that a family would interfere with the priest's work, but that turned out not to be the case. In fact, several advantages were seen in having a married priest; he was seen as more sympathetic and helpful with marriage problems, family concerns, and financial matters, and he was more "one of the people." One respondent felt that a married priest "helps to elevate our vocations as married people."[21]

In the United States, by papal permission a limited number of married Episcopalian priests are being accepted as priests in Catholic dioceses. The process was begun in 1981, and by summer 1986, 32 men have been accepted. Also 17 cases are awaiting decision in Rome and about 50 others are in various stages of preparation of papers.[22] The flow has been at the rate of about 6 a year. Two conditions have been set on accepting these priests, (a) that they not serve full-time in parish work (except in five parishes composed of former Episcopalians who became Catholic), and (b) that they not serve in the same cities where they were Episcopalian priests. The impetus for the process was a request by a coalition of Episcopalian priests who were Anglo-Catholic by theological persuasion and unhappy with recent trends in the Episcopal Church such as the change in the Book of Common Prayer and the ordination of women. (In recent years there has also been one married Lutheran minister and one married Polish National Catholic priest accepted, but independent of the Episcopal program.)

At a gathering of these priests in 1985 it was reported that they felt accepted by the other priests and the lay people. Most of them are serving in parishes on weekends, and their relationships with parishioners are good. Apparently most Catholic laity accept married priests as well as celibate, if they are effective in their ministry.[23]

We have heard reports that the presence of these former-Episcopalian married priests has upset other priests in the dioceses, since the other priests resent the permission to be married priests in the Catholic Church. This is an understandable reaction, since in our 1985 survey we found that 18 percent of the diocesan priests would certainly or probably marry if it were allowed.

(7) Adverse effects on the church's teaching on sexuality, matrimony, and the priesthood

This problem was mentioned by Archbishop Pilarczyk without elaboration, and we are uncertain what the specific difficulty is. If he thinks that optional celibacy would tend to elevate the marital state as equal to the celibate state for achieving Christian holiness, we would agree that this is plausible. Given the teachings of Vatican II regarding the marital state, this would not seem to be a theological problem. If he thinks that optional celibacy would tend to reduce clergy-lay distinctions in Catholics' minds, we would agree again that it is likely.

Potential theological problems must be investigated in depth, but we lack the competence to do it.

Two More Considerations

We looked into problems with clergy alcoholism in several denominations. The problems are serious in the Episcopal Church, as they are in the Catholic Church, taking a human and financial toll. In talks with Episcopal churchmen they judged that the problems are worse among unmarried priests than among married. The reasons are, first, that loneliness is greater among the unmarried, and loneliness seems to contribute to alcohol abuse, and second, that priests' wives are a big help in managing alcohol use and abuse. The wives don't have much effect on whether their husbands drink or not, but they control the amount and its effects. Some step in and force their husbands into rehabilitation programs if the problem is bad enough.

We asked three Episcopalian and Lutheran officials if they thought alcohol abuse among Catholic priests would increase or decrease if Catholics adopted optional celibacy. Two said it would decrease, and the third didn't know. Unfortunately we have no more definite information on this, since no careful research has been done. The most we can say is that *probably* the rate of alcoholism would decrease if there was optional celibacy for diocesan priests.

Lastly, there has been some speculation about how the Episcopalian oversupply of priests might relate to the Catholic undersupply, if there was optional celibacy. One conclusion seems convincing—that the flow of former Catholic priests into the Episcopal priesthood, which is largely because of marriage, would slow down or stop. Would there be a flow of Episcopalian priests, underutilized due to the oversupply, into the Catholic priesthood? We investigated this in a series of interviews and found that the amount of Episcopal oversupply is often misunderstood. In 1984 the Episcopal Church had 7,800 ordained priests serving churches and 500 others in the denominational pension system. In addition there were 3,000 retired and approximately 2,000 who have been ordained but are not employed in Episcopal ministry. This produces an estimate of 2,500 oversupply. One person we interviewed said that 2,500 is too low an estimate, that 4,000 is better. Paradoxically perhaps, there are job openings for full-time Episcopal priests with adequate remuneration which go begging, since no one wants them. They are either in rural areas or in inner cities, where the available priests don't want to go.

How many of the Episcopal priests in the oversupply, be it 2,500 or 4,000, would be interested in the Catholic priesthood, if celibacy were optional and if full-time parish ministry jobs could be found for them? The persons we interviewed speculated that the number would not be very high. Most of the people in the Episcopal oversupply are happily employed in other kinds of pursuits. The interested persons would be Anglo-Catholics theologically who are frustrated by the job pressures in the Episcopal Church stemming from the oversupply.

An additional consideration is that Episcopal dioceses screen candidates for postulancy and thereby cut down the number of persons finishing seminary and being ordained. This is done to ensure that newly-ordained persons are capable and suitable, also to manage the amount of oversupply of Episcopal priests. The amount of screening varies from diocese to diocese, entailing processes ranging from single discernment weekends to year-long series of meetings to evaluate expectations and motivations. Two persons we talked to estimated that over half of the persons beginning the screening process become discouraged and drop out. The question arises as to whether some of these people would be interested in the Catholic priesthood, if celibacy were optional. The numbers would probably be small, since under conditions of optional celibacy the Catholic dioceses would also enjoy large numbers of candidates and would begin their own screening processes. They would very likely be a bit suspicious of persons who had not made it through the Episcopalian screening process. So the Episcopal-to-Catholic flow would probably not be important.

It may be noted that neither the Episcopal Church nor any other mainline Protestant denomination have systems of vocation personnel like the Catholic Church now has. Under a policy of optional celibacy the diocesan vocation directors would essentially not be needed, except maybe to ensure the highest possible quality seminarians. There would be an oversupply of interested persons.

To sum up: if celibacy for diocesan priests were optional, the number of men interested in the priesthood would rise dramatically, enough to overcome the shortage. Some other problems would arise, such as a probable increase in priests' salaries and benefits, a more cumbersome system of assignment and deployment, clergy divorces, and some tension between married and celibate priests. Other problems may arise which are not visible now. More research is needed on these specific problems to see if any of them are as important as the obvious benefit of this option — that it would produce many more priests.

Option 7: Ordain women

One way to expand the number of priests is to ordain women. The idea has been debated at length, and the magisterium is opposed to it for theological reasons. Our discussion will not address the theological arguments but will look at only the social and institutional aspects of the proposal.

As we saw above in Table 19, 47 percent of all Catholic adults in 1985 endorsed the idea. Younger persons and more educated persons were disproportionately in favor; for example, 59 percent of those 39 and under favored it. Attitudes of Catholic campus ministry leaders were similar to those of all Catholics — 49 percent of them favored ordination of women. Priests were more hesitant — 38 percent favored it.

There has been a marked increase in support for ordination of women among Catholics; in 1974, 29 percent favored the idea in a nationwide poll, and in 1985 the figure in an identical poll was 47 percent. In both polls men were more in favor than women; in 1974 it was

35 percent of the men and 25 percent of the women, and in 1985 it was 51 percent of the men and 44 percent of the women. Thus it appears that the idea is experiencing broad increases in support among Catholics and that the support goes far beyond the women's movement. Probably the trend since 1974 is part of an overall shift in attitudes about sex roles in American society.

Attitudes of active, church-going Catholics are less favorable to women's ordination than attitudes of other Catholics. In the 1985 poll, only 22 percent of adult Catholics who attend Mass more than once a week favored women's ordination, and 40 percent of those who attend once a week were in favor. The recent Notre Dame Study of Parish Life, which surveyed registered Catholics in 36 parishes around the nation, found that a little more than one-third favored women's ordination. This is lower than the figure for all Catholics.[24]

How Many Candidates Are There?

Exact figures on the number of women wanting to be ordained are impossible to obtain. An estimate was made in 1985 by the Women's Ordination Conference, a group actively working for a change in church rules. They came up with a figure of 1,800 Catholic women interested in ordination.[25]

Another way of estimating numbers of available women is to look at the numbers of women entering the ministry in Protestant denominations — especially the Episcopal and Lutheran churches. In the Lutheran Church in America, after 15 years of allowing ordination to women, there were 363 ordained women among its active clergy in 1985, or 5 percent of the total.[26] In the Episcopal Church, which authorized women's ordination in 1976, less than a thousand of the approximately 13,500 clergy in 1986 were women.[27] This is about 7 percent. If the same rate of entry took place in the Catholic Church (let us say 5 percent in 10 years), it would amount to about 3,000 women priests in the first decade — not enough to make a great impact on the priest shortage. But a reasonable estimate is that the flow of women priests would increase with time, as has been true in Protestantism.

Figure 11

Percent Women Among Total Graduates of Ordination Programs, by Denomination of Seminary, 1976-77 and 1984-85

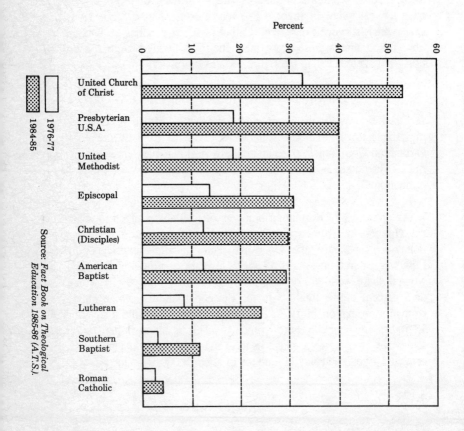

Source: *Fact Book on Theological Education 1985-86 (A.T.S.)*

How many Catholic women today are getting seminary training in ordination programs (M.Div. or B.D.)? Data is available only on the percentage of women in ordination programs by denomination of seminary, not by denomination of student. Data from the Association of Theological Schools shows very few women in Catholic seminaries earning the M.Div. degree, but rather large percentages of women in ordination programs in other seminaries. As Figure 11 suggests, 20 percent to 30 percent of all seminarians getting degrees in ordination programs in Protestant seminaries are women. A proportion of these women are Catholics, but no one knows how many. Catholic women are found in many Protestant and non-denominational seminaries. In 1983, Rosemary Ruether conducted an informal survey of registrars of several seminaries and found Catholic women in many different programs. She was not able to get data on how many.[28] Ruether found that it was fairly common for Catholic women who obtained M.Div. degrees to switch to a Protestant denomination to become ordained ministers.

Characteristics of Candidates

Two surveys of women desiring ordination have been done by the Women's Ordination Conference, one in 1978 (410 women) and one in 1985 (248 women). They give us a rough idea of the characteristics of women who would be the first Catholic priests if it were allowed. A majority in both surveys held advanced degrees, with 11 percent in 1985 holding doctorates. In 1978, 15 percent had or were pursuing the M.Div. degree, and in 1985 the figure was 25 percent.[29] In 1978 the most common occupation was teaching, whereas in 1985 the most common occupation was parish or pastoral ministry. This reflects the growing numbers of women in lay ministries today.

The proportion of women desiring ordination who are members of religious orders was 65 percent in 1978 but only 45 percent in 1985. Whether this drop of 20 points has any meaning is unclear; it may be an artifact of data collection methods. As a rule of thumb we could say that about half of the women desiring ordination are now members of religious orders. This proportion will probably move downward with time, since the number of women religious is declining and the number of lay ministers is rising.

There is a problem in using the results from this research for making inferences about hypothetical future women priests. The surveys were done on the assumption that *married* women could be ordained, so both celibate and married women are among the respondents. It would be more realistic to look at *celibate* women desiring ordination, either religious or lay, since a reasonable scenario of future events would suggest that they would be the first ones eligible for ordination. The most likely group, according to the persons we talked to, would be women religious. They are therefore of special interest to a research study such as ours, but the available research does not single them out.

Fran Ferder carried out an interview study of 100 women who signed a statement at a 1975 conference saying that they felt a call to ordination.[30] These women were similar to the larger samples described above, except that more were sisters (72 percent) and fewer were married (5 percent). The women were evaluated psychologically, using the same instrument which had been employed in a nationwide study of priests in 1972. The results were that these 100 women were more psychologically fit than the sample of priests. They were also evaluated for their potential as effective ministers, based on their current and past effectiveness in ministry, ability to relate well to people and communicate clearly, ability to show compassion, and quality of their faith life. The interviewers judged that 44 percent of these women "would definitely make effective ordained ministers, 33 percent would probably be good ministers, and the remainder would probably not be good ministers."[31]

Women's liberation did not seem to be the main motivation behind these women's quest for ordination. Although many of them expressed the hope that ordination of women would "automatically" change the present hierarchical structure of the priesthood and introduce more collegial ministry, the reasons most often cited for seeking ordination were more personal. The top three were simply that they felt called to sacramental ministry, they thought women were needed in the priesthood, and they thought they could serve others more totally if ordained.

The interviewers asked the 100 women about their hopes for the church in the future. The respondents supported the church's work for human rights in the world. They favored team ministry and greater lay participation. They saw the call to celibacy as separable from the call to priesthood, and "many members of religious communities would reject ordination if it were made available only to sisters, and not to single and married women who feel called."[32]

Above in Chapter 5 we looked at the results of the 1985 college student survey, when we were able to compare ecclesiological views of women interested in becoming ordained priests with men preparing for the priesthood. We found that the women would be quite innovative in their leadership, in contrast to the rather conservative men. The views of the two groups are not the same, and the introduction of women priests into the present crop of traditional seminary graduates would be a source of institutional ferment. In short, indications are that many of the women desiring ordination today could be expected to be critical of church policies.

A few reports have appeared concerning efforts toward women's ordination in other nations. Interest in women's ordination is highest in countries where women have gained the most political, economic, and educational rights. Local movements for ordination of women have developed in England, France, Switzerland, Belgium, and West Germany.[33] In 1970, Dutch bishops put forward an initiative on an ordained diaconate for women (it was never acted on by Rome). In 1971 a Canadian consultation of bishops and women leaders concluded that the church should accept "in principle" the ordination of women for ministry.[34] And according to a 1984 British Gallup poll, support for women's ordination ran at 37 percent among British Catholics, comparable to the level of support among American Catholics in that year.[35] In third world nations the issue is felt only by small elite groups.

Women Ministers in Protestant Denominations

Many of the Protestant denominations have a long history of ordaining women ministers. The United Church of Christ, American Baptists, and Disciples of Christ have ordained women ministers since the 19th century. In 1956 the United Presbyterian Church and United Methodist Church both approved full ordination for women, with the Presbyterian Church in the U.S. (in the southern states) following suit in 1964. Women were ordained in the American Lutheran Church and Lutheran Church in America beginning in 1970. The Episcopal Church officially admitted women to the priesthood in 1976. Groups not ordaining women today include the Missouri Synod Lutherans and Seventh-Day Adventists, although the latter allow women to play an associate pastoral role without authority to baptize or perform marriages. Southern Baptists leave ordination decisions to the discretion of individual congregations; the first woman was ordained in 1964, but due to a tradition of resistance to women ministers, few have been ordained since.[36]

A denominational decision to ordain women may cause great controversy, as exemplified by the Episcopal Church. Its first ordinations of women were done by three retired bishops in Philadelphia in 1974. They "broke ranks" in doing this, producing what were called eleven "irregular ordinations."[37] Official ordination of women to the Episcopal priesthood came two years later at about the same time that other divisive issues were being decided; these included changes in the prayer book and new denominational positions on divorce, abortion, and homosexuality. The combination of events, with women's ordination as probably the most emotional issue, drove about 5,000 dissidents to create the nationwide Diocese of the Holy Trinity as a refuge for 20 parishes that wished to disaffiliate from the Episcopal Church.[38] By

1986 over 30 married Episcopalian priests were ordained into the Roman Catholic priesthood, as we discussed earlier. About five new Catholic parishes were formed from the dissidents.

Since the first official ordinations of women in 1976, nearly 1,000 women have been ordained in the Episcopal Church. But the opposition still continues.[39] If the Catholic Church began ordaining women, a similar reaction could be expected in the U.S., and how it would be in the third world is hard to fathom. A change in church discipline of this magnitude would need to be approached carefully, with probably an initial time period allowing regional choice in the matter.

Research on Acceptance of Protestant Women Ministers

We have seen that 47 percent of American Catholics are in favor of ordination of women; the rest are not or are undecided. Protestants too are divided on the issue. A 1977 Gallup poll found varying degrees of acceptance of women ministers in different denominations. Opposition was highest in the denominations which have not ordained women or which have done so only for a short time. Mormons, who do not ordain women, had the highest rate of opposition (65 percent), followed by Baptists (northern and southern, 38 percent), and Episcopalians (28 percent), who had begun ordaining women only the year before. Among Methodists, who had begun ordaining women in the 1950s, opposition was only 15 percent.[40]

More recent studies of Protestant laity show that while opposition to women ministers is not high, still most laity prefer men in the pastoral role. A survey of lay leaders in nine mainline denominations found that 85 percent had no preference regarding the sex of an assistant minister, but 40 percent preferred a man as the senior pastor.[41] A study of Presbyterians found that 60 percent preferred a man as sole or senior pastor. Those persons not preferring a man do not thereby prefer a woman — they simply have no preference. The only position for which a large proportion of the Presbyterians preferred a woman was Minister of Education, a position in the traditionally feminine role of teaching.[42]

Several researchers have found that women ministers are perceived by laity as potential sources of conflict in their congregations, thus it is better not to raise the issue of hiring a woman to avoid stirring up trouble. Studies show that a majority of the laity in both Baptist and Presbyterian denominations feel concern that calling a woman minister would create tensions and even cause some people to drop out or stop their financial giving.[43]

Another concern of laity focusses not so much on the pastoral abilities of women ministers but on the conflict between the job and traditional feminine duties to home and children. For example, over 80 percent of the Presbyterians thought that a woman's temperament was just as suitable as a man's, but over half thought that married women with children could not fulfill their family responsibilities well if they were working full-time and that the women would be likely to experience emotional problems due to the demands of both jobs.

A third concern centers on the ability of women to handle organizational tasks. While most laity feel that a woman minister could perform as well as a man in helping with problems and crises, helping personal growth of church members, and providing good worship experiences, fewer are confident that a woman could do as well as a man in organization, coordinating church staff, and providing general leadership.

Among Presbyterians, persons with highly stereotyped attitudes toward women were the most likely to oppose women in ministry. Older age and male gender were also associated with opposition. In fact all Protestant research shows more opposition among men than among women, opposite to the situation with Catholics.[44]

In spite of these sources of resistance, there is no evidence that the advent of a woman minister causes declines in a church's participation or its revenues. A cross-denominational Protestant study comparing churches having men pastors with those having women pastors during the 1970s found that the presence of women pastors had no negative effects on membership and finances of churches or on denominational strength. [45]

It appears that women ministers do as good a job as men. At least we know that people with exposure to a woman minister usually have a more positive attitude than average toward women ministers. Carroll's nine-denomination study found that among women lay leaders who had been pastored by a man during the previous ten years, 55 percent preferred a man as senior pastor; among those who currently had a woman pastor, only 11 percent said the same thing. Among men leaders the pattern was similar but not as strong. Carroll also found that lay leaders rated man ministers and woman ministers about the same. In the area of church budget management the men got higher marks, but the women got higher marks in effectiveness at planning and leading worship and in teaching children. [46]

Experiences of Protestant Women Ministers

Protestant women ministers are a bit different in background from men ministers, and the differences are important to know. The women entered seminary, on average, at a later age. In the nine-denomination Carroll study, 25 percent of the women entered after age 29, compared with 13 percent of the men. Nevertheless, since women have been ordained for only a few years in many denominations, the average age of women ministers is lower than of men. Carroll found that 46 percent of the clergywomen were under 35, compared with 16 percent of the men.

With regard to marital status, women ministers were only half as likely to be married as men — 55 percent as compared with 94 percent for men. It is interesting that 60 percent of the clergywomen's husbands were also ordained, compared with only 4 percent of the clergymen's wives. The reasons the women ministers gave for desiring ordination were similar to the reasons given by Catholic women; most important was that they felt "called by God." [47]

In light of the lay attitudes presented earlier, we may expect that women ministers might have more difficulty than men in finding churches to call them. It seems to depend greatly on the hiring processes in the various denominations. Some denominations, like the Southern Baptists, leave both ordination and placement entirely to the discretion of the individual church, while others, such as the Presbyterians, Lutherans, and Episcopalians, control ordination via regional governing bodies but give each church authority to call the pastor of its choice. The United Methodist system is most similar to the Catholic system, in that bishops assign ministers to pastoral positions, usually after consultation with local churches and the ministers themselves. Carroll found that women ministers in the United Presbyterian and United Methodist denominations had the least difficulty with placement. The Presbyterians have a strong advocacy program for women ministers, and Methodist ministers, once accepted into a regional "conference," are guaranteed placement by their bishop.[48]

But in spite of the variations, research generally agrees that women ministers have more difficulty finding calls than men. A study of the Lutheran church in America is typical. The women got fewer calls on the average than men. Of those successfully placed, half of the men but only one-third of the women were sole or senior pastors. More women became associate pastors. Also women had to accept more part-time positions than men, and their placement took longer on the average.[49]

Studies have consistently shown that women earn less than men who are of the same age, with the same years of experience, and in the same positions. A 1982 survey in eleven denominations found that women ministers averaged receiving $4,000 to $6,000 less than men of the same age. The median salary for men under 35 was $18,000 - $20,000, but for women it was $14,000 - $16,000.[50]

Once the women ministers receive a call to a parish, they seem to have few problems and high levels of satisfaction. As we noted earlier, laity rate women as high as men in effectiveness at most ministerial tasks. In Carroll's study, 90 percent of both the men and women ministers felt liked, accepted, and appreciated by their parishioners, but women were more likely to feel a sense of accomplishment with their work. Women and men had similar proportions of persons who were considering leaving the parish ministry.[51]

Are women in denominations which appoint ministers to churches less well accepted than those in denominations in which lay committees select the ministers? A study of Methodist clergywomen (who are appointed by bishops) suggests that the answer is no. Once installed in a church, these women experienced very little problem with sexist attitudes. Over two-thirds found the parishioners helpful.[52]

Conflicts between personal life and pastoral obligations are often expected for women ministers, but apparently the problems are not insuperable. Carroll's research suggests that women ministers are successful at combining family life with ministry. While women ministers say that they have more difficulty rearing young children while working full-time as pastors than men do, women ministers are more likely to say their spouses are supportive of their career than are men. The high proportion of the married women ministers married to ministers accounts for their husbands being understanding about the demands of their work. Seventy-five percent of the women who are part of a clergy couple say their spouse is "never or rarely resentful" of the time and energy invested in ministerial work, compared with 57 percent of the women married to non-ordained spouses and 49 percent of the men.[53] Being married or single is unrelated to how easily clergywomen can manage personal and professional life, or to satisfaction with their ministry. But loneliness is a problem for single women. Younger age, combined with being single, led to loneliness, and Carroll noted that "young unmarried clergywomen in rural areas are most likely to feel lonely."[54]

A final question about women ministers is whether they tend to have a different style and emphasis in their ministry. Carroll found that men and women were no different in their self-described leadership style;

both saw themselves as fairly democratic. He also found that women ministers were slightly more likely than men to feel that the church should involve itself with social and political matters such as equality for women, blacks, and other miniorities. One study of several Methodist women pastors who had succeeded men found that church members perceived in them a more personal preaching style, greater approachability, and more willingness to include lay people in decision-making.[55]

Our review of Protestant data is helpful only insofar as the experiences of American Protestants can predict what the experiences of Catholics might be. Would Catholic laity be as accepting of women priests as Protestant laity are of women ministers?

No one knows, but my guess is that Catholics would be at least as accepting and maybe more so, for three reasons. First, the Catholic Church has a serious shortage of priests, and if it ordained women as priests many laity would be faced with a choice of accepting a woman priest in their parish or having no priest at all. Given this choice, a large number would accept the woman priest. Second, the mere passage of time probably enhances the acceptability of women in key leadership positions. Thus the resistance experienced by Protestant women ministers in the 1950s or 1960s is not likely to be as extreme in the 1980s solely because women are more commonplace now in many professional jobs, from lawyers to school principals to politicians. The hubbub occasioned by women running for state governor or U.S. senator has receded over the past 20 years, and today little is said about a candidate's gender but rather attention is devoted to his or her past record and views on the issues. Third, Catholics have a category of women not found among Protestants — religious sisters. I guess that acceptance of sisters as priests would come easier than acceptance of married lay women, because sisters are perceived as different than lay women, somehow intermediate between laity and priests. Also they are already trained, celibate, and in most cases living in religious communities. It is merely a guess, but it seems likely that they would find relatively greater acceptance as women priests. (These hypotheses are researchable by social science, and future research could tell us a lot.)

Option 8: Institute a term of service for the priesthood, or institute an honorable discharge

We have seen in Chapter 5 that the celibacy requirement is the most important characteristic of the priesthood deterring young men from entering it. In our 1985 college student survey the second most important deterrent was that "a life-long commitment is required" (see Table 15).

If the celibacy requirement did not exist, we estimated, on the basis of our college student survey, that the flow of men into seminaries would increase fourfold. This is a rough estimate. If the requirement of a lifelong commitment did not exist, there would also be an increase in interest, but we cannot estimate how much. Among men campus ministry leaders (the group we surveyed which included the most persons interested in the priesthood), 11 percent said they would be seriously interested in a vocation if an "honorable discharge" were available after 10 or 15 years of service. This compares with 35 percent who said they would be seriously interested if celibacy were not required. In our random sample the outcome was different (see Table 15), but the random sample contains so few people interested in vocations that it is less pertinent for us. Fee and her associates in 1979 found that 16 percent of Catholic men between 18 and 30 years of age would consider becoming a priest if a short-term commitment were possible — compared with 2 percent interested under the present rules.[56]

So the idea has a definite impact on prospective vocations. The most we can say with any confidence is that "if priests could have an honorable discharge, if desired, after 10 or 15 years of service" the number of young men interested would rise, maybe by 50 percent or 100 percent. This is a guess, the most that is possible given existing research. A rise of that magnitude would have a strong impact on the vocation situation, so the idea merits thought.

Fee and her associates posed the idea of a short-term commitment in their questionnaire with these words: "Serving as a priest for a short term agreement, two or five years at a time, for example." In our college student survey we asked about "an honorable discharge, if desired, after 10 or 15 years of service." We changed the language to make it less of a departure from present church discipline and possibly more realistic as a future option. The distinction between a "term of service" and an "honorable discharge," both of which ideas are drawn from the military, is not a big one in practice. The distinction between 2 to 5 years (Fee's formulation) and 10 to 15 years (our words) is much greater. The longer minimum period of service would seem more realistic for both the institution and the incumbent, given the long years of seminary training required for the priesthood.

There are important theological considerations and practical considerations. Theologically there are serious problems with this option, since it requires a change in the theological definition of ordination and holy orders. Over two-thirds of American priests believe that "ordination confers on the priest a new status or a permanent character which makes him essentially different from the laity within the church" (from the 1985 survey). And 57 percent believe that "since the priesthood is a lifelong commitment, there is almost never a good reason for leaving." Young and old priests have much different attitudes on these topics; for example, on the item saying "since the priesthood is a lifelong commitment. . . ," 40 percent of the priests 26-35 years old agreed, compared with 84 percent of those 66 years old or older. Theologically, once a priest is ordained, "the priestly character remains even though a priest may be forbidden to exercise that order."[57] Clearly the theological understanding of priesthood as taking on a special ontological nature militates against the idea of a term of service or honorable discharge.

The theological similarity between holy orders and matrimony is frequently emphasized when this topic is debated, and someone asks rhetorically if short-term marriage is also desired!

Practical considerations also need to be studied, of which we will note two. First, there is undeniably a youthful enthusiasm among many young men who enter seminary and the priesthood, which cannot be sustained over decades of life even under the best of circumstances, so one should expect a flagging of zeal among many priests during their careers. This is true of all occupations and professions. The question then becomes how to handle the situation if a priest sincerely wants to leave and if it seems to be in the best interest of the church too. All professions and occupations known to us, except for the Catholic priesthood, allow a departure in good faith. In terms of life commitments more broadly, the only clear exception is marriage. And the rising divorce rate in America tells us that many people find life-long marriage difficult to manage. The point here is not whether recent social trends are welcome or not welcome, but what is the best form of church structures for carrying out its overall mission.

Second, there are strong feelings among both priests and laity against the idea. There is more resistance to it among both priests and laity than to the idea of ordaining married men, ordaining women, or allowing resigned priests to return to priestly work (see Table 19). In addition, laity who are loyal Mass attenders resist it more than others; of those who attend more than once a week, only 23 percent say that the idea of an honorable discharge would help the church; of those who attend weekly, 42 percent say so; of those who attend less than once a month, on the other hand, 63 percent say so. Priests of all ages are more opposed to the idea than favor it; those age 25-39 include 30 percent who say an honorable discharge would help the church and 48 percent who say it would hurt; by comparison, among priests 70 or older, 9 percent say it would help and 78 percent say it would hurt. It is important to note that according to our surveys, the tradition of lifelong commitment is more strongly held than the tradition of celibacy. We did not expect to find this, nor did Greeley foresee it in his discussion of the idea.[58]

We find ourselves, therefore, in a situation not much different from that regarding married priests: a change in policy would produce more priests, yet it would be theologically alienating to many and would evoke dissent. But an additional element is present here — that a certain rate of departures will always occur, often in the best interests of both the church and the individual, and that there is no legal way to stop them. All American institutions assume that "if they want to go, you cannot hold them." Should they not somehow be allowed to go?

The experiences of the American Protestant mission movement will help illustrate cultural trends today. It is the closest analogy we know to the Catholic priesthood. The Protestant denominations sent thousands of missionaries into foreign mission fields in the 1920s and 1930s, and everyone assumed it was a lifelong commitment. The missionaries themselves, both single and married, assumed it, and the church boards assumed it. But officially the contracts were for definite terms of service, to be followed by furloughs, consultations, and decisions about additional terms. In the 1930s the term for Africa was normally three years, and for the Orient it was 5-7 years. These lengths of term were dependent on climate and hygiene factors. Missionaries who came home after one term or two and wanted to drop out of mission work were of course free to do so, and some did. There was no breach of trust with the denominational board when this was done, but there was some embarrassment with the congregations which had sent and supported the missionary, since everyone had assumed that it was for life. The lifelong commitment, that is, was a matter of mentality and expectation, even though there was never a contract or vow stating it.

This system gradually changed. The first changes came in the late 1950s and 1960s in the mainline denominations, as young missionaries preferred more and more to think not in terms of a lifelong career but of one or two tours of service. Soon assumptions about lifelong service were no longer made by either the denominational boards or the missionaries themselves. There was no change in the official policies, since they were already set up with definite terms of service separated by furloughs and meetings with the boards. In the conservative denominations the same thing happened, but later — in the late 1960s and 1970s.[59] Today most conservative boards recruiting and sending missionaries no longer expect a lifetime of service, but among the young persons entering missions under these boards the situation is mixed, with many fully expecting to serve in the foreign mission field until retirement. But it seldom happens; in the 1980s the conservative Protestant missions are finding that about one-half of the missionaries stop work after the first term (usually 3 to 5 years) or don't even finish the first term. Almost nobody continues after more than ten years. Mission work is now seen as for young adults mainly. The problem of "attrition" bothers these boards, and researchers are trying to understand what happened.[60]

When missionaries stop work after one or two terms they often give as reasons their concern about family life, Christian nurture of their children, and good high school and college education for the children. Another problem, less often voiced, is that they are burned out after a term or two; they have given it enough, they think, and now they want to stay home.

What brought about this change? The boards themselves did not desire it and even resisted it; even today it is not formally recognized by several of the boards, who continue to make speeches, print recruiting material, and officiate at commissioning services as if mission work is lifelong. Several boards explicitly distinguish short-term missionaries from lifelong missionaries when recruiting, training, and sending them, but in practice a vast majority of the "lifelong" workers return home long before retirement. So the source of the changes was outside the denominations and mission boards, not inside.

No one knows exactly what those sources are, but experts talk about three probable causes. First is the tendency of young adults today to act in terms of short-term commitment. As one expert put it, young people feel "try it, and if you don't like it, change." No one enters into a profession today with an expectation of lifelong commitment. Second is an increased concern about education of children and worry about losing children to the faith. Missionary families have always had a problem keeping their children in the faith, but more today seem to orient their lives with this in mind than earlier. (The strength of this reason is unclear.) Third is a change in the nature of missions in general. After the colonial period was over in the 1960s, many missionary boards sent missionaries only when the indigenous church leaders in the former mission lands requested them, and the requests were less and less for lifelong missionaries. The mainline denominations were the most concerned about relations with indigenous churches and changed the most in response to this; the conservatives changed little. But it had a genuine impact on the mentality of Protestants during the 1960s and early 1970s.

Option 9: Utilize some resigned priests as sacramental ministers

Over the last two decades the Catholic Church has lost many priests through resignation. One possibility for alleviating the shortage of priestly services would be to invite resigned priests back into church leadership. They are trained, experienced leaders who may be a potential resource to the church in carrying out its mission. To assess how effective this option would be, we need to know how many resigned priests there are, how many would be interested in returning to sacramental ministry, and how they would be received by the laity and other priests.

We must be clear on one point: most resigned priests are currently married and wish to remain so. Their interest in returning to church leadership would in almost every case be premised on permission to resume their ministry while being married. Therefore the question of utilizing resigned priests in church leadership includes the question of married priests. The few unmarried resigned priests who have desired to return to full sacramental priesthood have been able to do so by offering their services to one or another bishop with the understanding that bygones will be bygones; so no serious issue exists regarding them. But most are currently married; in the 1970 survey of resigned priests, 87 percent of all those resigned for four years or more were married.[61] Our discussion concerns only those who are married.

How many resigned priests are there? Since very few resigned prior to 1965, we limit our estimates to those resigning after 1965. Schoenherr estimates that between 1965 and 1975, 4,750 diocesan priests resigned.[62] Between 1975 and 1983 a further 2,066 diocesan priests resigned, according to Vatican statistics. In addition 4,757 religious priests resigned between 1966 and 1984.[63] Thus a conservative estimate of the number of priests who resigned since 1965 is 12,000 or 13,000.

Studies show that most of the resigned priests maintain some relationship to the Catholic Church. Very few resigned because of a loss of faith. They left mainly because they wished to marry or had problems with the authority structure of the church. In the 1970 survey, only 12 percent of the resigned priests said they resigned because of a loss of faith, compared with 63 percent who mentioned a relationship with a woman.[64] The reasons they resigned did not propel them out of the Catholic Church altogether. In 1970, 40 percent of the resigned priests still considered themselves Catholic within the structure of the church, and an additional 38 percent saw themselves as Catholic but outside the structure of the church. Forty percent said they attended Mass each week.[65]

In 1970 about 40 percent of the resigned priests said they "would be willing, under certain circumstances, to return to the exercise of priestly ministry." Only 10 percent of them would be interested in full-time ecclesiastical work; most said they would prefer a full-time secular job with part-time ecclesiastical work. About one-third desired to be involved in traditional parish ministry, but the majority preferred other forms of ministry such as education, counseling, social service, campus ministry, and chaplaincy.

CORPUS (Concerned Organization of Resigned Priests United for Service) is an organization which communicates with resigned priests and tries to speak for those wishing to serve the church in the future. Terry Dosh, the Executive Secretary, estimated that about 35 percent of the resigned priests would like to return to sacramental ministry in some form. Since he believes that about 17,000 resigned priests exist in the United States, that would represent 5,000 to 6,000.[66] The 1970 survey, which is the best available, indicates that only 10 percent would be interested in a return to full-time priesthood, with another 30 percent interested in part-time priesthood in combination with another job. Therefore, depending on which figures you use, between 4,800 and 6,000 resigned priests would like to render sacramental service to the church on a full-time or part-time basis.

Most of them are married, as we have noted. We have heard it said that the divorce rate among resigned priests is higher than average, but the available research indicates that this is not true. In the 1970 survey fewer than 1 percent were divorced. More detailed studies of the topic also show that the divorce rate is low. Hendricks-Rauch compared 445 resigned priest couples with couples in the general population and found that the resigned priests and their wives had a higher than average level of happiness. The older the couple at the time of marriage, the greater satisfaction they reported. About half of the wives in this study had been nuns.[67] Most resigned priests and their wives marry at much later ages than is typical of the general population, and all sociological research shows that older age at marriage is associated with greater marital success.[68]

One study of resigned priests' marriages debunked the stereotype of priests rushing out of the rectory into a hasty marriage. On the average, the priests knew their wives for three and a half years before marriage. While 25 percent married within three months of leaving the active priesthood, another 40 percent waited at least a year.[69]

Resigned priests seem to do well in secular occupations. A majority enter service fields such as teaching and counseling, and one study found that they see their new careers as a new form of ministry.[70] Thus a majority are not longing for a return to full-time ministry in the church.

The option of inviting resigned priests back into sacramental ministry to help ease the priest shortage faces two obstacles. First, most of the men are married. Second, resigned priests are viewed with some apprehension by many priests and laity. As we saw in Table 19, both priests and laity are more cautious about inviting married resigned priests to become active priests again than they are about allowing married men to be ordained. Sixty-three percent of the priests and 63 percent of the laity favor ordination of married men, but only 48 percent of the laity and 40 percent of the priests think it would help the church to invite ex-priests back to the active priesthood. In our interviews we have repeatedly heard strong feelings against resigned priests who were seen as having broken their vows and thus should not be trusted again. Also if married resigned priests were allowed to return to sacramental ministry without allowing other priests to marry, there would be an outcry from active celibate priests saying it is unfair to them.

All in all, the option of inviting resigned priests back to active ministry has problems, and it cannot do much to solve the priest shortage. As an option it seems viable only if there is a policy allowing ordination of married men; then new initiatives could be pursued which make use of this potential leadership resource.

7

Type D Options:
Expand the Diaconate and
Lay Ministries

An elementary principle of all organizational life is that if you cannot find traditionally-designated people to carry out a necessary function of an organization, you hunt for substitutes. If the function is really needed, someone must be found. In the Catholic Church, if you cannot find enough priests, you hunt for other people and find ways that they can carry out the necessary functions.

Here we will look at deacons and lay ministers from the viewpoint of the church's overall mission, and specifically of functions to carry out that mission. Secondary to this will be questions of status, theologically

or institutionally defined. As stated before, institutional church planning
is best served when the analysis is done first of all in terms of functions.
Then issues of status, recognition, or consecration will follow.

Type D options are based on the assumption that an increased supply of priests in the United States is not available. For the immediate future this assumption is certainly realistic. For the long run (with possible expanded criteria for ordination) it may not be. But since no
change in eligibility for the priesthood is being discussed by church
leaders today, Type D options are uniquely realistic. This chapter is the
most realistic of any in the book. It should be read as a road map of
what *will* happen, not just what *might* happen. But, like a road map,
there are many choices to be made even though the direction of movement is clear.

Three Clarifications

The topic is broader than our current interest, and some clarifica-
tions are needed. First, our interest is limited to the institutional church
and its needs. The Vatican II documents on laity stressed that laity are
first of all called to Christian witness in their workplaces. Engineers are
called to be Christian engineers, and politicians are called to be Christian politicians. This is an inspiring idea of unlimited potential power,
given the influence of Catholic laity in secular institutions today. We af-
firm this concept of lay ministry, sometimes called "workplace lay ministry" or "ministry in the world," but it is not our concern here. The
American bishops in their statement *Called and Gifted: The American
Catholic Laity* distinguished "ministry in the world" from "ministry in
the church."[1] They labeled lay persons carrying out professional ministry in the church "ecclesial ministers." Our discussion is limited to
these "ecclesial ministers," working mainly at the parish level.

Second, we emphasize that the restoration of the permanent
diaconate and the legitimation of expanded lay ministries by Vatican II
were not instituted just because of the priest shortage. These developments have theological legitimation on their own, and their value is not

contingent on any priest shortage, pro or con. Our present concern, nevertheless, is limited. We will look at deacons and lay ministers only from the viewpoint of the priest shortage.

Third, as stated above in the Introduction, we believe that parishes will continue to be the backbone of Catholic life and that social institutions as complex as present-day parishes require stable full-time trained leadership. With rare exceptions, parishes cannot be run with part-time staff, and they cannot be run with volunteers. This restricts our interest in lay ministries to paid positions, especially full-time paid positions.

New Research on Deacons and Lay Ministers

The 1985 surveys produced some new information on deacons and lay ministers. In the survey of student campus ministry leaders we asked whether some of the tasks priests now do could be reallocated to non-ordained staff persons, thus freeing the priests for spiritual leadership. The results are shown in Table 20. It lists fourteen tasks now often done by priests and asks if each should be done only by a priest or if it could be done by a deacon or lay person. The tasks do not include presiding at Eucharist, since by church law this must be done by a priest and cannot be delegated to anyone else. We assumed that almost all Catholics know this, hence it didn't have to be asked. The fourteen tasks listed may, under church law, be done by persons other than priests. The purpose of the survey was to tap *feelings* of lay people about allocating various tasks to others.

A vast majority of the students said that only priests should do two things — officiate at marriages (84 percent said this) and officiate at baptisms (75 percent said this). Also 45 percent said that only priests should preach at Masses. Besides these three functions, the students thought that priestly tasks could be done as well by other persons. If priests have too much work to do now, about half of the students said that two tasks should be done *only* by a lay person — supervising work on buildings and grounds (45 percent said this) and maintaining the financial books of the parish (44 percent said this).

Table 20

Attitudes of Student Campus Ministry Leaders on Priestly Tasks (Percents)

It has been suggested that if priests today have too much work to
do, some of their work could be done by deacons or trained lay
persons. Here are fourteen tasks often done by priests. Should
any of them by done by deacons or trained lay persons? Circle
one number after each.*

	Should be done only by a priest	Could be done by a priest, deacon, or lay person	Should be done only by a lay person
Visit the sick	8	91	1
Preach in Mass	45	54	0
Maintain the financial books of the parish	0	54	44
Do marriage preparation work	11	84	5
Officiate at marriages	84	15	0
Do baptismal preparation work	10	86	4
Officiate at baptisms	75	24	0
Teach the convert classes	13	82	4
Be responsible for C.C.D. programs	2	75	21
Organize the youth ministry and sports program	0	71	28
Organize and lead adult religious discussion groups	6	89	6
Organize charitable and social service work in the parish	2	77	21
Do marriage counseling	22	75	2
Be in charge of supervising work on buildings and grounds	1	52	45

* "Don't know" is 2 percent or less (not shown).

The main message of Table 20 is that, apart from marriages, baptisms, and preaching at Mass, most of the work currently being done by parish priests could be re-assigned to deacons or lay persons. And if priests are overworked, much of the work *should* be re-assigned, beginning with the supervision of buildings and grounds, maintaining financial books, organizing youth ministry and sports, coordinating C.C.D., and organizing charitable work. There is a basic acceptance among Catholics of the idea of hiring lay ministers for parish leadership.

Elsewhere in the 1985 surveys we asked more explicitly if a series of possible changes would help the church, hurt it, or have no effect one way or the other. Earlier we looked at some of the suggested changes, and Table 21 shows the results on seven suggestions involving deacons and lay ministers. The two columns labelled "Help" and "Hurt" give the percentages of persons thinking that each suggestion would help the church or hurt the church; the percentage saying that it would have no effect one way or the other or saying they didn't know is not shown.

The first two suggestions have to do with a great increase in permanent deacons and opening up the diaconate to women. All those sampled — priests, laity, and college students — agreed that both ideas would help the church more than hurt it. The least enthusiastic group was the priests, and among the priests there were mixed feelings about opening up the diaconate to women (43 percent thought it would help the church, 31 percent thought it would hurt). Also older laity, that is, people over 60, were less in favor of these ideas than other laity.

The next two suggestions refer vaguely to lay leadership without mentioning paid lay ministers. There was very strong support for both — making more influential roles for women in parishes, and giving laity more participation in decision-making. Among college students and younger laity it was almost unanimous that these ideas should be adopted.

Table 21

Percent Saying Possible Changes Would Help the Church or Hurt It

| | Priests | | Adults: Age | | | | | | Campus Ministry Student Leaders | |
| | | | 39 or under | | 40–59 | | 60 or older | | | |
	Help	Hurt	Help	Hurt	Help	Hurt	Help	Hurt	Help	Hurt
Permanent Deacons										
A great increase in the number of permanent deacons.	49	13	66	2	68	6	57	2	84	2
Open up the office of permanent deacon to women.	43	31	65	13	56	18	39	26	68	6
Lay Leadership										
More influential roles for women in parishes.	75	7	80	5	81	5	51	21	84	2
Greater lay participation in decision-making in parishes.	79	10	77	6	80	9	74	7	84	3
Full-Time Lay Ministers										
Hire full-time lay parish administrators in parishes.	63	15	59	10	51	25	47	25	72	6
Hire full-time lay religious educators and liturgical experts in parishes.	75	9	71	5	66	14	54	9	75	5
Hire lay marriage counselors or personal counselors in parishes.	73	8	77	9	76	13	56	8	67	10

The last three suggestions refer to hiring lay ministers, either parish administrators, religious educators, liturgical experts, or counselors. No assumptions were stated about whether the parishes had money to pay for them or what the costs would be. Again we see very strong support among all groups. The only group giving somewhat hesitant support is the laity 60 years old or older; on all three suggestions they are less certain than anyone else that the church would be helped.

Table 21 does not show age breakdowns among priests, but we looked at them and portrayed them in our data report #3. They are similar to the age breakdowns among laity, so that wherever older laity are hesitant about supporting one of the suggestions, older priests are too. One exception to the pattern was found, regarding "a great increase in the number of permanent deacons;" priests of all ages supported the idea to an almost identical extent, even though older laity differed from the other laity.

To sum up, all groups — priests, laity, and college students — support increases in deacons and lay ministers, and there is no evidence that one or another group is opposed. We have heard it alleged that priests are opposed to lay ministers, or that laity are slow to accept lay ministers, or so on, but none of these statements are supported by the nationwide surveys, making us conclude that none are true in general.

Table 22 provides information on the level of interest among Catholic college students in possible future work as lay ministers. In the sample of campus ministry leaders and in the random sample, all students not seriously considering becoming a priest, brother, or sister were asked a series of eight questions about their interest in lay ministries. The first four asked about full-time lay ministry careers, with the explanation that the wages would be slightly lower than in an equivalent secular job. To our surprise, the level of interest in lay ministry careers turned out to be very high. Over half of the campus ministry leaders

Table 22

College Students Interested in Lay Ministries (Percents)

	Campus Ministry Leaders		Random Sample	
	Men	Women	Men	Women
(For students not seriously considering becoming a priest, brother, or sister:)				
Some persons are seriously interested in serving the Church in a way different than being a priest, brother, or sister. Here are some opportunities for lay ministries. Each is full-time and has a wage slightly lower than an equivalent secular job. Would you be seriously interested? (Percent Yes.)				
Would you be seriously interested in a career as lay minister, serving the Church as an educator, counselor, or missionary?	45	59	32	45
How about a career as lay minister, working as an administrator?	32	34	33	37
How about a career as lay minister, working as a social worker or social action minister?	35	49	39	56
How about a career as lay minister, working as a youth minister or campus minister?	53	64	50	62
Here are some opportunities for paid part-time ministries.				
Would you be seriously interested in part-time paid work as an educator, counselor, or missionary?	63	74	45	57
How about part-time paid work as an administrator?	40	39	37	38
How about part-time paid work as a social worker or social action minister?	52	57	44	62
How about part-time paid work as a youth minister or campus minister?	74	78	63	68

would be interested in seriously considering careers serving the church as educators, counselors, missionaries, youth ministers, or campus ministers. In the random sample the level of interest was almost as high.

The last four questions in Table 22 asked about part-time paid work serving the church in various kinds of ministries. Interest was even higher, with three-fourths of the campus ministry leaders and over half of the random sample saying they would be seriously interested. Of the four kinds of ministries, the favorite would be youth ministry or campus ministry. Interest among women was higher than among men.

In sum, interest in lay ministries is high among Catholic college students. We were not able to survey Catholic adults on this topic, but probably interest would turn out to be high. We do know that a 1980 Gallup poll asked Americans 18 and over if they would be interested in either the full-time ministry or in some other form of religious work as a career. In the total population, 6 percent said yes, and among Catholics, 7 percent said yes. Interest increased with age, so that among people 50 or older, 9 percent said yes.[2] In the total population there is a high level of interest in religious work. It is a desirable career. There is no shortage of candidates for lay ministries, either full-time or part-time. Based on our college student survey in 1985, we estimated that the pool of young persons interested in lay ministries is about 50 times as large as the pool interested in the religious life. Even if all the persons who stated an interest in our college student survey turn out not to be really serious, still the pool of potential lay ministers is abundantly large, and churches can look forward to many good candidates for available positions.

In our college student surveys we were interested in discerning factors which encourage or discourage young people who might be considering working for the church, either in traditional religious vocations or in lay ministries. We asked four questions to tap the importance of four factors. See Table 23. To each of the four there were four responses, but only three are shown; "I don't know" is deleted. The first factor

Table 23

Four Factors Encouraging or Discouraging Interest in Working for the Church (Percents)

	Campus Ministry Leaders		Random Sample	
	Men	Women	Men	Women
When people think about possible religious careers and opportunities, they are sometimes influenced by conditions in the Catholic Church today. One condition is that the Church requires high standards of training for many ministries. Does this encourage you, discourage you, or have no effect on your interest in working for it?				
Encourage me	37	38	18	17
Discourage me	14	13	12	17
No effect	45	46	70	65
Another condition is that the Church has males in all of its top positions of leadership. Does this encourage you, discourage you, or have no effect on your interest in working for it?				
Encourage me	10	3	13	3
Discourage me	17	44	14	35
No effect	71	49	71	60
Another condition is that the Church sometimes takes unpopular stands on social or political questions today, for example, the arms race or the American economic system. Does this encourage you, discourage you, or have no effect on your interest?				
Encourage me	43	32	21	15
Discourage me	16	15	28	38
No effect	34	44	50	46
Another condition is that the Church usually pays lower salaries than persons would receive in similar jobs in secular organizations. Does this encourage you, discourage you, or have no effect on your interest?				
Encourage me	3	2	1	1
Discourage me	29	27	40	39
No effect	64	66	59	59

is that high standards of training are required for many ministries. We asked this because we were told that some young people are discouraged by the cost and time required for training and the difficulty of passing the courses. This turned out to discourage few of the respondents; on the contrary, it encouraged a large number of the campus ministry leaders. The second factor is that the Church has males in all of its top positions of leadership. This turned out to discourage a large number of the women -- 44 percent of the women campus ministry leaders and 35 percent of those in the random sample.

The third factor is that the church sometimes takes unpopular stands on social or political questions today. We asked this because of all the current discussion about the impact of the bishops' pastoral statements on the arms race and on the American economic system. Interestingly, this action by the bishops is more encouraging than discouraging for the campus ministry leaders, but vice versa for the random sample. Apparently the better informed Catholic students find more encouragement than others. The last factor is that the church usually pays lower salaries than people would receive in similar jobs in secular organizations. This turned out to discourage more than a fourth of the campus ministry leaders and about two-fifths of the random sample. We are left with the impression that the lower salaries paid by the church cause some possible candidates for such careers to turn away, but leaving more than enough for all of the church's needs.

To sum up: recent research shows that there is broad support among priests, laity, and college students for increasing the diaconate and lay ministries, and there are abundant numbers of candidates for future lay ministry positions. Since the number of people interested is so high, standards can be high in the training and selection processes.

We turn now to two specific options — expanding the diaconate and expanding lay ministries.

Option 10: Expand and develop
the permanent diaconate

The restoration of the permanent diaconate began in the United States in 1968, and the first class was ordained in 1971. Since then it has grown rapidly. At the end of 1985 there were 7,425 permanent deacons in the U.S., with another 2,264 in training.[3] We may reasonably expect the number to double in the next 15 years, barring a change in church policy. There are plenty of candidates.

The restoration of the diaconate was done quite apart from the priest shortage, but it is important with regard to the priest shortage, since it has two advantages. First, there are enough candidates that high quality standards can be maintained, and in the future they could be raised even higher. Second, deacons come virtually free of charge. A 1980 survey found that only 15 percent of them had received any money at all from the church in the previous year, and in no case did the amount exceed $1,000.[4] The only substantial costs of the diaconate to dioceses are training costs and administrative costs. Training costs are relatively low, since the courses are given on nights and weekends in existing facilities (mainly schools or seminaries), using part-time faculty. The costs are very much lower than the costs of seminary training for priests, and in addition the deacons themselves in many dioceses must cover part of the cost. In effect deacons cost the church practically nothing.

In the last few years a few deacons have been hired full-time by parishes and dioceses. In 1985 they numbered 221, or 3 percent of the total number, and the trend is gradually upwards. Most of these full-time deacons work for parishes, often in the field of Christian education. They are typically retired from other professions, and they are willing to work for much less than a professional wage.[5]

Most candidates for the diaconate come with long experience in parish involvement. Their formal training involved 2 to 3 years of part-time study until the middle 1980s, when it was raised to an average of 4 years. A college degree is not required; in 1985 it was reported that 57 percent of the existing deacons and 54 percent of the candidates lacked a college degree, and even 6 percent of the existing deacons had an 8th grade education or less.[6] It was a conscious policy to avoid having a definite educational requirement so that no underprivileged groups would be excluded. Today the training for the diaconate is being merged more and more with training for lay ministries. In 36 dioceses the diaconal program and the lay ministry program are the same, except that the diaconal program usually lasts longer.

Given the immensity of the total mission of the church and its need for devoted workers, if a large number of men are offering themselves for extensive training and service at little or no cost to the institution, it is only prudent to accept the offer, give them suitable training, and deploy them to do the work at hand. What institution would say no to such an offer? Deacons are an important resource to the church, potentially of great service in a time of priest shortage. But the promise is unfulfilled.

Issues in the Diaconate

The diaconate is under heavy fire in the United States today, as most people know. Only 144 dioceses out of 185 have diaconal programs. Everyone involved points out that the diaconate is only 17 years old and will undoubtedly need some adjustments as experience accumulates. So perhaps it is not surprising that strong feelings have developed pro and con. We will discuss them under three headings.

First, what can deacons do? Officially deacons are authorized to administer baptism, reserve and distribute the Eucharist, preside over marriages, officiate at funerals, read the Scriptures and preach, lead worship, direct the liturgy of the Word, and carry out acts of charity. They can therefore take over some of the liturgical tasks of priests and lighten their load. Except for 3 percent (as noted above), deacons are not full-time. The 1980 survey found that they devote an average of 13.7 hours a week to their ministry. This breaks down, on average, to 3.6 hours in liturgical service, 4.0 hours in ministry of the Word, and 6.1 hours in acts of charity. The main activities deacons actually do are distributing Holy Communion, participating in liturgies, and visiting the sick and aged.[7] A common complaint of priests is that deacons are not available enough to be very useful. Major program responsibilities cannot be delegated to them, so they end up being only "mini-priests" or "glorified altar boys" and feeling under-utilized.

Earlier we said that volunteers are not of foremost importance for coping with the priest shortage, since volunteers cannot carry enough responsibility to provide any worthwhile unburdening of priests. To some extent this is true of deacons too. A number of pastors complained to us that deacons aren't very helpful, since there is little they can do which represents a major relief for the pastor. The deacon works only a few hours a week, and he cannot be in a full staff relationship with the pastor and the other parish staff. So even though the deacon is empowered by church law to carry out some priestly functions, it doesn't work out well.

Second, the role of the deacon is inadequately defined. The problem is traceable to the definition of the office of deacon, which is stated in terms of a status, not in terms of a job to be done.[8] It is a theologically defined status without any training for a specific job. Specific assignments are to be negotiated in each work setting, but often the process is unsatisfactory. Some deacons find themselves in effect unemployed, since their supervising pastors fail to give them duties. The 1980 survey found that 54 percent of the deacons had no formal job descriptions, and 56 percent had no formal working agreements or contracts with parishes or dioceses.[9] In many parishes they didn't have much to do other than assist in liturgies. This led to loss of identity by deacons and cynicism among the laity about what is so special about them. Ernest J. Fiedler describes the problem of "liturgical deacons:"

> There are too many liturgical deacons, but I'm still strongly in favor of permanent deacons. Proper deacons. I am not in favor of purely liturgical deacons acting like disappointed or mistreated second-rate priests. I don't think their role at Mass

makes as much sense as a hill of beans if they cannot be recognized as men who spend their time in the service of the needy and alienated.[10]

Part of the problem stems from pastors, who have not been trained or accustomed to share leadership with deacons. In the 1980 survey, deacons said that conflict with priests was their number-one frustration. The bishops surveyed in 1980 also reported such conflicts; 32 percent said they knew of conflicts between deacons and laity, and 69 percent said they knew of conflicts between deacons and priests.[11]

Third, the diaconate experiences a measure of disapproval because it continues a clerical tradition which some Catholics think should be de-emphasized. It is open to men only (35 or older), and it includes an ordination ceremony and clerical garb. Catholic feminists feel discriminated against and ask why women can't be deacons too. The bishops' conferences in some nations have refused to institute the diaconate in their dioceses until it is open to women. This argument against traditional clericalism is voiced by Eugene Kennedy:

> The solutions (to the priest shortage) will not come from the golden age of clericalism, from, for example, the cadres of married deacons who have been ordained over the past fifteen years. Married deacons represent a past, temporary accommodation with a clerically dominated Church. As such, they are anachronistic and fit marginally, if at all, into the future. They will be remembered as a significant transitional presence which helped condition the Church for its greater lay character.[12]

None of these arguments diminishes the potential value of permanent deacons for taking over leadership tasks and thus reducing the pressures on priests. But extensive practical adjustments are needed. Some steps are already underway to overcome the present problems. For example, diaconal organizations are growing, and as of 1985, 86 dioceses had formed councils or associations of deacons for handling their problems.[13] The role of deacon needs more specification in a direction which coordinates with the role of priest and which genuinely serves the needs of the church. It is a management problem which needs to be solved to allow the diaconate to achieve its full potential.

Option 11: Expand and develop lay ministries

If enough priests cannot be found, perhaps trained lay ministers can be employed to take over responsibility for certain portions of parish life, thus freeing the priests for sacramental and liturgical ministry. Most American Catholics agree with this idea, as we have seen. Also there are many lay persons who would like careers in church work. Already many candidates for such jobs are available, and more would step forth if opportunities expanded. They are often trained and experienced people, with just as much theological training as priests. This option is of course a viable response to the problems of the priest shortage. It is already happening, and we have several research reports to let us know how it is going.

An important clarification here will prevent misunderstandings later. Lay ministers can be introduced to substitute for priests when, for example, the number of priests in a parish diminishes from 4 to 3 or from 3 to 2, and this normally has little impact on liturgical and sacramental life. Lay ministers can also be introduced when the number of priests drops from 1 to zero, that is, when the parish becomes "priestless," and this has an important impact on sacramental life. The latter case is much more consequential, and it has occasioned heated debate, for reasons we touched on in Chapter 4 above.

Lay pastoral administrators, often women religious, have proven to be effective leaders of such parishes. They live in the community, take part in the people's lives, and often develop strong bonds to the parishioners. They cannot celebrate the Eucharist and so visiting priests provide this service once or twice a month. On other weekends these lay ministers preside at services of Communion in which pre-consecrated hosts are distributed. The net effect is a separation of the pastoral leadership from Eucharistic leadership and a probable weakening of the sacramental nature of the church. We have quoted Peter Gilmour as saying that this form of lay ministry leadership in priestless parishes is probably transitory, not permanent, because of the other changes it sets in motion in these parishes. On this case we will not have more to say here; we will limit ourselves to lay ministries which do not directly impinge on sacramental life.

Two Surveys of Lay Ministers

Two useful surveys of lay ministers were done in 1981 and 1985, and we can get a picture of the role of lay ministers from the survey results. The 1981 survey was done by Thomas P. Walters of Detroit.[14] He set out to do a nationwide study of professional directors of religious education (DREs). Working through diocesan officers he compiled a national sample of people fitting these criteria: (1) The person has a Master's Degree in theology, religious education, or the equivalent, (2) has at least three years of experience, with demonstrated organizational skills, and (3) is a salaried, full-time member of a parish staff. In 1981 there were an estimated 4,685 people in the U.S. fitting these criteria. He asked the diocesan religious education directors to randomly select people they knew in their dioceses, then to send them questionnaires. This produced 693 completed questionnaires, possibly with a bias toward the more well-connected DREs.

Women made up 83 percent of the sample, and of the women, 53 percent were religious sisters and 47 percent were laypersons. Of the total sample, 1 percent were priests and 1 percent were deacons. Seventy-nine percent had a master's degree, and 2 percent had a doctorate.

Eighty-four percent of these people had written job descriptions, and 80 percent of these said that the job descriptions were "nearly" or "very" accurate. Seventy-two percent were directly responsible to the pastor for their job performance, 10 percent were responsible to the education commission, 8 percent to the pastoral team, and the other 10 percent to various individuals or groups (for example, associate pastor or school board). Most were responsible for the entire education program, including grade school and high school classes, adult education, and sacramental preparation (but not marriage preparation). Seventy-three percent had written contracts, from 1 to 10 years in length; 86 percent of the contracts were for one year.[15]

The professional DREs have high morale; 52 percent said their job satisfaction was "high," and another 40 percent said it was "moderate." Their morale is based on their satisfaction in sharing their faith and serving God, and they recognize that they are doing important work. Their main gripes are the lack of job security, the low salaries, the long hours, and the profession's present lack of identity within the church. Some are discouraged by lack of support from pastors, staff, and school principals.

Salaries are much higher for laity than for sisters. Among the laity, 4 percent earned over $20,000, 31 percent earned between $15,000 and $20,000, 44 percent earned between $10,000 and $15,000, and 21 percent earned less than $10,000.[16] The median was about $13,500. The median for religious sisters was about $6,500. In addition all received benefits, usually including paid continuing education, social security, a health plan, and retirement. Religious sisters received additional benefits — housing, use of a car, and travel allowance. Salaries among the laity were somewhat higher for married men than for others, since salaries took into account the living expenses of the persons; 71 percent of the married men made more than $15,000 a year as compared with only 41 percent of the single men, 37 percent of the single women, and 15 percent of the married women. Married women worked for less, since they were not the principal wage-earners of their families. Of the whole sample, 42 percent were somewhat or totally dissatisfied with their salaries, with laity more dissatisfied than sisters, men more dissatisfied than women. Walters concluded that the salaries were low because most of the lay DREs had spouses making good salaries, and they very much liked this kind of work.

The second survey was done in 1985 by Zenobia Fox for a dissertation at Fordham University.[17] She set out to get a sample of lay ministers who fit two criteria: (1) persons not belonging to any vowed religious community, and (2) employed full-time or part-time in ministry in a parish community. Teachers in Catholic schools were excluded from the survey, since Fox wanted to look only at the new emerging lay ministries. Also persons working for a volunteer program (such as the Jesuit Volunteers) were excluded. She chose nine representative dioceses where suitable lists were available and sent questionnaires to all the eligible persons on the lists. A total of 283 were completed and returned.

The great majority were women — 79.5 percent. Sixty percent of the women were full-time, and almost all of the men were full-time. The majority worked in suburban parishes, since those parishes had sufficient funds to employ lay ministers. Also 97 percent were non-Hispanic whites; Fox thought there was bias in the data, since she had evidence that Hispanics had tended not to respond to the survey, hence they were under-represented. Almost 70 percent were between 26 and 45 years old, that is, younger than the clergy. Sixty-four percent were currently married.[18]

Regarding their education, 1 percent had doctorates, 26 percent had Master's degrees, 46 percent had college degrees only, and the rest had less than college degrees or "other." At present 40 percent were enrolled in an educational program.

Of these lay ministers, 64 percent were full-time; less than 4 percent of the total group combined their ministry work with other salaried employment. Sixty percent have a contract, and 62 percent have a job description. Typically, they work more than 40 hours a week.

Turnover appears to be typical for such a profession. Fifty-two percent were in their first position in ministry, and those who were in their second (or more) job had stayed in their last setting an average of 3.8

years. Thirty-nine percent had been in their present position two years or less; 75 percent had been in the position five years or less.[19] Fox commented that since the "ministry explosion" began only in the middle 1970s, one should not expect that these lay ministers would have long histories of past positions.

A majority of the lay ministers had a past history of volunteer church work; 10 percent had been in other church work as a priest, seminarian, or religious. Median age was 39. In sum, most of the lay ministers had a history of church work before becoming professional ministers.

What kind of responsibilities did they have? About 57 percent were directors of religious education, 24 percent were coordinators of youth ministry (or youth ministry plus young adult ministry), 4 percent were "Pastoral Ministers," 3 percent were directors of music, 2 percent were directors of liturgy, 1 percent were directors of social ministry, and the rest had other titles or combinations of these.

Salaries for men were higher than for women. The approximate mean salary for full-time men was $18,200, and for women it was $13,800. The highest paid category was the pastoral ministers; 45 percent of them earn over $18,000.[20] Also the persons with higher degrees earn relatively more. For 62 percent of the respondents the salary is only one of two incomes supporting a family. Apparently persons whose income is not the only financial support for a family are willing to work for less salary. Most of the lay ministers receive benefits, such as continuing education funds and medical benefits. Less than half are in a retirement plan.

The respondents were asked, "All things considered, do you think your salary is a fair one?" Fifty-eight percent said no. But a total of 70 percent thought that the future would be better, since there is increasing attention to the need for a just wage, and the recognition of laity by the hierarchy is improving. On the other hand, 30 percent are not hopeful, citing the attitude of people about paying for religious leadership and the history of poor wages paid to women by the church.

How happy are these lay ministers? Forty-four percent said they are "very happy" in church work, and another 46 percent said they are "happy." If they were to leave their present job, most would continue in religious work. Forty percent would seek another parish job, 14 percent would seek a church job other than in a parish, 30 percent would leave church work, and the other 16 percent would do something different. If they left professional church work, 72 percent said they would continue as volunteers in the church. They like church work because they feel called to it, it utilizes their God-given gifts, and it is important.

What frustrations do they have? They ranked the desire to do other work, personal burnout, and inadequate salary as the biggest ones. For the men, inadequate salary and poor job security were more important than for the women. When asked how their work situations could be improved, the total sample ranked "having my efforts valued" as most important, followed by "having my role or function clarified."[21]

Authority in the parishes lies with the pastor; 86 percent of these lay ministers were hired by the pastor, and 79 percent said that the pastor has the authority to hire and fire them. In 21 percent of the cases the parish committee or council hired the lay minister, but only 5 percent have the authority to hire and fire him or her. Only 4 percent of the lay ministers are directly responsible to a lay committee or council.

Fox was interested in whether the lay ministers perceived the existence of due process procedures (defined as a formal procedure for seeking arbitration in a conflict over worker rights) in case they lost their job in a way they deemed unfair. Forty-seven percent said yes, 22 percent said no, and 29 percent didn't know. The lay ministers had little clarity about their rights, even though a majority knew of other lay ministers who had lost their jobs in ways they considered unfair. Fox concluded that better awareness of rights and due process is important not only for justice but also for avoiding adversarial attitudes between lay ministers and clergy.

Most lay ministers are found in larger-than-average parishes; 27 percent of the parishes have three or more full-time resident priests, 43 percent have two, 27 percent have one, and 4 percent have no priest at all. (These figures do not include priests-in-residence not active in parish leadership.) Also 40 percent of the parishes have one or more permanent deacons, and 63 percent have one or more sisters in parish work (not including schools). The majority of the lay ministers have other lay ministers as colleagues; the median number of lay ministers in these parishes is between 2 and 3. So we may conclude that most lay ministers are in large, well-staffed parishes, and only a few are in small or poor parishes. Generally they are not in situations facing a shortage of priests or sisters.

We should note another survey involving lay ministers but broader in its scope. It was done by Ann Patrick Conrad and Joseph Shields for the Archdiocese of Baltimore in 1982.[22] They surveyed pastors, associate pastors (priests or laypersons), deacons, salaried lay ministers, and members of parish councils in 153 parishes. A total of 78 pastors responded; in those 78 parishes there were 95 full-time lay ministers (religious sisters, brothers, and laypersons), but they were concentrated in a smaller number of parishes. Thirty-three percent of the pastors said that they wanted to hire lay ministers in their parishes but had no money to do so.[23] The pastors listed these functions as top priority for being handled by lay ministers: moderate youth clubs and organizations, coordinate and plan music for liturgies, conduct Baptismal preparation, conduct Eucharistic, Penance, and Confirmation preparation, and organize community service projects for youth. But they were hindered by the lack of money.

In sum, the nascent profession of lay ministry is attracting mostly women, and they are working mainly as directors of religious education. They have little job security, since most have contracts for only one year, and they work largely at the pleasure of the pastors. Not many are directly responsible to lay committees in the parishes. They are happy in their ministry, even though they complain about low wages, lack of support, and burnout. They are found mostly in larger and wealthier parishes.

Issues in the Development of Lay Ministries

We interviewed dozens of people concerning the development of lay ministries, and we asked what are the major factors hindering the development. Three were repeatedly mentioned. The most commonly emphasized was the lack of money; that is, lay ministers need to be paid a professional salary or at least something not far from it, and most parishes don't have the money. One person stressed that schools are competing with parish programs for the available money and until schools are financed differently, little money would be freed up for lay ministries.

We put a test question to many persons: "Suppose you were a bishop of a diocese with 200 priests. After several years, due to the shortage of priests, this number dropped down to 150, and meanwhile you replaced the 50 you lost with 50 professional trained lay ministers. Would the total cost go up or down?" Some instinctively said "up," arguing that the salaries of lay ministries are higher than the stipends received by priests. When we asked about the total costs of having priests in the diocese — including seminary training, rectory living, food and automobiles, health insurance, and so on, and when we mentioned that lay ministers are not subsidized in the same way, our interviewees concluded that they didn't know the answer. The question deserves research.

But the point here is merely that priests and lay ministers are supported in different ways, and this has implications. Priests come at a relatively low cost to parishes because many costs are subsidized from the diocese or are hidden. Lay ministers come at an apparently higher cost to parishes. Therefore lay ministers tend to be hired only by larger and more affluent parishes, as we have seen. The idea of having them fill in the gaps in parishes of all sizes, when priests are no longer available, is not financially provided for in most dioceses.

A related ambiguity exists regarding lay minister salaries. Since church work is a highly sought-after profession, many people are happy to work for low salaries if they are able to survive. For example, retired persons who are receiving a pension and married women whose husbands earn enough income for the household are able to work for less and often very happy to do so. This depresses the prevailing salaries for lay ministers, thus raising issues of economic justice for all other persons in the profession and influencing, to some degree, the type of persons the church hires. The situation is a dilemma which needs to be worked out.

The second hindrance to lay ministries is the attitude of priests, especially pastors. Many pastors resent the encroachment of laypersons on parish leadership, and many others feel uncertain and even threatened around lay ministers, especially women. Older pastors were typically not trained to work with professional staffs, and they don't trust non-priests in parish staffs. As the research shows, pastors are directly in charge of hiring and firing lay ministers in most parishes, and few lay ministers have any long-term job security in their positions.

The third hindrance mentioned to us was resistance among laity. Older laity are not accustomed to see laypersons — even women religious — in parish leadership roles, and they do not welcome or support any lay ministers who are appointed. This appears to be a transitional problem, since the 1985 surveys, discussed earlier in this chapter, found very strong support for increased lay ministries among all but the older-age Catholic laity.

We heard it argued that the growth of lay ministries has underlying revolutionary implications, in that lay ministers, unlike priests or deacons, are selected, supported, and fired by lay committees, or at least lay committees working together with clergy. Thus lay ministers represent an institutional innovation giving new powers to laity. But in reality the argument is weak, since it is not true that lay ministers are hired and fired by lay committees. If there is a trend in that direction, we would agree that an important institutional change will be taking place.

Finally, we have been in discussions in which two objections were raised to the growth of lay ministries. First was that it would give rise to "feminization" of the church, since lay ministers are predominantly women. It was argued that this might lower the participation of Catholic men in church life. Second was that lay ministers would become over-professionalized or over-clericalized, possibly creating distance between themselves and other laity or possibly reducing the motivation of laity to volunteer for church tasks with the feeling of "let the DRE do it" or "let Sister do it." Both arguments are difficult to evaluate, given experience so far, but both need study.

8
Conclusions

In the last four chapters we have looked at eleven options for responding to the priest shortage. We have weighed the research evidence and noted some implications of this or that line of action. Now in the final chapter we will go a bit beyond the factual data to venture some judgments about the eleven options. Our opinions and conclusions are not free of error, and if other people disagree with what we say, we would like to hear their arguments.

From the information available, some options appear to hold major potential for easing the effect of the priest shortage on the Catholic Church and Catholic community, while others have little potential. Our thoughts are summarized in Table 24. The three columns in the right-hand side of the table set forth our overall estimates on three crucial criteria. The first column states whether the option entails serious theological difficulties making it unrealistic in the current theological scene. Clearly two options, numbers 7 and 8, have such difficulties. Option 9, "utilize some resigned priests as sacramental ministers," is seen

Table 24

Summary Evaluation of Eleven Options for Responding to the Priest Shortage

	Are There Serious Theological Difficulties?	How Much Impact On the Priest Shortage?	Other Important Effects
1. Combine or restructure parishes, or re-educate Catholics to have lowered expectations of priestly services.	No	Low	Potential reduced appreciation of Sacraments
2. Re-assign or redistribute existing priests to get better utilization for parish leadership.	No	Low	–
3. Get more parish priests from religious orders.	No	Low	–
4. Get priests from foreign nations.	No	Low	Problems of acculturation
5. Recruit more seminarians.	No	Low	–
6. Ordain married as well as celibate men.	No	High	Higher quality due to numerous candidates
7. Ordain women.	Yes	Limited at first	More innovative priests
8. Institute a term of service for the priesthood, or institute an honorable discharge.	Yes	Medium	Higher quality due to numerous candidates
9. Utilize some resigned priests as sacramental ministers.	Some	Low	–
10. Expand and develop the permanent diaconate.	No	Low	–
11. Expand and develop lay ministries.	No	High	–

as having "some" theological difficulties. As outlined earlier, the principal difficulty resides in the fact that most resigned priests are currently married and wish to remain so; but this is a matter of church discipline, not doctrine, hence not a foremost obstacle. A second difficulty is the Vatican's attitude toward resigned priests, even if unmarried. The Vatican was not open to allowing them to return to priestly practice until recently, when it has shown signs of greater flexibility.[1] If the openness becomes more affirming, the theological difficulties for option 9 would reduce to those for option 7 (married priests), that is, not serious. Meanwhile the word "some" in the table seems more realistic.

The second column in Table 24 gives an estimate of the impact of each option. Can it make a noteworthy difference, or not? Options number 6 and 11 (ordaining married men and expanding lay ministries) seem to have the possibility of making the most difference. Option 6 (married men) would produce enough priests that the priesthood would expand until financial limits are reached. Since quality of priests could improve, with the availability of many candidates, levels of lay giving could reasonably be expected to rise, thus expanding the financial limits in the system.

Option 11 is the other possibility with major impact. It would produce many trained and committed lay leaders who can provide high-quality services. Numerous candidates are available, and with improved ministry in parishes lay giving could be expected to rise. Whether option 11 is a long-term solution is debatable. Persons who believe it isn't argue that the numbers of lay ministers can be expanded to an extent in parishes, but the total number which can be used is limited. The reason is that liturgical and sacramental duties must be carried out by priests, and even a large cadre of lay ministers cannot be useful in that respect. Thus lay ministers are no more than a temporary means to alleviate the priest shortage by unburdening priests of some of their non-liturgical tasks. But other persons disagree. They argue that the priest shortage will continue to deepen for a long time, and in the face of it, lay ministers will be urged by the faithful to carry out more and more liturgical duties in parishes. The recent Vatican adoption of the Communion Service for Sunday liturgy, which can be celebrated by a layperson and includes distribution of the Communion elements, exemplifies a trend toward lay leadership which will continue. Lay ministers are therefore not just a short-term measure to unburden priests but on the contrary they will, in the course of time, be urged into leadership roles virtually equal to priests. Church authorities will permit this to happen because of overwhelming pastoral needs. This second scenario contains numerous assumptions about future trends, but no one can call them unrealistic, and the scenario needs to be studied.

Options 7 and 8 would have smaller impact. Option 7 (ordaining women) would have a large impact in the long run, but at first the problems of acceptability of women priests would impede its effect. Option 8 (instituting a term of service for the priesthood) would probably produce a surge of men interested in the priesthood, but it is unclear if the re-enlistment rate would be high enough to sustain high numbers and high quality of priests; hence we have entered "medium" as its estimated impact.

From a realistic point of view, two options are most important — 6 and 11. They have a great potential impact on the priest shortage, and they are not blocked by serious theological difficulties. Also any future action should include continuation of the traditional opinion 5 (recruit as many seminarians as possible).

Option 7 (ordaining women) is more urgent than its practical usefulness in regard to the priest shortage would dictate, since the women's movement in the United States can be expected to grow. This will have a big impact on the Catholic Church whose extent is hard to estimate. The effect will be slow in coming, but its consequences will be great. We agree with Eugene Kennedy in his estimate of the issue's immensity:

Anybody who underestimates the intelligence, maturity, and determination of the Church's women, particularly its religious women, makes a mistake of enormous proportions. Mishandling or postponing the frank and open resolution of this issue will one day be judged a tactical error at the end of the century as grave as that made at its beginning through the repression of progressive scholarship and seminary education. Make no misjudgment: working out the conflict over an expanding role for women within it is the main business and moral obligation of the American Church in the next decade.[2]

We have not included the option of "doing nothing." This was done deliberately, since doing nothing has the effect of encouraging one or more of the eleven options. It does not serve to "stop everything" or "stop the clock."

In our interviews in the past two years we have been advised by a surprising number of people not to worry about the priest shortage. They told us that God will look after His church. We were told that "In the history of the church, it has never suffered for lack of priests" and that "God has always given the Church sufficient priests." One person said, "I have an idea that God will surprise us (by giving us more priests)." These statements imply that human beings should do nothing about the problem, and leave all to God. If church leaders do nothing, we can make reasonable predictions of what the priest shortage will lead to, but it is not within our province to judge the possibility that "God will surprise us."

In Chapter 4 we looked at some of the best scenarios available today. They indicate that Catholic laity will continue to increase in numbers and yet will stoutly resist any closing of parishes. As the number of available priests declines, laymen will exert pressure to get substitute leadership in priestless parishes in the form of lay pastors. The Eucharist will be less available, but the laity will be content with Communion services and other approximations. Parish life as we presently

know it will change in the direction of the developments in Latin
America, where the priest shortage has spawned new priestless communities of faith. In short, if we do nothing, the result will be option
number 11, the expansion of lay ministries, including lay pastors in
priestless parishes. This is not well understood today. Our view concerning what to do about the priest shortage is the same as that of
Archbishop John Whealon of Hartford:

> None of us can foresee the future, nor can we mistrust the Holy
> Spirit. But, looking at the attrition of priests in Europe, at the
> current decline of United States diocesan priests and at the
> even steeper decline in major communities of religious women
> and men, there is no doubt that much hard thinking, planning
> and even experimentation should be done *now* to prepare for
> the future.[3]

The Gerard Broccolo Thesis

Our discussion of options can be focussed by referring to a speech
given in 1985 by Rev. Gerard Broccolo. He is a priest of the
Archdiocese of Chicago, Director of the Ministerial Formation Department of the archdiocese, and a collaborator in the future planning
project, "Project 1990." He talked about the priest shortage and what it
may lead to:

> Now I am going to talk for a few minutes about being radical,
> and radical changes from tradition. The most radical change
> there can be is to have Christian communities without the
> centrality of the Eucharistic celebration. We must *not* lose that
> cornerstone of our Catholic Christian tradition for the sake of
> lesser "traditions." Eucharistic prayer does not mean Com-
> munion Service. We now have surfacing what is called the
> Communion Service: basically a Mass without a Eucharistic
> Prayer.[4]

He described the new Communion Service, which seems warranted for today's pastoral reasons, but which he called "a radical departure from our Catholic tradition." Then he described possible radical changes:

> I am going to suggest, in order of their intensity, four degrees of radical change, number one being the least radical, number two more radical, number three is a lot more radical, and number four the most radical. Degree number one of radical change: Bishops ordain people to the priesthood who are not celibate or not male, who thus could preside at Eucharist and other sacramental celebrations. That is the least radical possibility because it is a change of church discipline, not a change of church doctrine. It is a disciplinary change, not a doctrinal change, not a theological change...
>
> Degree number two of radical change would be that Bishops delegate others who hold public office to preside at Eucharist. The others who hold public office are permanent and transitional Deacons. For Bishops to delegate Deacons to preside at Eucharist would be a more radical change... In the early church, only Bishops presided at Eucharist. With a passing of time, Bishops delegated those of the second order of public office, Priests, to preside at Eucharist. Since Deacons have never before had the right or responsibility of presiding at Eucharist, that would be a radical change, more radical than the first, but still basically within the mainstream of our theological tradition.
>
> Level number three of radical change would have Bishops delegating those who do not hold public office (laity) to preside at Eucharist. This is semi-consonant with our theological tradition because the originator is still the Bishop who is delegating this person to preside in his place.

The fourth degree of radical change, and the most radical, would have the Bishops do *nothing*. Bishops doing nothing new allows one of two possibilities, either to have local Christian communities existing without Sunday Eucharist as central to their life; or, Christian communities depute their own leadership, which is rampant congregationalism.

The Catholic Church in this country falls into that last category. It is impossible to reconcile a congregational model with 2,000 years of a hierarchical tradition. It is not consonant. It is the most radical departure from our heritage. The irony is that the fear of the less radical change is allowing the most radical change. The most radical thing that could happen is to change the whole system. To have change within the system, or to have change within the structure, is less radical than changing our whole structure of church life.[5]

He closed with a comment on pragmatic accommodations:

We need to clarify the operative presuppositions that we have in moving into the future. That means, we have to come together and write vision statements, mission statements. We need to define our united sense of direction. If we do not do that we are going to back into our future, with extremely radical changes, under the rubric of pragmatic accommodations.[6]

Broccolo is an avowed institutional conservative, insisting that the Eucharist is constitutive of the Catholic tradition. It cannot be sidelined or changed. Therefore the church should not go the route of lay ministers and the Communion Service, but rather preserve the liturgical and sacramental structures intact by getting more priests wherever possible, including married men and women. Broccolo is extremely wary of the implications of the new Communion Service, preferring a rule to allow laity to celebrate Eucharist over widespread use of the Communion. From this point of view what seems gradual and pragmatic is actually radical and dangerous — and the ordination of married men and of women is the safest course. He agrees, incidentally, that "doing nothing" is equivalent to our option number 11.

We find his argument convincing, if one starts with the unchangeable Eucharist as the basis of all.[7] Others may disagree if they see intrinsic value in other basics, such as greater participation by laypersons, or more democratic structures, or whatever. (In this book we have stressed the central mission of the church.) Broccolo's preferred policies preserve the clergy-laity distinction and institutional power structure intact. His analysis needs to be taken very seriously and researched insofar as it is possible.

Concluding Personal Comments

The research project which produced this book was sponsored by the Lilly Endowment with the suggestion that it be practical, realistic, and helpful. At times we talked about the hoped-for book as a fact book or resource book which might make future debates more realistic. I have tried to carry out this mandate without boring anyone with uninterpreted research findings. I have made some political judgments, being guided by advisors and interviewees. They are always in the direction of gradualism and practical feasibility. Several times during the research I was admonished by friends that anything very radical would render the whole project suspect and thus useless; they said again and again that American bishops are conservative, especially now in this period of Vatican retrenchment, so don't be venturesome on institutional questions.

I have consistently held to the view that the priest shortage is an institutional problem, not a spiritual problem, and it can be solved through institutional measures. Therefore this book is an essay on institutional leadership, not on spiritual life, discipleship, or commitment. I am very much aware that the book pays little heed to the radical demands of the Gospel, especially in the domain of international justice. It does not call enough attention to Christian witness in situations where that witness is most inspiring and effective. It has an overall middle-class bias, not giving enough attention to the radical demands of the poor. My only excuse is that I have tried to be realistic. Debates about the priest shortage will take place on a practical, "political" (that is, church politics) level. Institutional changes at this level will occur slowly and haltingly.

Finally, I have held the view that the God-given mission of the church is basic. It is unchangeable, whereas the particularities of rules, disciplines, and procedures are not. On the contrary: rules, disciplines, and procedures need to be re-examined from time to time to see if they are still serving the central mission of the church or not. If they are a hindrance and not a help, they must be adjusted. This is true for seminary curricula, personnel policies, employment contracts, housing policies for clergy, and even celibacy. Particular parts of institutional church life have meaning only in relation to the church's central mission. As with individuals, so it is with institutions; as our Lord taught us: "By their fruits shall you know them."

Appendix A
Methodology Of 1985
Surveys

College Student Surveys

In autumn 1984 we decided that the project should include a random sample of undergraduate Catholics in all American colleges — Catholic and non-Catholic, and a random sample of undergraduate Catholics who are active leaders in campus ministries. After numerous consultations with survey experts I decided to use telephone interviews with the random sample and mailed questionnaires with the student leaders. Mailed questionnaires were preferable since they could be longer and they allow students to fill them out at leisure, but we doubted if we could get a defensible return rate with mailed questionnaires from a random sample.

I met with campus ministers in three local universities — University of Maryland, American University, and Catholic University, and arranged for pretesting with both student leaders and a quasi-random sample. Also I got names for telephone pretests from sociology classes at Catholic University. We did about 50 mailed pretests and 30 telephone pretests.

Dr. John Robinson of the Survey Research Center, University of Maryland, designed the sample. The colleges had to be located in clusters to save cost, and the Catholic college sample had to be large enough for separate analysis; we set as a goal 350 completions in non-Catholic colleges and 250 in Catholic colleges. Dr. Robinson's initial sample was composed of 27 colleges, 6 of them Catholic. After discussion we decided we needed a larger sample of colleges, so he drew a supplementary sample of 2 non-Catholic and 4 Catholic colleges, for a total of 33. Sample sizes in each were determined by Dr. Robinson according to how many Catholic undergraduates were enrolled in each. As a requirement of this process we telephoned the registrars of all 33 to ask for this information or at least an estimate.

The final list of 33 colleges was slightly different from the sample because of three replacements which were necessary. The final list, in ten clusters, was: (1) *Northern New York.* Siena College (RC); State Univ. College at Oneonta; State Univ. College at Plattsburg; Clarkson College of Technology. (2) *Southeast Pennsylvania.* St. Joseph's University (RC); LaSalle University (RC); Holy Family College (RC); Drexel University; Temple University; Univ. of Pennsylvania. (3) *North Carolina.* East Carolina University; U.N.C.-Charlotte. (4) *Mississippi.* Mississippi State University; Mississippi Univ. for Women; Univ. of Southern Mississippi. (5) *Northern Indiana.* University of Notre Dame (RC); Saint Mary's College (RC); Indiana University-South Bend. (6) *Central Illinois.* University of Illinois-Champaign; Illinois State University-Normal. (7) *Kansas.* Fort Hays State University; Kansas State University, Manhattan; Marymount College (RC). (8) *West Texas.* Hardin-Simmons University; University of Texas-El Paso. (9) *Southern*

California. California State University-Long Beach; California State University-Los Angeles; U.C.L.A.; Loyola Marymount University (RC); Mount Saint Mary's College (RC). (10) *Oregon.* Oregon State University-Corvallis; Lewis and Clark College; University of Portland (RC).

The replacements were in North Carolina and Oregon. The University of North Carolina at Wilmington had no campus ministry at all and thus was replaced by U.N.C. at Charlotte. In Oregon the University of Oregon-Health Services Center had no campus ministry and was replaced by Lewis and Clark College, and due to lack of cooperation Portland State University was replaced by Oregon State University-Corvallis.

Rev. Joseph Kenna, staff director of the Department of Campus Ministry, United States Catholic Conference, helped me contact campus ministers at all the colleges. I phoned them and arranged trips to each cluster. Between January and April I travelled to each cluster, met with the campus ministers, gathered lists of undergraduate campus ministry leaders, and set up the telephoning. I hired and trained interviewers to complete the task after I left.

A major difficulty was securing defensible lists for the random sampling. It occurred only in the non-Catholic colleges; in the Catholic colleges we were always able to draw random samples from total student lists or lists of all Catholic students. In seven of the non-Catholic colleges we called randomly down undergraduate lists, searching for Catholics and interviewing the ones we found. In ten we worked from printouts from registrar's offices giving names of students declaring themselves to be Catholics at registration. Some of these introduced little bias, since virtually all students had declared *some* religion at registration, but others were biased, since lower percentages (in a few cases less than half) had declared a religion. The bias was that our lists were overloaded with committed church-going Catholics. In four colleges we had only lists of Catholics which had been assembled through efforts of campus ministers. When using them we added snowball sampling by asking interviewees to name other Catholics they knew, and if the persons named were not on our list we attempted to include them. This succeeded occasionally. In two colleges we had to gather lists through other techniques. In one, helpful professors asked for Catholic volunteers in their classes to form our sample. In another (a college with very few Catholics) we had to use a snowball technique to find Catholics. When large biases were evident we under-sampled in those colleges and over-sampled the same number in similar colleges with less biased lists; this was done twice.

A second major difficulty was finding the students to interview them. We tried calling in afternoons, at night, and on weekends, with varying success. Refusals were low in number (less than 1 per 10 completions), but in some colleges phone numbers were often wrong or students could not be reached in repeated attempts.

We judged that the telephone interviews in 8 non-Catholic colleges contained definite bias toward over-representation of active church-going Catholics, so we down-weighted the respondents in them who attended Mass weekly (weight: .78) and up-weighted those who attended less (weight: 1.23). These weights were selected by comparing Mass attendance frequencies in our data with other college student surveys. Also we up-weighted the North Carolina data slightly (since the interviewer failed to complete the last two interviews), and we weighted all samples to make them half male, half female.

When reporting data on all Catholic undergraduates in both Catholic and non-Catholic colleges, we down-weighted the Catholic college data to make it comprise 10 percent of the total; this is because American Council on Education data shows that between 9 and 10 percent of all Catholic undergraduates in the U.S. are attending Catholic colleges.

We completed 607 phone interviews out of 609 prescribed by the sample design, and we received 610 mailed questionnaires from campus ministry leaders, or 87.5 percent of the 697 we mailed out. In one college there was no Catholic campus ministry but only an ecumenical campus ministry; we sent out no mailed questionnaires there. On the other campuses we mailed out an average of 21.8 questionnaires.

Survey of Adult Catholics

The adult Catholic survey had to produce reliable trend data by repeating earlier items in NORC surveys, so we needed a 1985 sample which exactly matched the 1974 NORC sample. I consulted with Dr. William McCready of NORC about the best approaches, and I got the technical report on the 1974 survey. A telephone survey seemed the best method, since modern sampling methods can avoid measurable bias in telephone surveys. After comparing prices and methods I selected the Gallup organization and purchased a random sample of 800 Catholics 18 or older in the contiguous 48 states.

The interview was pretested by my assistants at Catholic University, using names from three local Catholic parishes. Also the Gallup organization carried out its own pretests. The final survey was done in June 1985, with 801 completions. The data were weighted by the Gallup organization according to sex, region, race, age, and education to make the sample match the total U.S. Catholic population as defined by past accumulations of Gallup poll data.

Survey of Priests

The survey of priests had to produce reliable trend data based on the 1970 survey sponsored by the National Conference of Catholic Bishops and carried out by NORC. I formed a collaboration with Dr. Joseph Shields and Dr. Mary Jeanne Verdieck of Catholic University for the survey. We decided to use a questionnaire of 12 pages, much shorter than the 1970 version, which was 46 pages. Most of the space would be devoted to replication items. We planned to include all the 1970 variables used in the path models in the book (Greeley, 1972). We found we could include all except the Personal Orientation Inventory, a psychological test which was sent separately to a small subsample of priests in 1970.

We selected 1,200 as the sample size, a compromise between quality and economy but large enough for basic data analysis. The completion rate in 1970 was 71 percent, and we hoped to equal that.

We asked Rev. Colin MacDonald, Secretary to the National Conference of Catholic Bishops' Committee on Priestly Life and Ministry, if the committee would be interested in the survey. He said yes and later furnished us with letters of endorsement and assistance in convincing dioceses to participate. The chairman of the committee, Most Rev. Michael J. Murphy, gave us a strong letter of endorsement. The committee reviewed a first draft of the proposed questionnaire and suggested improvements.

We asked Dr. Richard Schoenherr, research director for the 1970 survey, for specific information about the 1970 sample. He sent details of the procedure and all names of dioceses and orders in the sample. The 1970 sample used an elaborate weighting formula so that smaller dioceses and orders could be oversampled for purposes of contextual analysis, yet overall frequencies representative of all priests could be produced. We decided against such a weighting scheme in 1985, and instead randomly sampled all dioceses and orders, choosing a 12.5 percent sample from their lists.

We did not need all 85 dioceses and 91 institutes sampled in 1970, so we randomly selected one-third of them within each stratum. The 1970 sample was a composite of 13 strata, mostly based on size but in the case of religious institutes also on basis of American or European formation. Our sample included 28 dioceses and 27 religious orders or provinces, all of which had been in the 1970 sample. We wrote to them in February 1985, asking for lists of priests and letters of endorsement to be included in mailings to the priests. Following the 1970 method, we asked that they include retired priests and priests serving outside the diocese, including overseas. All the dioceses complied except two. One was the Stamford Diocese of the Ukrainian Rite. Since it was small, and we already had a Ukrainian diocese in the sample, we did not replace it. The other was large, and we replaced it with a nearby diocese of the same size. Two small religious institutes refused to cooperate: both were replaced by other abbeys in the same orders.

One departure from pure randomness was made when we happened to select the Maryknoll Fathers as the representative American foundation. Since it is large and unusual in its emphasis on social mission, and since most of its priests are serving outside the U.S. in third world nations, we worried about skewing the sample. Also we worried about getting timely returns from around the world. So we took only half as many Maryknoll names as the method dictated and drew more names of American foundations to fill out the sample. We happened to get the Paulist Fathers and Josephite Fathers. By taking half-size samples from each we attained the correct numbers.

The sample size turned out to be 1,224. To each we sent an initial mailing, including an endorsement letter from the bishop or superior (or in a few cases from Bishop Murphy), then a week later we sent a reminder card to everyone. Three weeks after the initial mailing we sent a nearly identical second mailing, and three weeks after that we sent a third mailing.

The questionnaires had no names or identifying numbers; instead we provided postcards for the respondents to return separately, giving us their names and saying that they had returned the questionnaire. A total of 29 questionnaires were sent overseas, almost entirely to Maryknoll priests. Mailings went out in batches, since the lists of priests came in slowly. We began in April and finished the last diocese in August. Of the 1,224 questionnaires mailed, 6 were never delivered. We received

1,062 usable completed questionnaires (86.8 percent), 796 from diocesan priests (89.0 percent) and 266 from religious priests (80.6 percent). Cooperation was better in 1985 than in 1970.

We accidentally got a higher percentage of diocesan priests and a lower percentage of religious priests than in 1970, so for sake of comparability we weighted the data to reinstate the 1970 proportions (59.1 percent diocesan, 40.9 percent religious). The weights were .7863 for diocesan, 1.6426 for religious priests. When we used the 1985 data to compare with attitudes of laity, we weighted the data to produce the 1985 diocesan/religious ratio as given in the *Official Catholic Directory*— 61.2 percent diocesan, 38.8 percent religious. All analyses were done with weighted data.

Preliminary Reports

As data became available we proceeded with analysis, and between August 1985 and May 1986 we wrote five preliminary reports. They were printed in low quantities, sent to everyone involved in the project, and sold to others. They contained a broader range of analyses and data tables than are found in this book. The five are:

No. 1: Dean R. Hoge, "Attitudes of Catholic College Students Toward Vocations and Lay Ministries," August 1985. 43 pp. including tables.

No. 2: Dean R. Hoge, "Attitudes of Catholic Adults and College Students About the Priest Shortage and Parish Life," September 1985. 33 pp. including tables.

No. 3: Dean R. Hoge, Joseph J. Shields, and Mary Jeanne Verdieck, "Attitudes of Priests, Adults, and College Students on Catholic Parish Life and Leadership," January 1986. 31 pp. including tables and figures.

No. 4: Dean R. Hoge, Joseph J. Shields, and Mary Jeanne Verdieck, "Attitudes of American Priests in 1970 and 1985 on the Church and Priesthood," March 1986. 54 pp. including tables and figures.

No. 5: Dean R. Hoge, "Trends in Catholic Lay Attitudes Since Vatican II on Church Life and Leadership," May 1986. 38 pp. including tables and figures.

A Technical Appendix has been prepared to accompany this book. It includes details of the college student survey and the priest survey, all five preliminary reports, copies of the questionnaires and interview forms, and related material. Copies have been deposited in the libraries of Catholic University of America, University of Notre Dame, and Graduate Theological Union, Berkeley. Copies are for sale at twenty dollars each. Write to the Department of Sociology, Catholic University of America, Washington, D.C. 20064, and make out checks to Catholic University.

Appendix B

Table B-1

1	2	3	4	5	6	7	8	9	10
Year	Total Cath.Pop. from Official Directory	Percent Catholic from Gallup Polls	Total Cath.Pop. from Gallup Polls	Total Priests	Total Deacons	Priest.Cand. Seminarians Enrolled in Theologate	Cath. per Priest (from cols. 2 and 5)	Cath. per Priest (from cols. 4 and 5)	Cath. per Seminarian (from cols. 2 and 7)
1920	17,735,553			21,019		3,379	806		5,358
1922	18,104,804			22,049			784		
1924	18,559,787			23,159		3,860	765		4,891
1926	18,878,722			24,352			740		
1928	19,689,049			25,773			730		
1930	20,203,702			26,925			717		
1932	20,236,391			28,297		5,090	683		3,993
1934	20,322,594			29,619			655		
1936	20,735,189			31,108			637		
1938	21,451,460			32,668		5,237	627		4,087
1940	21,403,136			33,912			603		
1941	22,293,101			35,839			594		
1942	22,556,242			36,580			589		
1943	22,945,247			36,970			593		
1944	23,419,701			37,749			593		
1945	23,963,671			38,451		6,228	595		3,918
1946	24,402,124			38,980			598		
1947	25,268,173	20	27,379,000	40,470			596	646	
1948	26,075,697			41,747			597		
1949	26,718,343			42,334		5,665	603		4,901
1950	27,766,141			42,970			617		
1951	28,634,878			43,889			623		
1952	29,407,520	25	35,972,000	44,459			632	773	
1953	30,425,015			45,222		8,037	643		
1954	31,648,424			45,451			665		3,938
1955	32,575,702			46,970			663		

Year	Total Cath.Pop. from Official Directory	Percent Catholic from Gallup Polls	Total Cath.Pop. from Gallup Polls	Total Priests	Total Deacons	Priest.Cand. Seminarians Enrolled in Theologate	Cath. per Priest[a] (from cols. 2 and 5)	Cath. per Priest[a] (from cols. 4 and 5)	Cath. per Seminarian (from cols. 2 and 7)
1956	33,574,017			48,349			663		
1957	34,563,851	26	39,376,000	49,725		8,119	664	756	4,257
1958	36,023,977			50,813			677		
1959	39,505,475			52,689			716		
1960	40,871,302			53,796			726		
1961	42,104,899			54,682			735		
1962	42,876,665	23	40,876,000	55,581		8,480	737	702	4,965
1963	43,851,538			56,540			741		
1964	44,874,938			57,328			748		
1965	45,640,601			58,432		8,885	746		5,137
1966	46,246,175			59,193			746		
1967	46,864,910	25	47,400,000	59,892		8,159	747	756	
1968	47,468,333			59,803		7,511	758		5,744
1969	47,873,238			59,620			767		6,320
1970	47,872,089			59,192		6,426	772		7,450
1971	48,214,729			58,161		6,094	792		7,912
1972	48,390,990	26	52,325,000	57,421		5,804	805	870	8,338
1973	48,460,427			56,969			812		
1974	48,465,438	27	55,458,000	56,712		5,037	816	934	9,622
1975	48,701,835	27	56,030,000	58,909a		5,137	827	951	9,481
1976	48,881,872	27	56,576,000	58,847		5,279	831	961	9,260
1977	49,325,752	29	61,544,000	58,301	1,900c	5,346b	846	1,056	9,227
1978	49,836,176	29	62,188,000	58,485	2,498	4,800	852	1,063	10,383
1979	49,602,035	29	62,888,000	58,430	3,296	4,327	849	1,076	11,463
1980	49,812,178	28	61,344,000	58,621	4,093	4,187	850	1,046	11,897
1981	50,449,842	28	61,911,000	58,398	4,725	3,819	864	1,060	13,210
1982	51,207,579	29	64,820,000	58,058	5,471	4,109	882	1,116	12,462
1983	52,088,744	29	65,520,000	57,870	6,066	4,244	900	1,132	12,274
1984	52,392,934	28	63,774,000	57,891	6,702	4,170	905	1,102	12,564
1985	52,286,043	28	64,341,000	57,317	7,204	4,063	912	1,123	12,869

Table B-1 (continued)

Notes

Col. 2   Each figure is the one given in that year's Official Catholic Directory, even though actual data collection may have been a year earlier. Greek rite Catholic are included.

Col. 3   Gallup polls were less reliable in the 1940s and 1950s than today, as suggested by the variations in findings. The overall rise in percentage of persons with a Catholic preference is credible, given Catholic historical data. See the Yearbook of American Churches 1967, p. 219, and Demerath (1968). To smooth the curve we use 24 in 1952 and 1957. In addition we subtract one percentage point from every estimate because another reliable set of nationwide polls, the N.O.R.C. General Social Survey, has consistently reported lower estimates of Catholic preference, usually 1 to 3 points lower. Source: Emerging Trends, February 1986, p. 1

Col. 4   This is the product of the total resident U.S. population as given in Statistical Abstracts of the United States 1982-83, p. 6, multiplied by the percentage Catholic in Gallup polls (in column 3).

Col. 5   Total diocesan and religious priests including Eastern and Greek rite, from the Official Catholic Directory.

Col. 7   Data prior to 1979 are from Planning for the Future: Catholic Theology Schools, Formation Houses 1975-1984, published by the Center for Applied Research in the Apostolate, 1980, p. 34. Data after 1979 is from annual CARA Seminary Forum reports.

a   The increase from 1974 to 1975 in column 5 resulted from a change in reporting religious priests. An increase of about 2,250 occurred in 1975 apparently due to the inclusion of previously uncounted missionaries. The change is approximately .047 of the expected figure in 1975, judging from trends. Hence we multiplied all numbers of priests prior to 1975 by 1.047 when calculating columns 8 and 9.

b   The 1975, 1976, and 1977 figures are accidentally inflated by double counts of students living in religious houses of study and enrolled in cluster seminaries.

c   The permanent deacon program began in 1971, but the numbers were not listed in the Official Catholic Directory until 1977.

Table B-2

Priests (Diocesan and Religious) Per 10,000 Catholics

	1956	1960	1965	1970	1975	1980	1983
Western Nations							
Austria	11.1	10.6	11.1	9.3	9.0	9.3	8.9
Belgium	18.2	17.8	17.2	15.0	15.4	14.3	13.4
Canada	19.2	17.5	16.9	15.1	13.1	12.2	11.1
France	14.1	13.6	12.3	9.9	9.3	8.5	8.0
Great Britain	15.5	19.0	20.4	16.4	15.9	15.3	15.5
Germany (West)	a	a	a	8.2	8.2	8.2	7.8
Ireland	17.5	17.6	19.6	17.6	17.4	16.4	16.5
Italy	13.6	12.8	12.3	12.4	11.5	11.5	11.1
Netherlands	18.2	20.2	17.5	14.2	11.8	12.3	11.5
Spain	11.0	11.0	11.0	10.7	9.6	8.9	8.6
United States	14.5	13.2	12.9	12.1	11.7	11.6	11.0
Other							
India	12.5	10.7	11.6	11.2	11.0	10.4	10.0
Poland	5.9	5.2	5.6	5.8	5.8	5.9	5.9
Africa	b	6.0	5.4	4.3	3.3	3.0	2.6
South America	b	2.1	2.3	1.9	1.7	1.5	1.5

Source: 1956, 1960, and 1965 data is from The National Catholic Almanac (Paterson, NJ: St. Anthony's Guild, 1957, 1961, and 1966). Beginning in 1957 it summarizes statistics from various sources. 1970-1983 data is from the Statistical Yearbook of the Church for those years.

a Separate data for West Germany was not available before 1970; The National Catholic Almanac combined East and West Germany in earlier years.

b The National Catholic Almanac did not summarize data for continents in 1956.

Table B-3
Defections Per 1,000 Diocesan Priests

	1974	1975	1976	1977
Austria	6.2	3.9	3.8	4.7
Belgium	3.9	3.2	3.9	2.9
Canada	10.8	13.1	6.6	6.3
France	4.3	4.5	4.3	3.9
Germany (West)	4.6	3.7	2.6	2.0
Italy	3.1	2.7	2.9	3.3
Spain	9.8	11.1	8.8	11.4
United States	11.7	9.7	8.8	8.2
Poland	1.6	1.1	1.5	2.1

Source: Statistical Yearbook of the Church
        (annual).

1978	1979	1980	1981	1982	1983
3.3	.8	1.4	2.3	.9	.6
4.0	3.6	2.5	1.4	2.0	1.3
6.0	4.7	3.3	3.2	2.4	3.4
3.7	2.5	2.4	2.7	1.9	1.3
1.6	2.2	1.1	.8	1.2	1.2
3.0	2.9	1.7	1.7	1.3	1.0
9.6	8.2	7.8	5.8	4.4	3.4
7.2	6.4	4.7	4.9	4.8	3.9
2.7	1.5	2.0	.9	1.2	1.6

Table B-4

Attitudes of Priests, Adults, and College Students on Possible Changes in the Catholic Church (Percents)

	All Priests		All Adults		Campus Ministry Student Leaders	
	Help	Hurt	Help	Hurt	Help	Hurt
Permanent Deacons						
A. A great increase in the number of permanent deacons.	49	13	64	3	84	2
B. Open up the office of permanent deacon to women.	43	31	56	16	68	6
Parish Life						
C. Creation of more small groups in parishes to encourage face-to-face relationships.	72	6	78	4	86	1
D. Greater stress on obedience to priestly authority among the laity.	22	50	36	23	20	36
E. More influential roles for women in parishes.	75	7	74	8	84	2
F. Greater lay participation in decision-making in parishes.	79	10	77	7	84	3
G. More frequent informal relationships between priests and laity.	80	5	81	4	89	2
H. Allow periodic celebration of the Latin Mass if a parish desires.	38	22	67	4	54	8
Priests						
I. Allow priests to resign their priesthood with an honorable discharge, if they wish, after 10 or 15 years of service.	27	52	48	22	27	38

(continued)

	All Priests		All Adults		Campus Ministry Student Leaders	
	Help	Hurt	Help	Hurt	Help	Hurt
J. More recruitment of older men into the priesthood.	67	5	62	10	53	6
K. Allow priests to live where they wish, not just in rectories.	31	41	35	34	25	36
L. Allow parishes to help choose the priests who come to serve them.	40	37	55	22	46	29
Full-Time Lay Workers						
M. Hire full-time lay parish administrators in parishes.	63	15	55	17	72	6
N. Hire full-time lay religious educators and liturgical experts in parishes.	75	9	67	8	75	5
O. Hire lay marriage counselors or personal counselors in parishes.	73	8	73	9	67	10
Ex-Priests						
P. Invite ex-priests who are currently married to become paid lay ministers in parishes.	46	31	47	27	65	10
Q. Invite ex-priests who are currently married to become active parish priests again.	40	40	48	31	31	37

Table B-5

Attitudes of Men Interested in Vocations, Men Interested in the Priesthood If Celibacy Were Optional, and Women Interested in the Priesthood if Women Could Be Ordained (Campus Ministry Leaders; Percents)

	Men			Women	
	Inter. in Vocat. (N=32)	Inter. if Optional Celibacy (N=104)	All Men (N=242)	Inter. in Ordin. (N=49)	All Women (N=364)
Ethnicity: German, Austrian, Dutch, Swiss	35	20	21	16	20
Irish	23	24	18	29	22
Italian	12	9	12	8	8
Spanish, Portuguese, Mexican, Latin American, Caribbean	6	12	8	13	10
Other	25	36	41	34	40

On each issue, choose the statement closest to your opinion:

1. A. The Catholic Church should approve of individual variations in doctrinal beliefs among its members.	39	49	51	70	63
B. The Catholic Church should insist on strict standards of doctrinal beliefs among its members.	55	45	36	13	24
C. Cannot choose or don't know.	6	6	14	16	13
2. A. The Catholic Church should emphasize a way of life for Catholics which stresses distinctiveness from prevailing American life style in some ways, for example, sex and family.	78	75	67	51	53

(continued)

	Men			Women	
	Inter. in Vocat.	Inter. if Optional Celibacy	All Men	Inter. in Ordin.	All Women
B. The Catholic Church should emphasize a way of life for Catholics which is as close as possible to prevailing American life style.	7	13	15	26	26
C. Cannot choose or don't know.	15	12	18	23	22
3. A. For the good of the Church today we must first of all recruit many more priests to overcome the existing shortage in parishes.	42	28	20	14	15
B. For the good of the Church today we must first of all think of new ways to structure parish leadership, to include more deacons, sisters, and lay persons.	43	65	69	77	74
C. Cannot choose or don't know.	16	8	11	9	11
4. In the Church there is a special status and role of priests, as distinguished from lay persons. In the future should the Church put more emphasis on this special status and role of priests, or less emphasis on it? Or should the situation remain as it is?					
More emphasis	27	17	12	6	12
Less emphasis	21	27	27	50	27
Remain as is	52	53	56	37	56
Don't know	0	3	4	7	5

(continued)

Table B-5 (continued)

	Men			Women	
	Inter. in Vocat.	Inter. if Optional Celibacy	All Men	Inter. in Ordin.	All Women
5. The leadership in the Catholic Church is held mostly by celibate men. Some people believe this is a strength of the Church, and others believe it is a weakness. Do you think it is a strength, a weakness, or neither one?					
Strength	57	37	36	20	38
Weakness	4	26	25	48	30
Neither one	33	27	32	26	28
Don't know	6	10	7	6	4
6. Some people want the Catholic Church to put more emphasis on aiding poor and hungry human beings. Others want the Church to put more emphasis on providing counseling and spiritual guidance for all its members. Which of the two would you put as a higher priority, or would they be equal?					
Aiding human beings	4	16	19	18	21
Providing counseling	15	20	14	7	10
Both equal	81	63	66	75	69
Don't know	1	0	0	0	1
Percent saying "Strongly agree" or "Agree somewhat":					
7. Leadership in the Catholic Church should be restricted to bishops, priests, and deacons where possible.	58	58	55	40	42
8. Becoming a priest is not a good vocation for young people any more.	0	11	8	10	7

(continued)

| | Men | | | Women | |
	Inter. in Vocat.	Inter. if Optional Celibacy	All Men	Inter. in Ordin.	All Women
9. It would be a good thing if women were allowed to be ordained as priests.	18	45	48	89	50
10. It would be a good thing if married men were allowed to be ordained as priests.	43	59	54	67	49
11. The Catholic bishops should take public stands on some political issues such as the arms race or the American economic system.	61	70	63	64	49
12. The Church's teaching on matters of birth control and divorce should be brought more into line with current social practices.	30	39	37	67	55

Notes

INTRODUCTION

1. The three collaborators were myself, Rev. Raymond Potvin of The Catholic University of America, and Kathleen Ferry, graduate research assistant. Our advisors included Rev. Eugene F. Hemrick, Director of Research of the National Conference of Catholic Bishops/United States Catholic Conference; Rev. Paul Philibert, O.P., Associate Professor, The Catholic University of America; Rev. Robert Sherry, Executive Director, Bishops' Committee on Priestly Formation; Msgr. William Baumgaertner, Executive Director, Seminary Department, National Catholic Educational Association; and Rev. Adrian Fuerst, staff of the Center for Applied Research in the Apostolate.

2. Dean R. Hoge, Raymond H. Potvin, and Kathleen M. Ferry, *Research on Men's Vocations to the Priesthood and the Religious Life* (Washington, DC: United States Catholic Conference, 1984).

3. Between August 1985 and May 1986 we prepared five typewritten reports giving a full report on the new research findings. For details see Appendix A.

4. Eugene F. Hemrick and Dean R. Hoge, *Seminarians in Theology: A National Profile* (Washington, DC: United States Catholic Conference, 1985). A companion study was done by Rev. Potvin; see Raymond H. Potvin, *Seminarians of the Eighties: A National Survey* (Washington, DC: National Catholic Educational Association, 1985).

5. Richard A. Schoenherr and Annemette Sorensen, "Social Change in Religious Organizations: Consequences of Clergy Decline in the U.S. Catholic Church," *Sociological Analysis* 43 (Spring 1982), pp. 23-52. The projections are summarized in Hoge, Potvin, and Ferry, *Research on Men's Vocations.*

6. Hoge, Potvin, and Ferry, *Research on Men's Vocations*, p. 70.

7. Dean R. Hoge, *Converts, Dropouts, Returnees: A Study of Religious Change Among Catholics* (Washington, DC: United States Catholic Conference, 1981). Also see Dean R. Hoge, Gregory H. Petrillo, and Ella I. Smith, "Transmission of Religious and Social Values From Parents to Teenage Children," *Journal of Marriage and the Family* 44 (August 1982), pp. 569-80, and Dean R. Hoge, et al., "Desired Outcomes of Religious Education and Youth Ministry in Six Denominations," *Review of Religious Research* 23 (March 1982), pp. 230-54.

CHAPTER 1

1. The 1970 survey was reported in Andrew M. Greeley, *The Catholic Priest in the United States: Sociological Investigations* (Washington, DC: United States Catholic Conference, 1972).

2. Interviews, July 29, 1986 and September 24, 1986.

3. There are numerous by-products of the priest shortage, of which one may be noted here. The U. S. Army chaplaincy has a critical shortage of Catholic priests, and since not enough can be found to fill the jobs allocated to the Catholic Church by the Army, those slots are given over to Protestant bodies, whose representation in the chaplaincy is growing yearly. In 1979 the Army chaplaincy had 242 Catholic priests; in 1985 it had 228, and the best projection is that it will have 158 in 1990. See Rev. Leo J. O'Keeffe, "The Recruitment and Retention of Roman Catholic Priests for the United States Army," unpublished M.P.A. thesis, Auburn University, 1986.

4. Cited in George B. Wilson, "The Priest Shortage: The Situation and Some Options," *America*, May 31, 1986, pp. 450-3. Quote is on p. 450.

5. The surveys are identified in note 1 above. Whether a priest is considered "retired" or not depends on his response to a question about current position.

6. Greeley, *The Catholic Priest*, especially Chapters 13 and 15. Eugene C. Kennedy and Victor J. Heckler, *The Catholic Priest in the United States: Psychological Investigations* (Washington, DC: United States Catholic Conference, 1972). Eugene J. Schallert and Jacqueline M. Kelley, "Some Factors Associated With Voluntary Withdrawal from the Catholic Priesthood," *Lumen Vitae* 25 (1970), pp. 425-60. James N. Watzke, "Desocialization From the Priesthood: Critical Problems of Personal and Role Identity Among the Catholic Religious Professionals," unpublished Ph.D. dissertation, Harvard University, 1971. For a review of the literature on resigned priests see John E. Haag, "A Study of the Seminary and Priesthood Experience of Thirteen Resigned Roman Catholic Priests." D.Min. dissertation, Pittsburgh Theological Seminary, 1984.

7. See Joseph J. Shields and Mary Jeanne Verdieck, "Religious Life in the United States: The Experience of Men's Communities," ringbound report (Washington, DC: Center for Applied Research in the Apostolate, 1985). Also see Richard A. Schoenherr and Annemette Sorensen, "Decline and Change in the U.S. Catholic Church," Report #5, CROS (Madison, WI: University of Wisconsin, 1981).

8. Greeley, *The Catholic Priest*, p. 24.

9. Sister Marie Augusta Neal has gathered data on the number of American sisters who have left their orders. The trend line in the 1960s and 1970s is the same as in Figure 5. The number was 1,562 in 1965, then it rose to a high of 4,337 in 1970 before falling to 751 in 1980. The data was gathered in 1982. See Marie Augusta Neal, "Causes of Vocation Decline Among Priests and Religious Congregation Members," unpublished paper, February 1984.

10. "Seminarians' Increase Greatest in Adversity," *America*, May 10, 1986, p. 375.

11. Steve Askin, "Celibacy Prime Block to African Vocations," *National Catholic Reporter*, February 7, 1986, p. 7.

12. Central Office of Statistics of the Church, "Evoluzione del Numero e Della Distribuzione Territoriale dei Seminaristi Maggiori nel Periodo 1970-1982," unpublished report (Vatican City, 1984) .

13. See William Ferree, "An Atlas of the Vocation Crisis," unpublished report (Dayton, OH: University of Dayton, Institute for Consecrated Life, 1982).

14. Monique Brulin, "Sunday Assemblies Without a Priest in France: Present Facts and Future Questions," in Edward Schillebeeckx and Johann-Baptist Metz (eds.), *The Right of the Community to a Priest*, Concilium 133 (New York: Seabury, 1980), pp. 29-36.

15. Jan Kerkhofs, "Priests and 'Parishes' -- A Statistical Survey," in Schillebeeckx and Metz, *The Right of the Community*, pp. 3-11.

16. John Paul II, Sermon of May 10, 1981. Cited in *The Conclusive Document*. Statement of the International Congress of Bishops on Vocations, May 1981 (Boston: Daughters of St. Paul), p. 13.

17. *Ibid.*, p. 77.

18. Paul VI, "Message for Vocation Sunday," Dec. 30, 1976, cited in Robert G. Howes, "Priest Vocations: A Pastoral Plan," *The Priest* 39 (October 1983), p. 34.

19. Two addresses by Archbishop Pilarczyk of Cincinnati voice the feelings, by all accounts, of many American bishops. The addresses include the desire for more priests, a sober appraisal of the many difficulties lying ahead, and an institutionally conservative position regarding the theology of the priesthood. See Daniel Pilarczyk, "The Priest Shortage: Catastrophe or Opportunity?" *Origins*, October 17, 1985, pp. 303-6, and Daniel Pilarczyk, "The Changing Image of the Priest," *Origins*, July 3, 1986, pp. 137-46.

20. In a 1982 assembly of bishops in Collegeville, Minnesota, the bishops took a straw poll concerning issues they most wanted considered, and "vocations to the priesthood and religious life" came out in first place. Cited in Robert Sherry, "Vocations in an Age of Transition," *Origins*, June 2, 1983, p. 62.

21. Bishop James Malone, President of the National Conference of Catholic Bishops, discussed the vocation problem openly in his report to the Secretariat of the Extraordinary Synod of 1985. He mentioned cultural factors making young people today hesitant to make lifelong commitments, he mentioned the problem of celibacy, and he said that competing ecclesiologies created confusion. He recommended "renewed emphasis on the church as the mystical body of Christ." *Origins,* September 26, 1985, pp. 226-33.

22. On the question of how the shortage of vocations is felt as discouraging by priests see Thomas E. Holsworth, "Vocations: A Need for New Strategies," *The Priest* 39 (June 1983) , pp. 7-9, and Robert G. Howes, "Priest Vocations," p. 35.

23. Eugene Kennedy, *The Now and Future Church: The Psychology of Being an American Catholic* (Garden City, NY: Doubleday, 1984), p. 158.

24. One person, when reviewing the data, suggested that this item may contain bias, in that alternative A mentions "the existing shortage in parishes," while alternative B does not, and now we know that only a third of the adults have personally experienced any shortage of priests. Maybe this situation depressed the number choosing alternative A. To check, we looked at the responses of adults and college students who *had* personally experienced a priest shortage; it turned out that their responses were the same as the total samples. So there is little bias.

25. The question originally had a ninth part, "Merger of your parish with another parish," but it is not included here because the results seem misleading. The percentages who found it not at all acceptable were unexpectedly low, probably because the wording did not specify whether one's own parish or the other parish would disappear. By all accounts feelings run high when laity's own parishes are threatened with closing. Future research needs to study the topic with more precise questions.

26. Michael J. Behr, "Report Weighs Ministry's Future," *The Chicago Catholic*, April 12, 1985, p. 15.

27. *Ibid.*, p. 15.

28. Robert Sherry, "Shortage? What Vocation Shortage?" *The Priest* 41 (November 1985), pp. 29-32.

29. The estimate of Catholic giving is derived from data from the 1974 NORC survey of Catholics (adjusted for inflation), from the 1983-84 Notre Dame Study of Parishes, and from financial research on six parishes scattered across the country by Joseph Harris of Seattle, Washington. Most Catholic giving is reported by family; we have divided it by the commonly-used figure of 2.7 to get per-member giving; this is needed for comparison with the Protestant data which is always per-member. The Catholic data is per registered family or a maximally close estimate.

    Some persons have questioned the $125 figure, since it is lower than the Episcopalian and Lutheran figures. There is no doubt, based on other research, that Catholic giving is lower as a percentage of family income. A 1978 Gallup poll asked about percentage of income contributed to church. It found that 22 percent of Catholics reported giving 5 percent or more of their family income; among all Protestants the figure was 36 percent, and among Lutherans it was 33 percent. See Gallup Organization, *Religion in America 1984* (Princeton, NJ: Gallup Organization), p. 42. A 1984 survey by Yankelovich, Skelly, and White provides additional nationwide data; it asked for the amount of giving by the respondent's family to religious groups and also for family income. For Catholics the figures were $320 and $27,500; for all Protestants the figures were $580 and $26,400; for Lutherans the figures were $500 and $29,600; for combined Presbyterians and Episcopalians the figures were $790 and $35,300. See Virginia A. Hodgkinson and Murray S. Weitzman, *The Charitable Behavior of Americans: A National Study* (Washington, DC: Independent Sector, 1986), p. 5. The nationwide polls included no special definition of "registered" Catholics; apparently any respondent saying that he or she is Catholic was included. The $320 for Catholics in the 1984 survey divided by 2.7 equals $118.52 per Catholic, not far from our estimate. I wish to thank Rev. Francis Kelly Scheets, OSC, for helping assemble the Catholic financial data.

30. Joseph M. Champlin, *Sharing Treasure, Time, and Talent: A Parish Manual for Sacrificial Giving or Tithing* (Collegeville, MN: Liturgical Press, 1982). Phone interview, July 3, 1986.

31. Sherry, "Shortage?", p. 32.

CHAPTER 2

1. Jay P. Dolan, *The American Catholic Experience* (Garden City, NY: Doubleday, 1985), Chapter 5.

2. Andrew M. Greeley, *The American Catholic: A Social Portrait* (New York: Basic Books, 1977), p. 38.

3. Dolan, *American Catholic Experience*, p. 139.

4. *Time*, July 8, 1985, p. 27. On the second wave of immigration see Lionel Maldonado and Joan Moore (eds.), *Urban Ethnicity in the United States: New Immigrants and Old Minorities* (Beverly Hills, CA: Sage, 1985).

5. *Washington Post*, June 30, 1985.

6. *Time*, July 8, 1985, p. 36.

7. *The Lutheran*, February 18, 1986, p. 18.

8. Archdiocese of New York, Office of Pastoral Research, *Hispanics in New York: Religious, Cultural, and Social Experiences*, Vol. 1 (New York: Archdiocese of New York, 1982), p. 26.

9. Arnold M. Rose, *Sociology: The Study of Human Relations* (New York: Alfred Knopf, 1956), pp. 557-8. On assimilation see Milton M. Gordon, *Assimilation in American Life* (New York: Oxford University Press, 1964); William M. Newman, *American Pluralism* (New York: Harper and Row, 1973).

10. Dolan, *American Catholic Experience*, Chapter 11. Also see Joseph A. Varacalli, *Toward the Establishment of Liberal Catholicism in America* (Lanham, MD: University Press of America, 1983), Chapter 6; Lester R. Kurtz, *The Politics of Heresy: The Modernist Crisis in Roman Catholicism* (Berkeley, University of California Press, 1986).

11. Kennedy, *The Now and Future Church*, p. 179.

12. Allan L. McCutcheon, "Denominations and Religious Intermarriage: Marital Cohorts of White Americans in the Twentieth Century," paper presented to the Society for the Scientific Study of Religion meeting, October 1984, Chicago IL.

13. This statistic was calculated from data from the Association of Catholic Colleges and Universities.

14. *The Chronicle of Higher Education*, February 5, 1986, pp. 27-30. It is an important question why Catholic colleges and universities have not risen to eminence in American higher education, even though the wealth of the Catholic community has risen to a per-capita level equal to the Protestant community and many Catholic youth attend college and graduate school. In a recent study by the Conference Board of Associated Research Councils, Catholic institutions were rated almost entirely below the mean in research strength. Only a few graduate departments rose above the mean — two at Notre Dame and one at St. Louis University. See Andrew M. Greeley, *American Catholics Since the Council* (Chicago, IL: Thomas More, 1985), p. 145.

15. All surveys of Catholic attitudes in the last two decades show this. As an example, see my report #5 described in Appendix A.

16. Greeley, *American Catholics Since the Council*, p. 33.

17. Wade Clark Roof and William McKinney, *American Mainline Religion* (New Brunswick, NJ: Rutgers University Press, 1987).

18. See Benton Johnson, "Liberal Protestantism: End of the Road?" *Annals of the American Academy of Political and Social Science* 480 (July 1985), pp. 39-52.

19. See Dean R. Hoge, "Interpreting Change in American Catholicism: The River and the Floodgate," *Review of Religious Research* 27 (June 1986), pp. 289-99.

20. Greeley, *The American Catholic*, p. 44.

21. See Charles F. Westoff, "The Blending of Catholic Reproductive Behavior," Ch. 10 in Robert Wuthnow (ed.), *The Religious Dimension* (New York: Academic Press. 1979), pp. 231-40.

22. *Ibid.*, p. 234.

23. *National Catholic Reporter*, September 26, 1980, p. 7.

24. Greeley, *The American Catholic*, p. 129.

25. For a review of Catholic student value trends see David O. Moberg and Dean R. Hoge, "Catholic College Students' Religious and Moral Attitudes, 1961 to 1982: Effects of the Sixties and the Seventies," *Review of Religious Research* 28 (December 1986), pp. 104-17.

26. Greeley, *American Catholics Since the Council*, p. 98.

27. Duane F. Alwin, "Religion and Parental Child-Rearing Orientations: Evidence of a Catholic-Protestant Convergence," *American Journal of Sociology* 92 (September 1986), pp. 412-40.

28. Greeley, *American Catholics Since the Council*, pp. 47, 183.

29. George Gallup, Jr., and Jim Castelli, *The American Catholic People* (Garden City, NY: Doubleday, 1987), p. 105.

30. *Emerging Trends* (published by the Gallup Organization), May 1983, p. 5.

31. *Emerging Trends*, October 1983, p. 3.

32. Avery Dulles, *A Church to Believe In* (New York: Crossroad, 1983), p. 3.

33. The Parish Project, *Parish Life in the United States* (Final Report to the Bishops) (Washington, DC: United States Catholic Conference, 1982), pp. 18, 31.

34. *Ibid.*, p. 39.

35. The Notre Dame researchers issued a series of reports giving their findings; they numbered eight as of summer 1986. For information write the Notre Dame Study of Catholic Parish Life, 1201 Memorial Library, University of Notre Dame, Notre Dame, IN 46556. Also see the entire issue, *New Catholic World* 228 (November-December 1985) and David Byers (ed.), *The Parish in Transition: Proceedings of a Conference on the American Catholic Parish* (Washington, DC: United States Catholic Conference, 1985). More reports are in preparation.

36. David C. Leege, "The American Catholic Parish of the 1980s," pp. 8-22 in Byers, *The Parish in Transition*. Quote is on pp. 10-11.

37. Philip J. Murnion, "Parish Leadership," pp. 58-65 in Byers, *The Parish in Transition*. Figures are from p. 59.

38. Leege, p. 17 in Byers, *The Parish in Transition.*

39. *Ibid.*, p. 16.

40. Thomas Sweetser, *Successful Parishes: How They Meet the Challenge of Change* (Minneapolis, MN: Winston Press, 1983).

41. An exemplary study should be mentioned here, done in the Diocese of Rockford, Illinois: Michael J. Cieslak, "Parish Responsiveness and Parishioner Commitment," *Review of Religious Research* 26 (December 1984), pp. 132-47. Cieslak assembled data from all the parishes in the diocese to see what factors predicted high levels of Mass attendance, financial giving, and involvement in non-liturgical parish activities. He found that parishes which provide visible services to parishioners elicit higher levels of financial support. Also those parishes which are responsive to parishioner needs enjoy greater participation and commitment than others. This study supports the recommendations of the Parish Project.

42. See Dean R. Hoge, *Converts, Dropouts, Returnees,* pp. 171-2.

CHAPTER 3

1. I wish to thank Barbara Williams for extensive help in writing this chapter.

2. See John Seidler, "Priest Resignations in a Lazy Monopoly," *American Sociological Review* 44 (October 1979), pp. 763-83, for sociological implications of this point.

3. *Time*, December 21, 1970, pp. 16-22; Elmo R. Zumwalt, *On Watch* (New York: Quadrangle/New York Times Books, 1976), p. 271.

4. *Ibid.*, p. 183.

5. *Ibid.*, p. 192.

6. John V. Noel, Jr., *Division Officer's Guide*, 8th ed. (Annapolis, MD: Naval Institute Press, 1982), p. 189.

7. *Time*, December 21, 1970, p. 22.

8. Commander, Air Force Military Personnel Center, *New Directions: A Survey of Separating Officers.* Report, San Antonio, Texas, April 1985.

9. Interview with Major Greg Seidenberger, July 15, 1986.

10. Interview with Lieutenant Colonel Michael Gallagher, Officer Retention Unit, July 10, 1986.

11. Terry Deal and Allan Kennedy, *Corporate Cultures: The Rites and Rituals of Corporate Life* (Reading, MA: Addison-Wesley, 1982); Robert E. Kelley, *The Gold Collar Worker: Harnessing the Brainpower of the New Workforce* (Reading, MA: Addison-Wesley, 1985); Robert Levering, Milton Moskowitz, and Michael Katz, *The 100 Best Companies to Work For in America* (Reading, MA: Addison-Wesley, 1984); John Naisbitt and Patricia Aburdene, *Re-inventing the Corporation* (New York: Warner Books, 1985); William Ouchi, *Theory Z* (Reading, MA: Addison-Wesley, 1981); Tom Peters and Nancy Austin, *A Passion for Excellence: The Leadership Difference* (New York: Random House, 1985); Alvin Toffler, *The Adaptive Corporation* (New York: Bantam Books, 1985).

12. Kelley, *The Gold Collar Worker*, p. 93.

13. Levering, Moskowitz, and Katz, *The 100 Best Companies*, pp. 209-11.

14. *Ibid.*, pp. 172-4.

15. *Ibid.*, pp. 112-3.

16. *Ibid.*, pp. 96-7.

17. *Ibid.*, pp. 48-52.

18. Douglas T. Hall and Benjamin Schneider, *Organizational Climates and Careers: The Work Lives of Priests* (New York: Seminar Press, 1973); Bishops' Committee on Priestly Life and Ministry, *The Priest and Stress* (Washington, DC: United States Catholic Conference, 1982); Robert F. Szafran, "The Distribution of Influence in Religious Organizations," *Journal for the Scientific Study of Religion* 15 (December 1976), pp. 339-49; Robert F. Szafran, "Control Structures in Religious Organizations," *Journal of Sociology of Work and Occupations* 8 (1981), pp. 327-52; Stephen Soroka, "The Relationship Between Organizational Stressors and Priests' Perception of Stress," unpublished Ph.D. dissertation, Catholic University of America, 1985. Important consulting services on personnel practices

are now being offered by the National Association of Church Personnel Administrators, 100 East Eighth Street, Cincinnati, Ohio 45202.

CHAPTER 4

1. Archdiocese of Baltimore, Dept. of Personnel, *Project 83.* Photocopied report, January 1982. 25 pp.

2. Archdiocese of Baltimore, Dept. of Personnel, One-Priest Parish Task Force Report. Photocopied report, March 1984. 26 pp. Quote is on p. 17.

3. Archdiocese of Baltimore, Dept. of Personnel, *Report of the Advisory Panel on Parish Life.* Photocopied report, January 1986. 12 pp. Quote is on p. 4.

4. *Ibid.*, p. 4.

5. Interview with Sr. Sheila Kelly, Personnel Department, Archdiocese of Baltimore, August 4, 1986.

6. *Previews* (newsletter of the "For the Harvest" program) No. 6, September 1985, p. 3. Archdiocese of Cincinnati, Office of Planning and Research.

7. *Previews* No. 4, June 1985, p. 3.

8. Interview with Rev. Robert Schmitz, Office of Planning and Research, Archdiocese of Cincinnati, July 21, 1986.

9. James Parker, "Preparing for the Year 2000," unpublished paper. Portland, Oregon: Archdiocese of Portland, 1986, p. 2.

10. *Ibid.*, p. 6.

11. Interview with Rev. James Parker, July 21, 1986.

12. Sweetser, *Successful Parishes*, p. 4.

13. Francis Kelly Scheets, "The American Catholic Church — Alive and Well?" *The Priest* 38 (October 1982), pp. 40-5.

14. Steve Askin and Carole Collins, "African Catholics Gain Identity and Challenge Church," *National Catholic Reporter*, January 31, 1986, p. 23.

15. Raymond Hickey, "Priesthood and the Church of the Future," *The Clergy Review* 71 (May 1986), pp. 158-64. Quote is on p. 159.

16. The Parish Project, *Parish Life in the United States*, p. 73.

17. Suzanne E. Elsesser, "Parishes Without Resident Priests." Photocopied paper. New York: National Pastoral Life Center, 1986.

18. Peter Gilmour, "A Theological Reflection on Non-Ordained Persons Pastoring Catholic Parishes Without Resident Priests," unpublished D.Min. thesis (Mundelein, IL: University of St. Mary of the Lake, 1985). Also see four articles in the "Pastors Without Collars" series in the *National Catholic Reporter*, August 29 and September 5, 1986, telling of Gilmour's work and describing several priestless parishes. Gilmour's study will be available soon in book form: *The Emerging Pastor* (Kansas City, MO: Sheed and Ward, 1986).

19. The term "lay pastor," though widely in use, conflicts with canon law, since canon law requires that a pastor must be a priest. The new code, canon 517, makes official provision for a non-priest carrying out the principal pastoral ministry in a parish, but without giving the position a name. As yet no commonly accepted name has arisen.

20. Gilmour, "A Theological Reflection," p. 24.

CHAPTER 5

1. Department of Personnel, Archdiocese of Baltimore, *Project 83*, p. 17.

2. *New York Times*, March 20, 1985, "O'Connor Plans to Shift More Priests to Parishes."

3. Murnion, in Byers (ed.), *The Parish in Transition*, p. 60.

4. Interview with Dominic McNamara, Assistant to the President, St. Patrick's College, Meynooth, Ireland, October 24, 1986.

5. Interview with Rev. Silvano Tomasi, c.s., Director, Bishops' Committee on Migration and Tourism, United States Catholic Conference, July 23, 1986.

6. Interview with Msgr. James Kelly, Diocese of Rockville Centre, July 25, 1986. On Rockville Centre also see Vincent J. Dunigan, "The Church's Need of a Lay Ministry to Provide Sacramental Service," *The Priest* 36 (April 1980), pp. 29-33. Other information came from interviews with Msgr. Colin MacDonald, Executive Director, Secretariat on Priestly Life and Ministry, National Conference of Catholic Bishops.

7. For a review of the research see Hoge, Potvin, and Ferry, *Research on Men's Vocations.* Also see Potvin, *Seminarians of the Eighties;* FADICA, *Laborers for the Vineyard: Proceedings of a Conference on Church Vocations* (Washington, DC: Foundations and Donors Interested in Catholic Activities, 1983); Howes, "Priest Vocations;" Holsworth, "Vocations."

8. Joan L. Fee, Andrew M. Greeley, William C. McCready, and Teresa A. Sullivan, *Young Catholics* (Los Angeles: Sadlier, 1981).

9. *Ibid.,* p. 133.

10. *Ibid.,* p. 150.

11. All the differences mentioned here are significant at .05 by t-test, 2-tailed, indicating that they are real differences and not just a result of fluctuations in the data. Also we have some evidence that the students interested in vocations hold different attitudes than current Catholic seminarians in the theologate. In the 1985 random sample of seminarians in theology, 54 percent agreed with the statement, "Women should be allowed to be ordained priests in the Catholic Church;" this compares with 18 percent who agreed with a similar statement among the men student leaders interested in a vocation. On another item, 21 percent of the seminarians agreed with the statement, "I feel leadership in the Catholic Church should be restricted to bishops, priests and deacons where possible;" among men student leaders interested in a vocation the figure was 58 percent. On both measures the seminarians are more open to broader participation in church leadership than the college men interested in a vocation. (For the seminary data see Potvin, *Seminarians of the Eighties.*) Why is this? From the data available we do not know; possibly seminary training has had some effect, or possibly tomorrow's

seminarians will be less in favor of broad participation in church leadership than today's. This finding took us by surprise, and it deserves more research.

12. A clarification of the groups may be helpful. A total of 32 men are interested in a vocation now, and an additional 104 would be interested if celibacy were optional. In this section we compare the 104 with all 242 men in the leadership survey.

13. See Joseph Perreault, "The Encouragement Factor: How Important Is It?" *The Priest* 39 (January 1983), pp. 42-3. For more data on encouragement as a factor perceived by seminarians see Hemrick and Hoge, *Seminarians in Theology*, pp. 23-5 and Potvin, *Seminarians of the Eighties*, pp. 23-9.

14. These estimates are based on data from Hoge, Shields, and Verdieck, Report #4, described in Appendix A.

15. Sherry, "Shortage?", p. 30.

16. The number of ordination annually in the United States is not reported anywhere, so we must rely on estimates. We do know that in 1985 there were about 4,063 seminarians in theology, of whom 20 percent were in their final year, or about 813; see Hemrick and Hoge, *Seminarians in Theology*, p. 66. Schoenherr and Sorensen reported that there were 593 ordinations to the diocesan priesthood in America in 1980, and they projected 463 for 1985; see Schoenherr and Sorensen, "Social Change," pp. 33, 36. Of the seminarians surveyed in 1985, 74 percent were headed for the diocesan priesthood, implying that the projection for 1985 for all priests, based on Schoenherr's estimate, would be about 625 (463 divided by .74). The estimates do not agree, and we use 815 as a reasonable preliminary estimate.

17. FADICA, *Laborers for the Vineyard*, pp. 49, 118.

18. Hemrick and Hoge, *Seminarians in Theology*, p. 15.

19. See David Mills, "Higher Callings: With Fewer Youths Wanting to Be Priests, Seminaries Woo Adults," *Wall Street Journal*, October 10, 1983.

20. Hemrick and Hoge, *Seminarians in Theology*, pp. 30-3.

21. Potvin, *Seminarians of the Eighties*, p. 19.

22. *Ibid.*, p. 53. A 1981 study came to the same conclusion—that there is no evidence to question recruitment of older men to the priesthood. See Thomas H. Hicks, "A Study of the Background, Level of Job Satisfaction, Maturity, and Morale of 'Delayed Vocation' Catholic Priests." *Review of Religious Research* 22 (June 1981), pp. 328-45.

CHAPTER 6

1. I wish to thank Kathleen Ferry for extensive help in writing this chapter.

2. This estimate assumed 64,341,000 Catholics of whom 70 percent are registered, that the registered ones now contribute $125 per year, also that 20 percent of contributions are used to support schools. If costs are similar to the Lutheran Church in America (see Table 4), about 74,000 priests or lay professionals could be supported.

3. Pilarczyk, "The Changing Image of the Priest," p. 145.

4. *Church Pension Fund 1983 Annual Report*, Episcopal Church (New York: Episcopal Church Center), p. 15.

5. Constant H. Jacquet, Jr., "Clergy Salaries and Income in 1982 in Eleven U.S. Denominations," pp. 265-9 in C. H. Jacquet (ed.), *Yearbook of American and Canadian Churches 1984* (New York: National Council of Churches).

6. Diocese of Richmond, *Report of the Task Force on Salaries and Stipends*. Mimeographed report (Richmond, VA, 1976).

7. David and Vera Mace, *What's Happening to Clergy Marriages?* (Nashville: Abingdon, 1980), p. 76.

8. Interview with Dr. Jackson Carroll, Methodist researcher and co-author of *Too Many Pastors?* (New York: Pilgrim Press, 1980), on September 12, 1986. Also Bishop Alexander Stewart informed me that in the Episcopal Church today, changes in rectorships occur every six years on the average.

9. Letter from Most Rev. Daniel E. Pilarczyk, September 8, 1986.

10. Interview with Rev. Roy Oswald, Senior Staff, Alban Institute, Washington, DC, August 8, 1986.

11. Richard A. Goodling and Cheryl Smith, "Clergy Divorce: A Survey of Issues and Emerging Ecclesiastical Structures," *The Journal of Pastoral Care* 37 (December 1983), pp. 277-91.

12. Ira W. Hutchison and Katherine R. Hutchison, "The Impact of Divorce Upon Clergy Career Mobility," *Journal of Marriage and the Family* 41 (November 1979), pp. 847-55.

13. Shirley Foster Hartley, "Marital Satisfaction Among Clergy Wives," *Review of Religious Research* 19 (Winter 1978), pp. 178-91.

14. Raymond Hickey, "Priesthood and the Church of the Future," *The Clergy Review* 71 (May 1986), pp. 158-64.

15. Joseph H. Fichter, *America's Forgotten Priests: What They Are Saying* (New York: Harper & Row, 1968), p. 176.

16. Interviews with Fr. Basil Rodzianko, Former Bishop, Orthodox Church in America, and Fr. Dmitry Grigorieff, Dean of St. Nicholas Cathedral, Washington, DC, Orthodox Church in America, November 6, 1986.

17. Dr. Loren Mead, Director, and Dr. Robert Gribbon, Senior Staff, of the Alban Institute, Washington, DC; Rev. Preston Kelsey, Head of the Board of Theological Education, Episcopal Church; Rev. Craig Casey, Vice President and Manager of the Pension Fund, Episcopal Church; Rev. Joseph Wagner, Director of the Division of Professional Leadership, Lutheran Church in America; Dr. Jackson Carroll, Protestant researcher, Hartford Seminary; Rev. Donald Smith, General Director, Vocation Agency, Presbyterian Church, USA; Rev. Howard McCuen, Jr., Data Coordinator, Vocations Agency, Presbyterian Church, USA.

18. Hartley, "Marital Satisfaction Among Clergy Wives," p. 188.

19. William Douglas, *Ministers' Wives* (New York: Harper & Row, 1965), pp. 33ff.

20. John Scanzoni, "Resolution of Occupational-Conjugal Role Conflict in Clergy Marriages," *Journal of Marriage and the Family* 27 (August 1965), pp. 396-402; Mace and Mace, *What's Happening To Clergy Marriages?*

21. James O'Brien, "Ordaining Married Men: The Australian Experience," *The Clergy Review* 67 (November 1982), pp. 406-411. Quote is on p. 410.

22. One Episcopalian official mentioned that the movement of 32 Episcopalian priests to the Catholic Church is less important than the many Catholics who have become Episcopalian priests. During the same period of time over 200 Catholic priests became Episcopalian, mostly because of marriage. In the words of Dr. Loren Mead of the Alban Institute, "Many of them are good priests."

23. Interviews with Rev. James Parker, assistant to Cardinal Bernard Law for administering the processing of Episcopalian applicants, July 7 and August 12, 1986. Also interviews were done with Rev. Thomas Bevan and Sister Sheila Kelly, Archdiocese of Baltimore; Rev. Richard Hynes, Executive Director of the National Federation of Priests' Councils; Dr. Loren Mead and Rev. Roy Oswald, Alban Institute, Washington, DC; and Rev. John Doaker, Coordinator for Ministerial Development, Episcopal Church.

24. Leege, "The American Catholic Parish in the 1980s," p. 22.

25. Mark Neilsen, "Though Ordination Remote, Women Persevere in Cause," *National Catholic Reporter*, November 8, 1985, p. 8.

26. Martin Smith, *Fifteen Years After the Ordination of Women in the LCA*. mimeographed report (Philadelphia: Division for Professional Leadership, Lutheran Church in America, 1985).

27. Barbara Leix Braver, "Anglicans Can Foresee Women as Bishops," *Christian Century*, April 23, 1986, p. 406.

28. Rosemary Ruether, "Give Women a Chance or They'll Go Elsewhere," *National Catholic Reporter*, October 21, 1983, p. 13.

29. "Project Priesthood Statistics," report (Mt. Rainier, MD: Quixote Center, 1978); "Ordination Reconsidered: Project Priesthood '85," report (Fairfax, VA: Women's Ordination Conference, 1985).

30. Fran Ferder, *Called to Break Bread?* (Mt. Rainier, MD: Quixote Center, 1978), p. 30.

31. *Ibid.*, p. 31.

32. *Ibid.*, p. 56.

33. Constance F. Parvey, "Stir in the Ecumenical Movement: The Ordination of Women," Appendix to Brita Stendahl, *The Force of Tradition* (Philadelphia: Fortress Press, 1985), p. 160.

34. Constance F. Parvey (ed.), *Ordination of Women in Ecumenical Perspective.* Faith and Order Paper 105 (Geneva: World Council of Churches, 1980), p. 12.

35. "British Favor Women Priests," *Emerging Trends*, June 1984, p. 5.

36. See Jackson Carroll, Barbara Hargrove, and Adair T. Lummis, *Women of the Cloth* (San Francisco: Harper & Row, 1983), p. 102.

37. Braver, "Anglicans Can Foresee Women as Bishops," p. 406.

38. Georgette Jasen, "The Split in Episcopal Ranks," *The Wall Street Journal*, November 9, 1977, p. 26.

39. Patricia Scharber Lefevere, "Women Episcopal Priest Takes Vows Over Hecklers," *National Catholic Reporter*, December 13, 1985, p. 2.

40. Gallup Organization, "Religion in America, 1977-78," *Gallup Opinion Index* 145 (Princeton, NJ: American Institute of Public Opinion, 1978), pp. 110-2.

41. Carroll, Hargrove, and Lummis, *Women of the Cloth*, pp. 144-5. The nine denominations were: American Baptist, American Lutheran, Lutheran Church in America, Christian Church (Disciples), Episcopal, United Church of Christ, United Methodist, United Presbyterian, and Presbyterian Church, U.S.

42. Edward C. Lehman, Jr., *Women Clergy: Breaking Through Gender Barriers* (New Brunswick, NJ: Transaction Books, 1985), p. 41.

43. Lehman, *Women Clergy*; also see Edward C. Lehman, Jr., *A Study of Women in Ministry* (Valley Forge, PA: Judson Press, 1979).

44. Lehman, *Women Clergy*; Carroll, Hargrove, and Lummis, *Women of the Cloth*; unpublished data from the Lutheran Listening Post, Panel II, October 1982.

45. Marjorie H. Royle, "Women Pastors: What Happens After Placement?" *Review of Religious Research* 24 (December 1982), pp. 116-26.

46. Carroll, Hargrove, and Lummis, *Women of the Cloth*, p. 156. A similar finding occurred in a 1976 survey of Catholics — that Catholic laity who had experienced women as altar servers, homilists, or ushers were more likely to support the ordination of women. See Maureen Fiedler and Dolly Pomerleau, *Are Catholics Ready?* (Mount Rainier, MD: Quixote Center, 1978), p. 36.

47. Carroll, Hargrove, and Lummis, *Women of the Cloth*, pp. 215, 251; Harry Hale, Jr., Morton King, and Doris Moreland Jones, *Clergy women: Problems and Satisfactions* (Lima, OH: Fairway Press, 1985), p. 24.

48. Carroll, Hargrove, and Lummis, *Women of the Cloth*, p. 113.

49. Smith, *Fifteen Years After the Ordination*, pp. 5-7.

50. Jacquet, "Clergy Salaries and Income in 1982," p. 267.

51. Carroll, Hargrove, and Lummis, *Women of the Cloth*, p. 200.

52. Hale, King, and Jones, *Clergywomen*, pp. 73ff.

53. Carroll, Hargrove, and Lummis, *Women of the Cloth*, p. 193.

54. *Ibid.*, p. 199. Also see Mary-Paula Walsh, "Role Conflicts Among Women in Ministry," unpublished Ph.D. dissertation, Catholic University of America, 1984, for a discussion of this issue among Presbyterian ministers.

55. Susan Murch Morrison, "Ministry Shaped by Hope . . . Toward Wholeness: The Woman as Ordained Minister," unpublished D.Min. dissertation, Wesley Theological Seminary, 1979, p. 106.

56. Andrew Greeley, "Proposed: Limited Terms of Priesthood," *National Catholic Reporter*, February 25, 1983, pp. 10-14.

57. James H. Provost, "Employing Dispensed Priests for Ministry," *The Priest* 34 (October 1978), pp. 29-33.

58. Greeley, "Proposed: Limited Terms of Priesthood." This pattern of attitudes does not hold true for Catholics in England and Wales, according to a 1978 survey. Frequent Mass attenders favored 5 or 10 year terms of service for priests more than married priests, part-time priests, or using married ex-priests as part-time priests. The figures were 49 percent in favor of terms of service, 35 percent for married priests, 35 percent for part-time priests, and 30 percent for use of married ex-priests. Two other options received much stronger endorsement than any of these: more use of deacons and lay parish assistants. See "The Roman Catholic Church in England and Wales," *Pro Mundi Vita Dossiers* (Europe/North America Dossier 11, December 1980), p. 6.

59. Interview with Dr. Norman Horner, former Associate Director of the Overseas Ministries Studies Center, Ventnor, NJ, July 17, 1986.

60. Interview with Robert Coote, Assistant to the Director, Overseas Ministries Studies Center, Ventnor, NJ, July 17, 1986.

61. Greeley, *The Catholic Priest*, p. 285.

62. Schoenherr and Sorensen, "Decline and Change in the U.S. Catholic Church," p. 27.

63. Shields and Verdieck, "Religious Life in the United States," p. 11.

64. Greeley, *The Catholic Priest*, p. 281. On reasons for resigning see James N. Watzke, "Desocialization From the Priesthood: Critical Problems of Personal and Role Identity Among the Catholic Religious Professionals," unpublished Ph.D. dissertation, Harvard University, 1971; Robert Patrick Nestor, "A Qualitative Reason Analysis of Dissatisfaction With the Roman Catholic Priesthood Among Those Who Resigned Between 1968-78," unpublished Ed.D. dissertation, Boston University School of Education, 1979; John E. Haag, "A Study of the Seminary and Priesthood Experience of Thirteen Resigned Roman Catholic Priests," unpublished D.Min. thesis, Pittsburgh Theological Seminary, 1984.

65. Greeley, *The Catholic Priest*, pp. 292-3.

66. Interview with Terence Dosh, Executive Secretary of CORPUS, July 21, 1986.

67. Maureen Hendricks-Rauch, "A Study of the Marriages and Marital Adjustment of Resigned Roman Catholic Priests and Their Wives," unpublished Ed.D. dissertation, University of Northern Colorado, 1979.

68. Daniel Moga, "Mid-Life Marriage of Catholic Clergy," *Counseling and Values* 22 (1978), pp. 71-9. Similar findings were reported in Greeley, *The Catholic Priest*, and Hendricks-Rauch, "A Study of the Marriages."

69. Moga, "Mid-Life Marriage of Catholic Clergy," p. 74.

70. Greeley, *The Catholic Priest*, p. 299. Also see George E. Reinheimer, "A Comparative Study of the Vocational Interests and Values of Roman Catholic Priests Active in the Ministry and Roman Catholic Priests Who Have Left the Ministry," unpublished Ph.D. dissertation, St. John's University, 1973.

CHAPTER 7

1. National Conference of Catholic Bishops, *Called and Gifted: The American Catholic Laity* (Washington, DC: United States Catholic Conference, 1980).

2. "Many Interested in Career in Religion," *Emerging Trends*, February 1980, p. 2.

3. Samuel M. Taub, "Annual Report on the Permanent Diaconate in the United States, 1985." Photocopied report (Washington, DC: United States Catholic Conference, 1985).

4. Bishops' Committee on the Permanent Diaconate, *A National Study of the Permanent Diaconate in the United States* (Washington, DC: United States Catholic Conference, 1981), p. 14.

5. Interviews with Samuel M. Taub, Executive Director, Bishops' Committee on the Permanent Diaconate, August 14 and September 17, 1986.

6. Taub, "Annual Report, 1985," p. 2.

7. Bishops' Committee, *A National Study of the Permanent Diaconate*, p. 14.

8. On this issue see Joseph A. Komonchak, "The Permanent Diaconate and the Variety of Ministries in the Church," pp. 12-38 in Bishops' Committee on the Permanent Diaconate (ed.), *Diaconal Reader* (Washington, DC: United States Catholic Conference, 1985); Philip J. Murnion, "The Diaconate in the Context of Today's Ministry," also in *Diaconal Reader*, pp. 66-75; Tim McCarthy, "Deacons: To Be, or What To Be," *National Catholic Reporter*, March 15, 1985, pp. 15, 26-7.

9. Bishops' Committee, *A National Study of the Permanent Diaconate*, p. 14.

10. Ernest J. Fiedler, "Permanent Deacons Shouldn't Play Priest," *U.S. Catholic* 51 (May 1986), pp. 15-16. Quote is on p. 15.

11. Bishops' Committee, *A National Study of the Permanent Diaconate*, p. 41.

12. Kennedy, *The Now and Future Church*, p. 171.

13. Taub, "Annual Report, 1985," p. 6.

14. Thomas P. Walters, *National Profile of Professional Religious Education Coordinators/Directors* (Washington, DC: National Conference of Diocesan Directors of Religious Education, 1983). An earlier survey was done in 1976, but it is less useful for our purposes: United States Catholic Conference, *A National Inventory of Parish Catechetical Programs* (Washington, DC: United States Catholic Conference, 1978).

15. Walters, *National Profile*, p. 18.

16. *Ibid.*, p. 61.

17. Zenobia V. Fox, "A Post-Vatican II Phenomenon: Lay Ministries: A Critical Three-Dimensional Study," unpublished Ph.D. dissertation, Fordham University, 1986.

18. *Ibid.*, p. 156.

19. *Ibid.*, p. 165.

20. *Ibid.*, p. 178.
21. *Ibid.*, p. 202.
22. Ann Patrick Conrad and Joseph J. Shields, *Career Lay Ministers in the Archdiocese of Baltimore: An Assessment of Future Roles and Functions.* Ringbound report (Washington, DC: Center for Applied Research in the Apostolate, 1982). For a commentary on the Baltimore study see H. Richard McCord, "Research on Lay Ministry," pp. 94-5 in Bishops' Committee on the Laity (ed.), *Gifts: A Laity Reader* (Washington, DC: United States Catholic Conference, 1983).
23. Conrad and Shields, *Career Lay Ministers in the Archdiocese of Baltimore*, p. 17. Another diocesan study of lay ministers was done in the Archdiocese of Seattle in 1985. See Mary Beth Celio, "The Changing Shape of Ministry in the Roman Catholic Church," paper presented to the Religious Research Association meeting, October 26, 1985, Savannah, Georgia; also Mary Beth Celio, "Women in Ministry in the Roman Catholic Church," paper presented to the same meeting.

CHAPTER 8

1. Gerard Fuller, OMI reports, "Apparently to inject a little mercy into his approach in the matter of laicization, John Paul II is now inviting and readily allowing priests who have left to return to priestly practice with little or no ecclesiastical red tape." See his article "Paternalism Won't Solve Priest Problem," *National Catholic Reporter*, September 5, 1986, p. 18.
2. Kennedy, *The Now and Future Church*, p. 177.
3. Archbishop John Whealon, personal statement, in Bishops' Committee on the Laity, *Gifts: A Laity Reader*, p. 21.
4. Gerard T. Broccolo, "Can We Have Prayer Without Father?" *Journal of the Catholic Campus Ministry Association* 1 (Spring 1986), pp. 22-4. Quote is on p. 23.
5. *Ibid.*, p. 23.
6. *Ibid.*, p. 24.

7. Gerard Austin makes a similar argument in an article on liturgy. He opposes the increased acceptance of the Communion service: "Receiving a previously consecrated host is a fine thing, but it is not what celebrating the Eucharist is about. My fear is that we will eventually have a generation of Catholics who will have lost sight of the difference. Ordained priests will travel about, consecrating and filling tabernacles with hosts to be given out at services of the Lord, even on Sundays. If this is done long enough, our people will get used to it, and not even realize that they have been denied their right to celebrate the Eucharist." Gerard Austin, O.P., "Spirit Through Word," Ch. 1 in Gerard Austin, O.P., Theresa F. Koernke, I.H.M., Mary Collins, O.S.B., and Louis Weil, *Called to Prayer: Liturgical Spirituality Today* (Collegeville, MN: Liturgical Press, 1986), pp. 11-27. Quote is on p. 16.

INDEX

(NOTE: Information presented in Tables or Figures in the text is indicated in the index by the use of *bold italics* for page numbers.)